ADVANTAGE INDIA

Anindya Dutta is an international banker-turned-entrepreneur working in the area of sports-led leadership development. He has spent the best part of three decades working in major financial markets—London, Hong Kong, Mumbai and Singapore. Anindya is deeply interested in sports history and is a sportswriter by vocation.

Anindya's first book, *A Gentleman's Game* (2017), was followed by his widely acclaimed and bestselling account of the greatest bowling spells in the history of cricket, *Spell Binding Spells* (2017). His next book, *We Are the Invincibles* (2019), a fascinating account of Bradman's 1948 team's tour of England also received critical acclaim.

Wizards: The Story of Indian Spin Bowling published by Westland Sport in 2019 won the Cricket Book of the Year Award at the Ekamra Sports Lit Fest.

Besides penning books, Anindya is also a columnist for *Sportstar, Hindustan Times, ESPN Cricinfo, Cricket Monthly, Cricket Soccer, Roar, The Cricketer Magazine, The Print, Firstpost, News9 Live* and *Fountain Ink*.

Delicately maintaining his work–write balance—entrepreneur by day and writer by night—Anindya lives in Singapore with his hugely supportive wife Anisha and canine daughter Olu.

Praise for *Advantage India*

'This is the breeziest history of any sport ever written. ... the story of Indian tennis is told in [an] engaging fashion with anecdote after anecdote bringing out the thrills and excitement of the sport while giving us more than a glimpse into the careers and achievements of old gladiators who have long departed ... The book is a must-read for all tennis lovers.'

—Deccan Chronicle

'... a much-needed addition to a rather empty cupboard of books written on the premier racquet sport.'

—The Hindu

'*Advantage India* by Dutta introduces readers to former greats of the game, the journeymen and the millennials of Indian tennis. It covers all the major players, their achievements and their place in the pantheon of the sport in the country. The book is a tribute to all the Indian lawn tennis players since 1885 ... The greatest success of Dutta, a seasoned author and columnist, lies in getting the players to talk about their peers.'

—The Tribune

'Anindya Dutta's new biography of the colonial game in India throws light on the earliest and lesser-known heroes of the sport'

—Mid-Day

ADVANTAGE INDIA

The Story of Indian Tennis

ANINDYA DUTTA

First published by Westland Sport, an imprint of Westland Publications Private Limited, in 2021

Published by Westland Sport, an imprint of Westland Books, a division of Nasadiya Technologies Private Limited, in 2023

No. 269/2B, First Floor, 'Irai Arul', Vimalraj Street, Nethaji Nagar, Allappakkam Main Road, Maduravoyal, Chennai 600095

Westland, the Westland logo, Westland Sport and the Westland Sport logo are the trademarks of Nasadiya Technologies Private Limited, or its affiliates.

ISBN: 9789395767859

10 9 8 7 6 5 4 3 2 1

Typeset by SŪRYA, New Delhi
Printed at Saurabh Printers Pvt. Ltd

This book is dedicated to Anisha—my friend, philosopher, partner-in-crime, bedrock of support and fount of inspiration for these past twenty-seven years.

May the decades ahead be even more magical together.

CONTENTS

ABOUT THE UPDATED EDITION

When I sat down to research and write *Advantage India*, I knew I was working on a largely unchronicled sport in the country. What I didn't know, however, was that the stories that would emerge would go beyond tennis and into the very heart of the history of the nation. Much less did I gauge the overwhelmingly positive reception the book would receive from those associated with tennis in India—players, critics, fans, writers and journalists.

I was humbled by the praise for the book from those who had been writing on Indian tennis for decades longer than I had. A book review (among the many that the book has garnered) that particularly pleased me was penned by one of India's most respected journalists R. Mohan, and started with the words, 'It is the breeziest book on sports ever written', and after chronicling the journey of some of the characters of the sport I had written about, ended by calling it 'a must read for all tennis lovers'.

I was equally overwhelmed by the words of appreciation from some of India's greatest tennis players—Mahesh Bhupathi, Sania Mirza, Ramesh Krishnan, Enrico Piperno and Somdev Devvarman. Particularly unexpected were Bhupathi's closing words at the COVID-19 impacted virtual launch of the book to the global audience: 'I would like to thank Anindya on behalf of all players for writing the history of our sport which we did not know.'

So why this edition and what's different about it, readers may well ask.

Why—In early 2020, Westland, the publishers of this book, were abruptly shut down by their owner, Amazon. The reincarnated Westland, under new ownership, is now back to doing what it does best—publishing good books. What that did is allow us to present this new and updated version of the book.

What's Different—The chapter on one of the most fascinating players in the history of this sport—Sydney Jacob, has been significantly expanded with stories, insights and photos that I did not know the existence of until Jacob's grandson, Philip, living in distant Ireland, read a review of the book on an American sports site and reached out to me. He then opened up Sydney Jacob's personal scrapbook with rare photos no one else possesses, and provided valuable insights that only family can possess.

I also got opportunities to speak to several of the players and their families to glean more insight into their careers after they read the book and filled in some gaps. That has immeasurably enriched the book. My thanks go out to all the players who took the trouble to do so.

Finally, I took the opportunity to update the chapters on the players who are still active on the circuit, or have recently retired (or like Paes and Bhupathi, who in recent interviews have revealed a bit more about their lives) as this edition goes to press.

History is never static, so I continue to believe that while this book is perhaps the first reference tome for tennis in India, others will follow in time. That will be hugely beneficial for the future of the sport in India, and there will be none happier than I if that happens.

May the stories never dry up.

INTRODUCTION

'You want to have a coffee with Vijay today?' was the cryptic text I received one morning six years ago from Shiraz, an old friend. As far as I knew, Shiraz was in Bangkok where he lived, and I was at work in Singapore. But I did know which Vijay he was referring to.

We had spoken a few days earlier and he had casually mentioned that he was working on a business venture with Vijay Amritraj. It turned out that both were in Singapore that day and Vijay had an hour free between meetings and was happy to say hello if I could make it to the Four Seasons at 3 p.m.

'I'll be there,' I replied.

That one hour turned into two and a lifetime of memories.

'This is our second meeting,' I told him as we sat down and ordered coffee, 'the first was when I was ten and you ruffled my hair and gave me this at the Madras Gymkhana Club in 1977.' Vijay sat there shaking his head as he held my first autograph book open to a page that read: 'Love, Vijay Amritraj.' Then he looked up with a smile and to my utter disbelief, recited the exact scores of each match that he had played that year in the Davis Cup tie against Australia.

I knew the scores because it held special significance for me. It had been my first glimpse of international tennis, sitting with my father on the temporary bamboo stands at the Gymkhana grounds, listening to him recount the exploits of the legendary Ramanathan Krishnan, seated on the team bench across the court.

It was also the day I had fallen hopelessly in love with the sport that I would only start playing a few years later when we moved to Cochin (now Kochi). There, a close friend, Arun Varadarajan, who had made it to the semi-finals of the junior Nationals that year, insisted I join him on the clay courts of the Lotus Club where he practised. But even then if someone had told me that I would end up writing the story of Indian tennis four decades later, I would have laughed in his face.

Fast forward three decades and four books later. A weekend conversation took place between my editor for *Wizards: The Story of Indian Spin Bowling* (whose manuscript he has just read for the first time)—Karthik Venkatesh—and myself, and he asked what I wanted to write on next. 'Indian tennis,' was my answer. 'But remember, Nadal is not Indian,' he teased me, knowing much of my work on tennis until then had been a series of pieces over the years on Rafael Nadal. We laughed and left it at that. A month later, I was at breakfast in Copenhagen and got a call from Karthik. 'Congratulations! You are going to be writing the story of Indian tennis. We will discuss terms when you get back.'

And thus began a fascinating roller coaster journey that culminated in the book that you hold today.

I didn't quite realise how daunting a task writing this story was going to be until I immersed myself in the research.

Unlike cricket, tennis has virtually no recorded history in the country before the arrival of Ramanathan Krishnan in the 1950s other than a book written by a retired bureaucrat, P.K. Datta, and published by the government of India in 2001, titled *A Century of Indian Tennis*. That book is largely a quick compendium of bare statistics and often cryptic comments on players rather than a history of the sport. A hundred websites and books have since copy-pasted the work instead of making an attempt at building on the invaluable work that he did. The result is a sport whose history had gaping holes that were waiting to be filled.

The months that followed were to reveal to me long-forgotten tales that are inextricably linked to the fabric of Indian society. It was to take the story of the sport in India back to the early dawn of tennis as we understand it today. It was also to bring to life characters who had significant roles to play on the court, and very often off it—roles that were to influence Indian history itself.

The stories of Sydney Montague Jacob and the Jallianwala Bagh massacre, and that of Mohammed Sleem, barrister-at-law and the greatest Indian tennis player of the pre-independence era, fascinated me, particularly the details and links I managed to unearth to bring these men's stories to life. The interactions and conversations with some of India's best tennis players of the past seven decades would turn out to be much more than interviews, as they gave freely of their knowledge and insights into the sport itself, and that has enriched this book.

For later generation readers and fans who have grown up watching Indian tennis reach great heights in the doubles format, the section on Indians and doubles will hopefully be an insightful and nostalgic page-turner. The section on women's tennis in India will, I hope, be as much of a revelation to readers as it was to me when I wrote this book. The fact that Sania Mirza, indubitably India's greatest contribution to the world of women's tennis and the unique phenomenon that she is, was passed on the baton from a series of lesser known but illustrious predecessors so that she could accelerate and anchor the team to a glorious finish, may come as a surprise to fans unfamiliar with the long history of the women's sport in India.

As you read this story, I hope the same sense of pride fills you as it did me when I wrote it. India may not have a Grand Slam singles champion yet, but there is far more to this story of tennis than that. The achievements of the generations of players who have wielded their racquets in their quest for national and personal pride is staggering, the stories of their sacrifices for the tricolour enormously moving, and every step they have taken on this journey has moved the story of Indian tennis towards an ever more glorious future.

THE ORIGINS OF TENNIS

(Tennis is) a perfect combination of violent action taking place in an atmosphere of total tranquility.

—Billie Jean King

7 JULY 2008, CENTRE COURT, WIMBLEDON

Roger Federer and Rafael Nadal meet for the third successive time at the Centre Court of Wimbledon for an almost ridiculously hyped and anticipated match. Nadal is on a twenty-three match winning streak. Twice, Nadal has had the summit in sight, and twice, Federer has thwarted his attempt to ascend that final step. In fact, Federer has won the Championship five times in a row going into the match. One more, and he will surpass Bjorn Borg's long-standing record.

Midway through the eventual four hours and forty-eight minutes of the encounter, when the third set tiebreaker starts with Nadal up 6-4, 6-4, it looks like the Spaniard has finally found a way to conquer the Swiss peak. But what follows is a reminder of the reason why Federer has remained unbeaten at Wimbledon for so long.

Time after time, on crucial points, Federer renders Nadal helpless with punishing aces. He sends down a flurry of down-the-line returns, perhaps twenty-five of them through the match, each more mind-blowing than the last. Two spirit-crushing tiebreaks later, in each of which Nadal had the chance to finish the match and Federer refused to yield, incredibly, the two find themselves tied 7-7 in the final set.

As the digital clock shows 4.48, the time that has elapsed in the match, it's yet another match point with Nadal serving 8-7 up. Federer, having played some unbelievable shots on the forehand throughout the match, hits a return into the net. Nadal wins 6-4, 6-4, 6-7,6-7, 9-7.

He vaults into the Players' Box, picks up a Spanish flag and walks along the roof above the TV commentators to reach the Spanish royalty. Then it's back on court to celebrate the first Spanish victory at Wimbledon since Manuel Santana in 1966. It won't be the last.

Bruce Jenkins sums it up in his *San Francisco Chronicle* story the next morning: 'There will never be another scene quite like it, or another match, for that matter. Wimbledon closed down a 132-year era Sunday night with the greatest tennis match ever played.'

THE BEGINNINGS

It is a fact that but for a broken lawn roller at the All-England Croquet Club 132 years before Rafael Nadal and Roger Federer were to play the greatest tennis match of all time on its manicured lawns in 2008, the Wimbledon Championships would not have come into being. Indeed, tennis as we know it today, played on rectangular courts, with racquets and a bouncing ball, may not have existed at all.

The All-England Club started out as a croquet organization, and the Wimbledon Tennis Championships were organised there in 1877 to help raise funds to repair the broken pony roller that kept the grass flat at the original Worple Road site of the Club in south-west London. The sub-committee that met to take that fateful decision was to change the setting, the framework, and the rules of the game, and forever alter the course of sporting history.

As Honor Godfrey, the curator of the Wimbledon Museum, recounts about that first championship, 'Everybody who entered the championship paid a guinea (worth about $80 now) entrance fee, and the spectators who came to watch the final paid a shilling each (about $4) and they saw Spencer Gore beat William Marshall in the final.'[1]

The origins of tennis, however, go much farther back than that fateful day when the sub-committee met in 1877. There is some evidence that the Greeks, Romans and Egyptians played an ancient version of the game, thousands of years ago. But the more traceable history of the sport goes back to between the eleventh and twelfth centuries to a French sport called 'Jeu de Paume' (game of the palm).

French monks began to play the game against monastery walls or over a rope hung in the courtyard, and at this time the ball was struck with the hand, hence the name Jeu de Paume. Every time the ball was served, the monks would shout 'tenez' (French for 'to take'). Eventually, the word would morph into 'tennis' and the sport had a name that would outlast its origins.

The next stage in the evolution was when a leather glove was worn to protect the battered hands, either with webbing between the fingers or a solid paddle, and eventually a webbing was attached to a handle. By the sixteenth century, the use of the hand and the glove had completely stopped, and a wooden racquet frame with sheep gutting (in all likelihood first seen in Italy) was in common use. During the same period, the wooden ball had been replaced by a leather one filled with cellulose, and finally there was a three-ounce cork ball.[2]

In the meantime, the sport had spilled beyond the monastery walls into the courtyards of European nobility. It had stopped being called Jeu de Paume and became known as 'Real Tennis' (or Royal Tennis) as it was taken up by the French royal family.

From leisure to death, tennis was a part and parcel of French life at the time. Julian Norridge in his book, *Can We Have Our Balls Back Please*, writes: 'In 1316, Louis X (known in history as the Quarrelsome) met an untimely end because of the sport. The story goes that he played an energetic game in the Forest of Vincennes and immediately afterwards drank a beaker of cold water or cold wine, depending on which version of the story you follow, lay down to rest and caught a chill from which he died.'[3]

Norridge goes on to say: 'The rules were first codified by a master professional (such people existed by then and had their own Corporation) called Forbet in 1592. A visitor to France in 1596 reported that there were at least 250 well-appointed courts in Paris and that 7000 people made their living from the game. This was out of a city population of 300,000.'

By this time there were about eighteen hundred indoor courts across Europe, and in the 1530s, Henry VIII, across the English Channel, had built the first tennis court at Hampton Palace. That court was replaced by a similar one in 1625, which continues to exist today.

The Venetian ambassador at the court of Henry VIII wrote eulogistically about him around 1519: 'His Majesty is twenty-nine years old and extremely handsome; nature could not have done more for him; he is much handsomer than any other sovereign in Christendom; a great deal handsomer than the King of France; very fair, and his whole frame admirably proportioned ... He is extremely fond of tennis, at which game it is the prettiest thing in the world to see him play, his fair skin glowing through a shirt of the finest texture.'[4]

One can only assume that the flattery got him the concessions he needed for Venice, but for us it plays a larger role in showing the status of the sport in the royal courts of the time.

But the tennis that was played in the royal courts and monasteries would look very unfamiliar to today's viewer. It was played on narrow, indoor courts, where the ball was played off the walls with roofed galleries and a number of openings. Players won points by hitting the ball into netted windows beneath the roof, with the net being five feet high on the ends and three feet in the middle, which created a pronounced droop.[5]

The tennis court of the time was undoubtedly the scene of many intrigues and treaties, given the composition of players—mostly of European nobility. Ironically, however, it was on a tennis court that the seeds of an epochal event in history, the French Revolution, would be sown. That story is worth re-telling.

Before the French Revolution, French society (other than royalty) was divided into three 'Estates'.* The First Estate comprised the clergy, the Second Estate, the nobility and the Third Estate the rest of France (about 98 per cent of the population), that had virtually no say in the running of the country. France was in the throes of fiscal and agricultural crisis, and although an assembly had been called for between the three estates, no decisions were being taken.

On 20 June 1789, the Third Estate, assembling for a meeting, found the chamber door locked and guarded by soldiers. Fearing a royal attack from King Louis XVI, they went away and reassembled at a tennis court near the Palace of Versailles. There, 576 of the 577 members took an oath immortalised as the Tennis Court Oath, '... not to separate, and to reassemble wherever circumstances require, until the constitution of the kingdom is established'.

The oath signified for the first time that French citizens formally stood in opposition to Louis XVI, and the National Assembly's refusal to back down forced the king to make concessions.

A month later the Bastille (the French fortress that acted as a political prison) was stormed, triggering the French Revolution. Forty-five days later, feudalism was abolished in France, and two months after the Tennis Court Oath had been taken, the 'Declaration of the Rights of Man and of the Citizen' came into being as a document that would

---

*The broad order of social hierarchy

become the Bible for individual rights and freedom for future generations.

The French Revolution culminated in the execution of Louis XVI in January 1793 and would alter the course of modern history, acting as the trigger for the decline of absolute monarchies across Europe and the rise of republics and democracies.

And it all started on a tennis court outside the Palace of Versailles.

It was, however, in the Victorian age that tennis came into its own and started its journey towards being the sport that we know today. In March 1874 the London-based *Court Journal* reported news of a new game likely to replace the croquet of which everyone had tired. 'Sphairistike'* or lawn tennis was just the thing for those in search of 'novelty', and, continued the report, '... it has been tested at several country houses, and has been found full of healthy excitement, besides being capable of much scientific play'. Equipment for the game was for sale as a box set, 'not much larger than a double gun case' and 'contained bats and balls and a portable court'. Thus was the birth of lawn tennis announced to a public ready to fall for the charms of a game that, from its birth, combined thrills, social cachet and commercial possibilities.[6]

A decade earlier, in the 1860s, Major T.H. (Harry) Gem and Mr J.B. Perera had laid down the first lawn tennis court in Edgbaston, and in 1872 the first lawn tennis club had been founded at the nearby Leamington Manor House Hotel.

But it was in 1874, when Major Copton Wingfield designed the boxed lawn tennis set which could be easily

---

*Greek for 'the art of playing ball'

laid out on Victorian lawns, as a business venture to revive the fortunes of his landed family, that the game attracted a wider audience. The box included vulcanised rubber balls (vulcanisation had recently been invented by James Goodyear, purely by accident, as major inventions are wont to happen). Wingfield marketed the box at five guineas and publicised it via the *Court Journal, Army and Navy Gazette, The Field* and *Vanity Fair*. While he didn't invent the game (the name by then shortened in common use to 'Sticky' from the unpronounceable 'Sphairistike'), the Major certainly helped spread the word.

Wingfield's marketing had an immediate impact. The Prince of Wales led the way in purchasing a set, and most royal families of Europe followed. More than a thousand sets were sold, and since the Major had not renewed the copyright, other manufacturers took over.

Having patented the idea, and satisfied himself it worked, Walter Wingfield walked away from the sport without any further attempt to monetise his contribution to it. His personal life would not be a happy one with his wife suffering from mental illness and all his three sons dying young. But before he passed away in 1912, Wingfield would invent a new bicycle, and a pipe tobacco mixture—'Wingfield'—that continues to be on sale today, bearing the name of the man who first spread the word about the sport we all love.

Meanwhile, in 1868, the All-England Croquet Club had been founded and the physical premises were established the following year in Wimbledon. Sadly, by that time, croquet as a sport was already in decline and the croquet lawns were taken over by the 'Sticky' sets.

As Elizabeth Wilson explains in *Love Game*, 'So rapid was the advance of lawn tennis that in 1877 the All-England Club staged its first tournament there. By this time a new set of rules had been established. The MCC (the Marylebone Cricket Club), as the most important official body overseeing any sport, had been asked to reconcile the differences in the rules between the game played by Gem and Perera and that of Wingfield. A sub-committee opted for the rectangular court, rather than the hourglass-shaped one of Wingfield's game, and, even more significantly—and against the recommendations of the MCC—adopted the traditional tennis system of scoring rather than the cumulative method used in the game of rackets (and most other sports). So, within a decade, first the MCC and then, decisively, the All-England Croquet Club, had taken control of the game.'[7]

An intriguing but important development took place as the MCC sub-committee met to decide on the court, a story that merits recounting. A member of the sub-committee spoke up to say that he had discovered a better ball. Finding Wingfield's vulcanised rubber ball difficult to control, especially in the wet English weather, he had asked his wife to cover one in white flannel. Thus came about the birth of the modern tennis ball.

With that first successful tournament organised on what would become the hallowed turf of Wimbledon (although the actual location of the club would change later), with the dual purpose of reversing the fortunes of a club started for a sport (croquet) that had suffered a premature demise and finding money to fix a broken pony roller* for its substantial lawns, tennis had arrived.

---

*The famous roller is preserved and can be seen at the Wimbledon Club.

Coincidentally, that very year, the very first cricket Test match had been played between England and Australia at Melbourne, a rivalry that would, a few years later, come to be known as the Ashes.

Over the next century, Wimbledon and Ashes would become the highlights of the English summer, and London the most desirable destination for sports lovers around the world.

TENNIS—IT WAS DIFFERENT

It's important to understand why lawn tennis took off and survived as a sport where many others failed. Timing, as they say, is everything.

Victorian England was the wealthiest country in the world, its apparently inexhaustible wealth coming from colonial expansion had given rise to an upper middle class that, along with the nobility, had plenty of leisure time and expendable income.

In such a situation, lawn tennis quickly became fashionable and turned into a desirable social occasion. Lieutenant Colonel Osborn, a fan of the new sport, wrote in 1881: 'The scene should be laid on a well-kept garden lawn. There should be a bright warm sun overhead ... Near at hand, under the cool shadow of a tree, there should be strawberries and cream, iced claret mug, and a few spectators, who do not want to play but are lovers of the game.'[8]

But there was an equally important reason for tennis gaining in popularity at the time.

The Women's Suffrage movement, that demanded voting rights for women, had gained momentum in England, and become a national movement in the Victorian era. In 1872, five years before the first Wimbledon tournament, the National Society for Women's Suffrage had been formed. Very quickly, it had widened its demands to include education as well as the vote and property rights, and generally called for widening of opportunities for women in society.

One of the things that was at the core of this attempt was the playing of sport, as girls' schools and university colleges were founded. Tennis benefited from this, for it was the only sport of the period where men and women shared the pitch, partnering each other, two on each side of the net. In the relative 'safety' of the suburban garden lawn, old prejudices and chaperones were dispensed with, and the sport flourished.

What added to the allure of the sport was the unique scoring system and the endless possibilities of coming back and pulling off unlikely victories. The origin of the scoring system has never quite been agreed upon by scholars. The closest any explanation comes to sounding plausible is the one propounded by French scholar Jean Gosselin in 1570. He opined that it came from a physical sextant, an instrument very familiar to navigators and surveyors of the time.

A sextant is an instrument with an arc of sixty degrees, each degree made up of sixty minutes, each minute of sixty seconds. So sixty was a special number in the medieval age. A tennis game was divided into four points, each point worth fifteen, thus making up sixty.

To make it even more complicated, the French added the concept of deuce. When both (or both sets of players) reached 40 (no one has an explanation why 45 was contracted to 40, but it's just accepted for some reason), the French said 'a deux', and you had to play advantage and game. When the game became popular across the Channel, the English corrupted the world to 'deuce'.

About why tennis starts with 'Love' (why not, the romantics could well ask), Julian Norridge in *Can We Have Our Balls Back Please* reminds us of one theory (among the many): 'The most amusing explanation is that it is a corruption of the French word 'l'oeuf' meaning egg, in the same way that a nought in cricket was called a 'duck's egg', quickly abbreviated to duck. There's no evidence but it's a nice thought.'

Elizabeth Wilson in *Love Game* has a more romantic take on it: 'Love', the word, is at the centre of tennis. It is embedded in the unique and eccentric tennis scoring system. Love meaning nothing—zero. Playing for love. That it was, uniquely, a sport in which women and men played together made it a 'love game' in a social and romantic sense.'

In addition to the (arguably) bizarre scoring system, tennis, unlike most sports, has no fixed duration, and like Roman gladiatorial contests (albeit without the bloodshed and gore) was originally designed to continue until one of the players (or a set of players) was victorious. The concept of a tiebreak, whether at 6-6 or 12-12 (as introduced at Wimbledon in 2019), was still several decades in the future.

These two aspects made for some very enjoyable contests on Victorian lawns, and the popularity of the game quickly skyrocketed. This being the age of Britannia ruling the seas, the word did not take long in spreading across the far-flung empire.

But we get ahead of ourselves. First, there was Wimbledon.

WIMBLEDON—PUTTING THE SEAL OF PERMANENCE TO TENNIS

In the summer of 1877, when the (now renamed) All-England Croquet and Lawn Tennis Club announced the first national lawn tennis championship open to all amateurs, to be held just five weeks later from 9 July, it was greeted with much enthusiasm.

Twenty-two players signed up for the first historic tournament, and two hundred spectators paid a shilling each to watch them. The players were in white flannel shirts and trousers, many of them in caps, with a tie and a belt around their waist. The majority of the players had honed their skills in 'real tennis' and had the tendency to slice the ball after allowing it to bounce. On the fast grass courts, and the net, which at the time was three feet at the centre and five feet at the sides, passing shots were pretty nigh impossible to implement. Instead, it was an old Harrovian* rackets** player, Spencer Gore, who beat W.C. Marshall in the final 6-1, 6-2, 6-4. Gore's tactic of forcing his opponent on the defensive, then rushing to the net and volleying a winner, would come to embody the essence of the grass court game.

The next year Wimbledon introduced an 'All Comers' Round', the winner of which would meet the reigning champion. Patrick Hadow, a coffee planter from Ceylon, holidaying in England, decided to try his hand at the new

---

*An alumni of the old sixteenth century public school, Harrow School, located in North-West London

**Rackets or racquets is an indoor racket sport played in the United Kingdom, Republic of Ireland, United States and Canada.

sport, and progressed rapidly to face Gore. Frustrated with Gore's volleys and unable to play the passing shot, Hadow invented the lob, an entirely new stroke, thus negating the chance of volleying. With it, he overcame Gore 7-5, 6-1, 9-7.

It then took three years of boring baseline rallies (there was no other known way to counter both the volley and the lob) before William and Ernest Renshaw were to change the face of the sport and launch it on the path of modernity it finds itself on. They invented the overhead serve and the smash.

The Renshaw brothers were magnificent tennis players and were accused of resorting to brute force and ignorance by opponents who could not keep up with them. From 1881, William would win six championships and his brother Ernest filled in for him the year William pulled out with the first known case of tennis elbow.

Generations later, when net heights were less skewed and magnificent passing shots had become possible, future champions would combine the innovations of volleying by Spencer Gore, the lob by Patrick Hadow, and the overhead service and smash by the Renshaw brothers to allow the sport its full expression.

By 2008, when Rafael Nadal and Roger Federer played out their classic encounter, delivering each stroke with brushes of their genius, tennis had indeed been elevated to an exquisite art form, fittingly, on the green canvas of Wimbledon where the first outlines had been drawn that warm summer's day of 1877.

THE BEGINNINGS OF THE SPORT IN INDIA

INDIAN TENNIS
THE JOURNEY BEGINS
1885–1947

TENNIS COMES TO INDIA

It was fortuitous for the sport that modern tennis arrived at a point when Britannia ruled the waves. The earth was becoming a smaller place, and with the British Army and Civil Service spread out across the colonies, it was inevitable that the officers and bureaucrats would find means of entertainment that connected them with the home country. It thus came about that less than a decade after the first Championship at Wimbledon, India hosted her first tournament.

In 1885, barely seven years after Spencer Gore won the first Wimbledon Championships, the lawns of the Gymkhana Club in Lahore were transformed, with a carnival-like atmosphere heralding the inaugural Punjab Lawn Tennis Championships.

Trevor Douglas David Berrington, a twenty-six-year-old civil servant, came through a tough field to become India's first tennis champion. While he will always be remembered for this moment in India's sporting history, Berrington's role in subsequent events beyond the court is largely forgotten.

Trained at the Royal Indian Engineering College for the Telegraph Department at Cooper's Hill, Berrington was posted in Rawalpindi when he won the tournament at Lahore, and became the chief superintendent of the Postal Department in the Punjab in 1900. From here the rise was swift and he was appointed the director-general of the Telegraph Department in 1907.

Berrington would be in the thick of the action immediately as telegraph signallers and subordinate staff went on a coordinated nationwide strike in Rangoon, Moulmein, Calcutta, Allahabad, Agra, Bombay and Karachi. The Swadeshi Movement, set off by the partition of Bengal in 1905 was in full swing at the time, and the strike coincided with the first arrests of the leaders of the network of revolutionary organisations.

It has been suggested that the timing of the strike which caused information panic was deliberate rather than coincidental. If that is indeed so, Trevor Berrington clearly holds a place in Indian history that is greater than merely being its first tennis champion.

Two years after Berrington won at Lahore, Calcutta hosted the first Bengal Lawn Tennis Championships (BLTC) in 1887, which was to become an annual event. This tournament, organised by the Calcutta Cricket Club,[9] was played on courts marked out in the outfield of the Eden Gardens. Interestingly for the times, while the Calcutta Cricket Club itself was only open to the British, the BLTC was open to everyone. The eventual winner was, however, another British civil servant, L.C. Ogbourne. While Indian participation was not discouraged, it would be another two decades before an Indian made a real impact on the sport.

The year 1887 was important not only because the Calcutta event allowed all and sundry to participate, but because that same year, the event at Lahore introduced the first ladies singles event. Remarkably, this was also the same year that the ladies event was first staged at Wimbledon. A year later, the Punjab Lawn Tennis Championships went a step further and introduced the mixed doubles event.

For the next two decades, while Indians honed their skills on tennis courts around the country, these two championships remained the main events on the Indian tennis calendar.

THE ARRIVAL OF THE INDIAN MEN

Little has been known and written, until now, about the first two Indian men who receive mention in the early accounts of the sport. The facts that have emerged from researching this book shed new light on their careers, and confirm them as the earliest torch bearers of Indian tennis.

The mysterious B. Nehru who entered the Wimbledon Championships in 1905 as a British player and received a bye into the second round of the main draw qualifies as the first player of Indian origin at a major championship.* Nehru played two tournaments before Wimbledon, making it into

---

*This is the first time research has unearthed the fact that B. Nehru did play at Wimbledon and hence is confirmed as the first player of Indian origin to appear at a major championship. Thus far, Sardar Nihal Singh was credited with this feat.

the second round of the North London Championships (also called Gipsy) on grass. There he lost to E. Stanley of Great Britain 0-6, 3-6. He then went on to the Queens Club Tournament on grass and lost to John Flavelle in the first round, 1-6, 0-6, 1-6. At Wimbledon, for reasons unknown, he gave a bye to his opponent Robert Hough, but reached the Wimbledon Plate (the loser's consolation section) second round, before losing to Wilberforce Eaves. Eaves would go on to win the bronze medal at the London Olympics in 1908.

Three years later, the second Indian, Sardar Nihal Singh, not only entered but played in the main draw of Wimbledon, as he would do for three consecutive years. Singh is said to be of royal lineage, some accounts maintaining he was the son of Maharajah Sirdar Gulabh Singh. What is confirmed from the archives is that he did lose in the first round of the main draw at Wimbledon in both 1908 and 1909. In 1908, it was to Henry Wilson-Fox, 9-11, 2-6, 4-6. Wilson-Fox, a barrister-at-law, would go on to become a very influential journalist and eventually a British member of parliament representing the Conservatives.

The final year of Singh's appearance, 1910, saw him march into the third round where he lost a close encounter against Scottish player Geoffrey Dorling Roberts, 4-6, 5-7, 4-6. That year also saw Singh's best-ever tournament result when he made the semi-finals of the East Surrey Championships, a pre-Wimbledon event of the time.

Perhaps inspired by the examples of Nehru and Singh, the first crop of Indian players who made a real impact on the international arena would emerge immediately after this, from the domestic circuit back home.

Sardar Nihal Singh

In 1910, the first All-India Lawn Tennis Championships was played at the Gymkhana Club in Allahabad between the seventh and twelfth of February. While the surface on which it was played and the cities that staged it would undergo several changes as would its name, the championship itself would continue to be staged for the next seventy-two years.

In the men's finals, Edmund Atkinson defeated Lewis Seymour Deane, 7-5, 7-5, 7-5, in three closely fought sets.

LEWIS SEYMOUR DEANE

Lewis Seymour Deane, born in Meerut on 12 March 1882, is an important character in early Indian tennis, whose contribution has thus far remained largely unrecognised.

In 1909, the year before he made it to the finals of the All-India Championships, Lewis Deane, a banker then based in Allahabad[10] (registering himself as an Indian rather than British) had become the first Indian (born) tennis player to win the Punjab Lawn Tennis Championships, or indeed any major tennis tournament held in the country. But he narrowly lost to Edmund Atkinson in Calcutta at the Bengal Lawn Tennis Championships the following month, and would fail to defend his Punjab title in 1910, losing once again to the same opponent.

Deane would have to wait for five long years before his next triumph at the 1915 Bengal Championships when he defeated Francis Boxwell in a five-set encounter, 6-0, 4-6, 6-1, 4-6, 6-4.

In 1918, Deane had been promoted to the rank of captain in the 3rd Punjab Rifles,[11] but had not been involved in the war. His tennis career would continue to flourish in the meantime.

In 1921, Lewis Deane was to be part of an important moment in Indian tennis history. Playing alongside compatriots Mohammed Sleem, Ali Hassan Fyzee and Sydney Jacob, Deane shocked a strong French team and helped his country make it into the semi-finals of the Davis Cup. The famous victory had been possible largely through the efforts of Deane and Sleem. It was India's maiden entry into the

Davis Cup competition, and would immediately make the nation a serious contender for the future.

Deane participated at the 1911, 1921 and 1923 Wimbledon Championships, and failed to get past the first round in singles on each occasion. The best stretch of his tennis career was yet to come.

In 1921, after his early loss in the Wimbledon singles event, thirty-nine-year-old Deane paired with ICS officer and fellow Indian-born Englishman, Sydney Jacob, and stormed into the semi-finals of the Wimbledon doubles, thus becoming the first Indian pair to reach this stage. Here they lost narrowly after an exhausting five-set battle to the English brothers Arthur and Gordon Lowe.

Two years later, Deane once again reached the men's doubles semi-finals, this time partnering compatriot Hassan-Ali Fyzee. But once again, this is as far as he would go, losing to the English pair of Leslie Godfree and Randoph Lycett, the ultimate champions that year.

Lewis Deane then went a step further the next day. Partnering Dorothy Shepherd-Barron of Britain, Deane reached the Wimbledon mixed doubles final, becoming the first Indian tennis player to do so. There, the Indo-British pair lost to the British-American pairing of Randolph Lycett and Elizabeth Ryan (who was to win the women's doubles that year, partnering the legendary French player Suzanne Lenglen), 6-4, 7-5.

1923 would be Deane's career peak in terms of international competitions. He continued to reach the finals and the semi-finals of the major Indian events until finally laying down his racquet after losing to Edward Bobb at the All-India Championships in 1926. He was by then forty-four years old.

Lewis Deane, the first Indian-born tennis champion and playing throughout under the flag of the country of his birth, passed on in 1934 at Delhi, aged fifty-two.

THE FYZEE BROTHERS

Long before Vijay and Anand Amritraj took the country by storm with their achievements on the court, another pair of Indian siblings had made the world sit up and take notice of their prowess in the doubles format.

Born in Bombay four years apart in 1879 and 1883 respectively, Ali Azhar Hassanally (Hassan-Ali) Fyzee and Ali Athar Hassanally Fyzee were two of eight children brought into the world by Haji Hassanally bin Feyzhyder and Amirunnissa Fyzee. The Fyzee brothers were destined to form part of India's early group of world class tennis players.

Dr Hassan-Ali Fyzee

Ali Azhar Hassanally Fyzee (widely known as Hassan-Ali) was sent by his father to England to study medicine. Having duly qualified as a doctor and set up a practice, Hassan-Ali found himself excelling in the trio of racquet sports—tennis, badminton and table tennis, all three of which he had taken to playing socially at medical school.

In 1909, at the age of thirty, he made his first foray into competitive tennis at the Southfields tournament where he reached the quarter-finals, repeating the feat next year at the British Covered Court Championships. He also appeared at Wimbledon the same year, and made it to the second round of the event in 1910.

Playing largely in Britain, over the course of a career that eventually lasted nineteen seasons between 1909 and 1933 (with gaps due to the First World War), Hassan-Ali reached the finals of twenty-one singles events, winning ten of them. When he walked off the tournament court for the final time, he was fifty-four years old. His 65.7 per cent (223-116) win record in tournament singles continues to stand out among Indian tennis players a hundred years later.

In 1921, Hassan-Ali and his brother Athar-Ali joined Mohammed Sleem, Lewis Deane and Sydney Jacob as a part of India's first-ever Davis Cup team. Hassan-Ali did not play in the quarterfinals where India beat the formidable French team 4-1 on clay in Paris. His brother Athar-Ali partnered Lewis Deane to win one of the doubles encounters.

In the semi-finals, against a rampaging Japanese team on the grass courts at Lake Forest near Chicago, Hassan-Ali was brought into the mix given his years of experience of the surface in England. Unfortunately, the Japanese were too strong and experienced for the Indians, with Hassan-Ali losing both his singles and a hard-fought five-setter doubles match partnering Deane, coming back from two sets down to level scores but unable to capture the fifth. Over the course of the next six years, Hassan-Ali was to play eleven Davis Cup ties for India, winning four out of seventeen singles and six out of elven doubles matches.

Tennis was, however, far from being the only sport that this remarkable medical man excelled in. Hassan-Ali made his first international appearance in badminton at the All-England Championships in 1923 at the age of forty-four. Marching into the quarter-finals with his deft placements and consistency, Hassan-Ali eventually bowed out to the speed and finesse of Ireland's Frank Devlin, then twenty-three years old. Devlin would go on to win eighteen All-England titles (across formats) between 1925 and 1931 and become the second most successful player ever in the history of the Championships. Two years later, Hassan-Ali once again played the All-England Championships, but at forty-six, fast-paced competitive badminton was becoming more difficult to keep up with, and he lost to Arthur Kenneth Jones of England, that edition's doubles winner.

Badminton done, table tennis beckoned.

The following year, in 1926, Hassan-Ali joined his brother as a part of the Indian squad at the first World Table Tennis Championships in London. The team of six players—Hassan-Ali Fyzee, Athar-Ali Fyzee, T.A. Dawn, Peermahomed, W. Ernest and S.R.G. Suppiah won the bronze medal in the team championships. In the singles, Hassan-Ali reached the quarter-finals, beating his brother, but lost to eventual finalist Mechlovits of Hungary (the Hungarians dominated table tennis at the time). Compatriot Suppiah went one better, bowing out to Mechlovits in the semi-finals.

That year, Hassan-Ali was appointed the president of the Table Tennis Federation of India, and would continue to be an administrator of the sport for some time to come, holding posts in the International Table Tennis Federation.

Dr Athar-Ali Fyzee

Following in the footsteps of his brother, Ali Athar Hassanally Fyzee (often called Athar-Ali), four years younger, also qualified as a doctor and started playing competitive tennis in 1909 at the age of twenty-six. He would continue to appear on the circuit until 1934, when he retired at the age of fifty-one. By then, he had won thirteen tournaments of the sixty that he had participated in, including fifteen appearances at Wimbledon. Remarkably, between 1910 and 1920, Athar-Ali did not play any competitive tennis, choosing to concentrate on building a medical career.

Back playing the sport he loved, Athar-Ali, appearing after his decade-long self-imposed exile, helped India beat France to make the semi-finals on her maiden Davis Cup appearance. He was also a part of the team that reached the quarter-finals the following year. In 1923, he had his best result at Wimbledon, reaching the third round. He then played for India at the 1924 Olympic Games and won the team bronze for India at the World Table Tennis Championships in 1926 for good measure.

The two remarkable brothers—both doctors by profession, both proficient at the highest levels of multiple sports, passed away in London within a year of each other, Hassan-Ali in December 1962 and Athar-Ali in November 1963. Their names may have been largely lost to history, but accounts of the exploits of the Fyzee brothers deserve to be revived, for they together brought India into the global limelight in multiple sports at a time when the native talents of the nation had been largely overshadowed by the sporting prominence of the colonial masters.

*The 1925 Indian Davis Cup team. Sitting: Dr A.A. Fyzee,
Sydney Jacob, Jagat Mohan Lal. Standing: Dr A.H. Fyzee*

COTA RAMASWAMI

One of the most remarkable early men of Indian tennis,
and indeed sports in India, was Cota Ramaswami. Hailing
from an illustrious sporting family in Madras, and son of the
'Father of South Indian Cricket', Mothavarapu 'Buchi Babu'
Naidu, Ramaswami remains the only international sportsman
to represent India both in tennis and in cricket.

Buchi Babu co-founded the Madras United Club (MUC),
and was captain of the cricket team until his untimely passing
in 1908. He encouraged the best young up-and-coming
players from the local colleges to join the club, imported
all the equipment for them and paid for it personally, and

encouraged them to become good cricketers. Ramaswami recounts an early lesson from his father in his autobiography, *Ramblings of a Games Addict*, 'When the Madras Cricket Club (MCC) asked my father to play a match, he told them that he would do so only if his team members were allowed to use the pavilion and have lunch with them. It was only after they had agreed, he consented to play against them. After that, all other clubs were also allowed to use the pavilion.' Unfortunately, both his parents passed away in 1908, relatively young, within months of each other. Brought up by a guardian, Ramaswami and his two brothers (he was the youngest) went through school and college, excelling in cricket and hockey.

In 1919, he was accepted by both Oxford and Cambridge, but chose to join Pembroke College in Cambridge which had a strong sports culture. At Cambridge, by the time the first term ended, Ramaswami found the only sport that he could participate in during the winter was tennis, played on the hard courts just outside the university. He soon made his way into the university's tennis team.

At the end of the summer term and about ten days before the all-important Oxford-Cambridge match, an open university championship was held for the Doherty Cup. Ramaswami became the first freshman and the first Indian to win the Doherty Cup. This was to change the course of his tennis career. Over the next year and more, Ramaswami notched up impressive victories, earned his full Blue in 1921, and was soon playing tournaments around England including his first Wimbledon Championships.

By 1922, his improvement on the circuit had been noticed, and Ramaswami found himself a part of the Indian Davis

Cup team alongside the Fyzee brothers. In the first round, India beat Romania 5-0 on grass at the Beckenham Cricket Club in England. The Fyzee brothers played the singles, while Ramaswami partnered Hassan-Ali in the doubles, beating the Romanian pair 6-2, 6-4, 6-0.

In the quarter-finals a month later, the Indians ran up against Spain. Leading Spain was its first great tennis player, Manuel Alonso Areizaga, Wimbledon finalist the previous year, and four-time quarter-finalist at the US Championships. India lost 1-4, but the lone victory came in the doubles (a pattern that readers may note would often repeat even a century later). It was Ramaswami, playing some brilliant tennis alongside Hassan-Ali Fyzee, who made this possible. Exhibiting scintillating strokes and fighting every step of the way for national pride, Fyzee and Ramaswami prevailed 3-6, 7-5, 11-9, 8-10, 6-4.

Ramaswami never played Davis Cup for India again, thus becoming one of the few Indians to have an unblemished record in the competition. Appeared twice, won twice.

There were, however, other life experiences to be had from the tennis that remained to be played.

In May 1923, a combined Oxford and Cambridge University team visited the United States to play Harvard, Yale, Princeton, Stanford and Texas at Newport, Rhode Island. It was Ramaswami's first brush with racism in a white world he had thought was his to waltz into, given his privileged upbringing and experiences in Europe. He describes in his autobiography, *Ramblings of a Games Addict*, his experiences in New York:

'In the reception office (of the Vanderbilt Hotel), we were given our room numbers and keys and shown the lift by which we could go. As soon as I reached it, the man in charge looked at me and told me that the lift for me was on the other side. When I went there, I found that the lift was intended for coloured servants working at the hotel. I was, therefore, put out and complained immediately to Jim Lowry, our captain. He informed the manager who profusely apologised and pleaded ignorance on part of the lift man.'

The world outside the hotel was no less complicated. 'I had asked the hotel management to reserve a seat in the stalls of the best theatre in New York. They did so and gave me the ticket two days in advance. On the day of reservation, I presented the ticket at the entrance. The ticket examiner looked at me and saying there was some mistake went away with my ticket and came back again with another and showed me a different entrance, which I found, was intended for negroes.' Ramaswami goes on to lament: 'When such humiliating experiences were narrated, our hosts would not believe that such things could happen.'

Back in England by end of July 1923, he stayed in London to prepare for the final examinations at Cambridge. At the end of September, Ramaswami was invited by an England international, D.M. Greig, to join him as a doubles partner at the Roland Garros Covered Court Championships. There was, however, a small problem. Ramaswami's passport was still in Cambridge, and to make it to Paris, they had to leave the same day. The solution is testimony to the efficacies of the long-standing Indian practice of 'jugaad',* and what transpired would be unimaginable in today's world.

---

*Translates loosely to finding an innovative solution

Ramaswami writes: 'He (Grieg) said that the passport officers could not make out the difference between one Indian and another so I might borrow someone else's passport. It was, indeed, a very risky thing to do but I asked Dr (Hassan-Ali) Fyzee to lend me his passport which he readily gave. The tournament was a big one and Cochet, Lacoste, Borotra and Brugnon, the well-known "Four Musketeers of France" were playing. Greig and myself were beaten in the semi-finals by Lacoste and Borotra. I returned to London by air and till I passed through the passport offices in Paris and London, I was feeling extremely nervous and guilty. Fortunately, the passport officers automatically passed me and I felt so happy and relieved when I reached my destination. I profusely thanked Dr Fyzee for his passport and returned it to him.'

Returning to Madras after his graduation, Ramaswami received an appointment as the assistant director of agriculture in 1924.

A year later, while working in the South Arcot district, he went out fowl shooting with two other local government officials. Walking to retrieve a fallen fowl, he suddenly heard the sound of another shot, and looking down found a deep wound between his right elbow and wrist. The shotgun in the hands of one of his colleagues had gone off accidentally. Rushed to hospital, it was found that the bones had compound fractures and about sixty lead pellets were embedded in the bones between the wrist and the elbow. Although the arm did heal eventually, competitive tennis was now only a pipe dream. But there was a second sporting career he was destined to have.

In November 1926, Ramaswami came into the limelight playing against Bombay for the MUC. Soon after, when

Arthur Gilligan's team came to play in India, the Hindus, a team that played in the Bombay Quadrangular (the predecessor of the Ranji Trophy), requested his services. While he did not set the world on fire, the first step towards international cricket had been taken.

A full decade after he had played against Gilligan's team, on 26 July 1936, against all odds, at the age of forty, Cota Ramaswami would walk out to bat at Old Trafford wearing an Indian cap. With scores of 40 and 60 in the two innings of his first Test match, playing in two of the three Tests India played on that tour, Ramaswami emerged with a magnificent batting average of 56.66, the highest for an Indian batsman on that tour. He never played for India again, though.

Cota Ramaswami is a man often forgotten in the pages of Indian sporting history. That is travesty indeed, for a 100 per cent win-loss record in Davis Cup matches combined with a Test batting average of 56.66 should justly have made him an icon of Indian sports to be remembered and honoured.

Sadly, but perhaps fittingly, the final chapter of the Ramaswami story would be as unpredictable as the life that he led. In 1985, aged eighty-nine, Cota Ramaswami, still firm and erect in posture, walked out of his Chennai home and disappeared. He was never seen again. Through his disappearance, as in his life, Cota Ramaswami would remain an enigma.[12]

S.M. 'Rainbow' Hadi

Following in the footsteps of Ramaswami came another remarkable sportsman whose life and career would parallel Ramaswami's in many ways.

Syed Mohammad Hadi was born in 1899 in Hyderabad. His father, Captain Syed Mohammed, an officer of the Paigah army in Hyderabad State, died when Hadi was just two years old. The family of Sir Asman Jah, the former prime minister of Hyderabad State, adopted Hadi, and he grew up alongside Nawab Moin-ud-Dowlah, who would go on to become a leading patron of sports in Hyderabad.

Very early on, the Jah family realised that Hadi had an extraordinary aptitude for sports. He had learned horse riding and become an accomplished polo player. At the same time he represented Nizam College in football and also displayed an aptitude for cricket. Appearing at the Hyderabad Tennis Tournament in 1921 more as a lark than with any serious intent, Hadi emerged the winner, defeating local rival Zainul Abijin, 6-2, 6-1. The family arranged for him to be educated in England so he could give full expression to his athletic abilities.

Arriving in Cambridge, Hadi enrolled at Peterhouse and immediately displayed his proficiency at tennis. Gathering that his game was perhaps of a higher standard than he had realised, Hadi took the decision to work at becoming a Cambridge Blue.* During his time there, playing alongside Ramaswami, he helped Cambridge beat Oxford as well as several visiting teams from leading American universities. Not only was he awarded the Blue for tennis, but he also earned university colours in hockey, football and table tennis.

---

*Athletes at the University of Cambridge may be awarded a full blue (or simply a blue), half blue, first team colours or second team colours for competing at the highest level of university sport, which must include being in a varsity match or race against the University of Oxford. A full blue is the highest honour that can be bestowed on a Cambridge athlete.

A reflection of how close Hadi and Ramaswami were at the time is reflected in the fact that the latter repeatedly refers to 'my brother S.M. Hadi' in his book when describing his own tennis career during the period.

Matt Worth writes about Hadi in a 2016 article in the Cambridge newsletter, *Varsity*: 'The wardrobe in his room at Peterhouse must have been bursting with light blue jackets, as he shone at polo, tennis, soccer, field hockey, cricket and table tennis. A particularly fine tennis player, it is at the racquet game that his sporting career perhaps hit its greatest heights, as he played at Wimbledon five times, reaching the doubles quarter-final in 1926. He also represented India at the 1924 Summer Olympics and in the Davis Cups of 1925 and 1926. The run of representative appearances for his country must have more than made up for his frustration at being denied the Light Blues' tennis captaincy on account of his nationality.'

Hadi's best run at Wimbledon would come in 1924 when he entered the third round. Here, in a hard-fought encounter, he lost 5-7, 3-6, 3-6 to Jean Rene Lacoste. Lacoste eventually finished runners up that year, losing to fellow musketeer, Jean Borotra, in a gruelling five-set match, 1-6, 6-3, 1-6, 6-3, 4-6.

The same year Hadi represented India at the Paris Olympics and bowed out to eventual quarter-finalist Richard Norris 'Dick' Williams of the United States. Williams was a fascinating man. He had been a two-time US and one-time Wimbledon singles champion, besides picking up four Grand Slam doubles and mixed doubles titles. And he had done all this after surviving the sinking of the R.M.S. Titanic in 1912.

1924 was the only Olympics Hadi played in, and it was unfortunate he had come up against a player of Williams' pedigree so early in the draw. But in the doubles event, Hadi went a step further.

The main doubles pair for India at the Olympics that year was the formidable combination of Sydney Jacob and Mohammed Sleem. They did not, however, progress beyond the first round, and instead, marching into the quarter-finals was the unfancied duo of Hadi and young Daniel Rutnam. Rutnam, a cricketer and tennis player of Ceylonese origin, would also later represent India at Wimbledon and go on to become a senior civil servant of the Ceylon Civil Service.

In the quarter-finals, the inexperienced duo ran up against the world's top doubles combination of the age, France's Jean Borotra and Rene Lacoste. A 2-6, 2-6, 3-6 result was not unexpected, thus putting to rest India's chance of a first Olympics tennis medal, for which the country would have to wait another seventy-four years and the arrival of a certain Leander Paes.

As if his proficiency in tennis was not enough to get along with, back in India, in the midst of his tennis career, Hadi made his first-class debut in cricket for Hyderabad against the Maharajkumar of Vizianagram's XI in the Moin-ud-Dowlah Gold Cup semi-final of 1930-31, the trophy named after his childhood friend, played at Secunderabad.

Four years later the 'Cricket Championship of India' kicked off in 1934 for the cup that would forever carry the name of India's first cricketing superstar—K.S. Ranjitsinhji. In the third match of the first ever Ranji Trophy Championship, facing Madras' score of 301, Hadi walked in to bat with his team tottering at 12/3. He made 132 not out in his team's score of 227, becoming the first ever centurion in the history of the Ranji Trophy. Not only was this his maiden first-class century, but it was also his debut in the tournament.

Hadi's grand nephew, Abbas Ali Baig, appropriately enough holds the distinction of being Indian cricket's youngest and indeed, the first century-maker in Test cricket while making his debut abroad. Baig had unexpectedly been drafted into the Indian team for the Test match midway through the series, while studying at Oxford University in 1959, and had stroked his way to a magnificent 112.

In doing so, Baig carried on the family tradition so to speak, moving the bar just a bit higher to Test cricket. A charming, handsome man (as he continues to be today at the age of eighty), Baig also holds the distinction of being the first Indian cricketer to be kissed on a cricket pitch (in Mumbai) during a Test match.

The charm clearly flows in the family genes. Baig tells me a story about his mother's uncle that bears this out in ample measure. While at Oxford, young Baig would spend the two weeks of Wimbledon, riveted to his seat in a coveted Centre Court box. He recalls, 'Hadi had an admirer called Lady Swaythling who had a box in her name at Wimbledon Centre Court to which I got invited throughout the tournament. [I] got to witness some memorable matches including [the] Hoad–Rosewall final.'[13]

What Baig may not have fully appreciated was that Hadi's 'admirer', Lady Swaythling, had been an important person in Britain during the two world wars. Born in Belfast, Northern Ireland, in 1879, she married Louis Montagu when she was nineteen. As Lord and Lady Swaythling, they were leading members of the Anglo-Jewish community and leading figures in English society. Lady Swaythling had a lifelong friendship with Queen Mary and donated her time and money generously and worked tirelessly for causes that helped uplift lives of women. She also donated a country house, and later, their own home for use as a sanatorium for the injured, and herself took care of them, to the extent that she became know as the 'British godmother' among American naval enlisted men.[14]

Even after he retired from active life on the courts and fields, Syed Mohammed Hadi continued to be deeply involved in sports. Along with a few others, Hadi founded the Hyderabad Cricket Association and Hyderabad Football Association in 1934, with himself as the first secretary. He became the director of physical education in Hyderabad and later, joint secretary of education in the Indian government. He was National Commissioner of Boy Scouts of India and when the All India National Council of Sports was founded in 1959, he became the first secretary. The runners-up trophy of the Moin-ud-Dowlah Gold Cup tournament is now called the S.M. Hadi Memorial Trophy.

Abbas Ali Baig recounts to me an amusing anecdote that occurred towards the end of Hadi's life that truly sums up the colourful life of the man.

Towards the end of the 1960, Hadi had a visit from an astrologer who convinced him that the end of his client's life was near and predicted an exact date and time of his demise. Months of preparation ensued, and friends and family gathered around for his passing. The only thing that passed, however, was the time determined by the astrologer.

Baig was unable to recall what ensued thereafter between the soothsayer and his customer. Hadi would live on for another year or so before the almighty finally found time for him.

Although he passed on in 1971, Syed Mohammed Hadi lives on fondly in the minds of Indian sports lovers as 'Rainbow Hadi', the man who played seven sports—cricket, tennis, hockey, football, table tennis, chess and polo—some more proficiently than others, but each of them competitively, and with tremendous passion and dedication. Never again would the nation be blessed with an all-round sportsperson of such class.

OTHER EARLY STARS OF INDIAN TENNIS

While Deane, Sleem, Ramaswami, Hadi and the Fyzee brothers, along with the two stalwarts the following chapters are dedicated to, were the outstanding stars of the Indian tennis firmament at the time, there were indeed others in the 1920s and '30s who deserve honourable mention.

One of the members of the 1925 Davis Cup team was **Jagat Mohan Lal.** He was a doubles specialist winning the All India Lawn Tennis Championships in 1925, partnering Jasbir Singh (the victory that put Lal into the Davis Cup team), and the Punjab Championship four times with Mohammed Sleem (1924-26, 1930). He also reached the fourth round in singles at Wimbledon in 1925.

Sohan Lal of Lahore, from all contemporary accounts, was a gritty fighter, refusing to give up points even under extreme pressure. This would help him pick up two Punjab Championships singles titles in 1932 and 1933 before winning his maiden All India Championships in 1934. With little international tennis being played at the time (India skipped the Davis Cup between 1935 and 1937), and it being easier for the London-based players to travel to the Davis Cup ties when India did indeed play, Lal and his contemporaries like **P.L. Mehta**, the All India Championships winner in 1929, never got a chance to represent their country.

The Bobb Brothers from Allahabad, born into an Anglo-Indian family, were two of the best players of those two decades. **Stanford Wilson (S.W.) Bobb** played a doubles tie for India in the Davis Cup in 1926. On the domestic circuit, he won the All India Championships twice—singles in 1921 and doubles in 1926.

His younger brother, **E.V. Bobb**, an English teacher at a Bombay school, was a more accomplished player. He was ranked no. 1 in India in 1934-35 and again in 1936-37, winning the All India Championships on five occasions in 1926, 1927, 1930, 1933 and 1937. He played two Davis Cup ties in 1928 with a 1-4 win-loss record.

D.N. Kapoor, with one of the most devastating forehands and aggressive approaches of the time, won the All India Championships singles and doubles titles in 1931. He followed up by defending his singles title the next year, defeating another prominent player of the time, **Ahad Hussain**, both years, renowned equally for his tennis and his Urdu poetry. Kapoor also won the mixed doubles in 1932, partnering Jenny Sandison.

Krishna Prasad, an Oxford Blue, played for India in the Davis Cup in 1927 and 1932. A doubles specialist, he won the All India Championships doubles title in 1921 and the mixed doubles titles in 1923 and 1926 besides picking up the Bengal Championships in 1926. He then passed the Indian Civil Services examination and had a long career with the ICS before retiring as director general of posts and telegraphs.

Hira Lal Soni was a member of the Indian Davis Cup teams of 1928 and 1930. He also won three Punjab Championships doubles titles, one partnering Mohammed Sleem and the other S.L.R. Sawhney. Soni's teammate in the 1930 Davis Cup squad was **Atri Madan Mohan** from Lahore, a Cambridge Blue. Madan Mohan won the Punjab Championships singles title in 1930.

Another doubles specialist who paired with Sawhney to win the Punjab Championships in 1936 was **Krishnaswami**. Much of his tennis was played in Ceylon and the south Indian tournaments.

The final player on this list, **S.L.R. Sawhney**, Soni's doubles partner, deserves more than a passing mention. He was no. 2 in India, behind the mighty Ghaus Mohammed, between 1937 and 1939 and remains the only man to play for India in the Davis Cup both before and after independence, in 1938 and 1948 respectively. In later life, as an administrator, Sawhney would hold the post of the AITA Secretary in 1958–59.

MOHAMMED SLEEM
THE FIRST INDIAN TENNIS SUPERSTAR

'Aren't you too old to play tennis?' I asked him. 'I play only doubles, two sets. But I think I can take you on for a singles match.' He was in his eighties and I still in my forties. 'Dinner's on the winner,' he said. He had no difficulty in beating me 6-1, 6-3.

—Khushwant Singh

In 1915, when Lewis Deane, fresh from his triumph at Calcutta at the Bengal Lawn Tennis Championships, reached the finals of the Punjab Championships at Lahore after a hard-fought five-set victory in the semis, he may well have been forgiven for considering that this tournament too was in the bag. Deane's nemesis, Atkinson, three-time winner and defending champion, had been knocked out in the semis by a relatively unknown local twenty-three-year-old Punjabi boy, Mohammed Sleem.

On 13 February 1915, with an effortless 6-3, 6-2, 6-3 straight sets victory in Lahore over Lewis Deane, Mohammed Sleem became the first native Indian to win a major championship in India and stamp his name firmly in the annals of Indian tennis. His would be a journey that would inspire players for generations to come.

Born in Multan in 1892 into a wealthy family from Lahore, Mohammed Sleem was sent to Cambridge to study law by his father Sheikh Mohammed Umar. Sleem practised criminal law in England as a barrister, having been inducted into the Lincoln's Inn in 1910, at the remarkably young age of eighteen.*

Sleem spoke his mother tongue Punjabi fluently, and would become equally proficient in Urdu in the coming years given his successful law practice at Lahore. But English was what he was most comfortable in, given his upbringing and education, and England was where he would thrive in the initial years, first as a lawyer and then as a tennis player.

Tennis had been a passion from childhood and Cambridge gave Sleem the opportunity to hone his game. The first tournament at which Sleem played was the London Covered Court Championships at the Queen's Club in April 1913, losing in straight sets to Alfred Beamish on the club's wooden surface, in the second round. Repeated (but unsubstantiated) references talk of Sleem also participating that year at a minor grass court tournament at Craigside that he is supposed to have won.[15]

The Punjab Championship in 1915 would be Mohammed Sleem's first major victory. The following year he again beat Deane, this time in the semi-finals, over four sets and went on to defend his title, snuffing out the challenge of Sydney

---

*The Honourable Society of Lincoln's Inn is one of the four Inns of Court in London to which barristers of England and Wales belong. It is recognised to be one of the world's most prestigious professional bodies of judges and lawyers.

Jacob, another up and coming Indian player, in the final. In 1919, Sleem won his fifth successive title at Lahore, this time beating Jagat Mohan Lal in the final. Over the next decade and more, he would add three more championships at Lahore.

Mohammed Sleem in 1921

THE PEAK YEARS, 1921–1924

By 1921 Sleem had long been a force to reckon with in India, and that year he decided he was ready for the big stage. England beckoned.

That summer Sleem reached the finals of the Queen's Club Tournament before losing to the legendary Japanese player Zenzo Shimidzu, ranked no. 4 in the world. Shimidzu had been a Wimbledon finalist the previous year, and would make the semi-finals again a few weeks later. Interestingly, Shimidzu was at the time working for Mitsui & Co. and was based in Calcutta.

Appearing then for the first time at Wimbledon, Sleem did well to get to the fourth round where he lost to American player Francis Townsend (Frank) Hunter. In a remarkable first set, Sleem, displaying brilliant touch tennis, had prevailed 6-2 over a stunned Hunter. But his more experienced opponent came back strongly to win in four closely fought sets. Hunter would go on to win an Olympic gold for the United States in 1924, reach three Grand Slam singles finals and pick up five Grand Slam doubles and mixed doubles titles before he turned professional in 1931.

Just a few weeks after his fourth-round loss at Wimbledon, Sleem joined Lewis Deane, Dr A.H. Fyzee and Sydney Jacob as members of the first Indian team to play the Davis Cup. The venue was Paris, the opponents the formidable French on their favoured surface, clay.

Sleem was at the top of his game and won both his singles encounters. Three-time French Championships finalist and France's no. 1 player Jean-Pierre Samazeulth had beaten Sydney Jacob in the opening singles, but went down in straight sets to Sleem. Lewis Deane won both his matches and India breezed past the shell-shocked French into the semi-finals.

'Big' Bill Tilden, one of the greatest tennis players of all time, wrote in his book, *The Art of Lawn Tennis*, 'India sprang a sensation by defeating France in their match in Paris. Sleem, Jacob and Deane showed great promise for the future.'[16] Tilden would go on to call Sleem the 'best baseline player in the world'.

Two weeks later the semi-finals of the competition were played at Chicago in the United States, on grass. India lost 0-5 to the extremely powerful Japanese team. Notwithstanding the loss, this had been a superlative performance from Sleem and his teammates in their first-ever outing for the country, and it firmly put India on the tennis map.

The best run of Sleem's career continued at the Sussex Championships in September 1921 when he emerged victorious against fellow Indian Cota Ramaswami in straight sets, 6-4, 6-3, 6-0. There is a back story here worth recounting.

A few weeks before proceeding to Paris for the Davis Cup encounter with France, Sleem visited Cambridge, where he had once been a student. A match was arranged between him and Ramaswami, the current tennis star of the university. We have a wonderful account of the encounter in Ramaswami's autobiography.

He starts by describing Sleem's game (one of the few descriptive accounts that survive): 'He [Sleem] was a slim but strong and wiry man who had plenty of stamina and played tennis more with his brains than with the racket. He had a very unattractive and ugly style and most of his strokes went two feet above the net and they were not too hard. His services looked simple and slow but he placed them deep and intelligently. He had wonderful control of his ground strokes and whenever he wanted and found it necessary, he would hit the ball hard and place accurately.'

Ramaswami goes on: 'Sleem agreed to play against me and all the Indian students turned up in large numbers to watch the game because they thought I would beat him easily. I was also very confident of beating him because watching him play from outside, it looked to me that I could sweep him off the court by my hard services and ground strokes and crisp volleying at the net. I strutted on to the court like a proud peacock while Sleem stepped in meekly.' The match, however, was not destined to go quite along the lines young Ramaswami had planned.

'When the game started, I was trying to show off by hitting the balls hard while he was just hitting the balls back softly. I served first and I tried to serve hard but he was returning them effortlessly and winning point after point by making me commit mistakes. I did not bother at first because I thought that when I warmed up and got going, I could win points as I liked but before I knew what was happening, he had taken the first set without conceding a single game. I was then getting worried because I thought I was letting down my admirers and so with added vigour, I tried to blow him off court in the second set, but the harder I hit the easier it was for him not only to return the ball but to place in such a way that I could not send my next return effectively. If I rushed up to the net, he passed me with great ease and if I stayed back and played a baseline game, he relished it more because he went on returning the ball steadily as though the balls were hitting a wall and coming back while I could not keep up a rally more than two or three times. It was obvious that while I was impetuous, inexperienced and immature, he was like an iceberg, very calm, deliberate, calculating and precise. He beat me 6-0, 6-0, 6-0 and I walked out of the court crestfallen, humbled and humiliated.'[17]

Two weeks later, Sleem won the Hendon tournament at the London Country Club, this time on clay, against Sydney Jacob. A week later, it was the turn of Walter Crawley of England to suffer a defeat at the hands of the rampaging Sleem at the Welsh Covered Court Championships in Craigside. In less than two weeks, the hapless Crawley was to go down again to Sleem in four sets in the finals of the London Covered Court Championships, the tournament that had marked the beginning of Sleem's tennis career in 1913.

By the close of the year, an unofficial ranking placed Mohammed Sleem at no. 7 in the world,[5] the highest any Indian would achieve for the next three decades until Ramanathan Krishnan burst onto the scene.[18]

Continuing his rich vein of form, Sleem went on to win, what would remain his only All India Championships in 1922, defeating Harry Samuel Lewis-Barclay in the final. Lewis-Barclay had served as a captain in the Australian Imperial Forces in the First World War, and transferred to the Indian Army in 1917. He went on to play at five Wimbledon Championships, reaching the quarter-finals in 1925. Besides tennis, Lewis-Barclay was also a gifted opening bowler and twice dismissed MCC captain Arthur Gilligan, when his team visited India in 1926.

In September 1924, Mohammed Sleem was again in his elements as he swept into the finals of the South of England Championships. There he met Britain's Francis Gordon Lowe.

Lowe had been the Australasian Championships winner in 1915, had won the Queen's Club thrice and the World

Covered Court Championships in 1920. He had been a semi-finalist at Wimbledon the previous year. But that September day of 1924 he ran into a Mohammed Sleem in sublime touch on the grass courts of Eastbourne. Sleem prevailed in straight sets, 6-2, 6-1, 6-1.

A week later, Sleem, in what would be his last championship victory outside India, won the Gleneagles Championships at Scotland on clay defeating Francis Marion (Frank) Bates Fisher of New Zealand in straight sets.[19] It is worth spending a moment on his colourful opponent.

By the time he came up against Sleem, Fisher was already forty-seven years old and had been an Australasian Championships (the predecessor of the Australian Open) finalist in 1906. He had fought in the South African Boer War in 1902, and between 1905 and 1914 he had been a Member of Parliament from Wellington. During this stint he had earned himself the sobriquet of 'Rainbow Fisher' by virtue of having changed political parties thrice during the period. After the First World War, Fisher stood for election in England as a Conservative candidate in Cheshire, and lost. Giving up on politics for good, Fisher went back to his interrupted tennis career at the age of forty-two. Clearly a gifted player, he went on to reach the second round of Wimbledon four times between 1919 and 1923, and in 1927, aged fifty, he finally bid adieu to the sport after his loss in the second round of the French Open.

1924 was the peak of Sleem's career. Earlier that year he had made it to the third round of Wimbledon before losing to Patrick Spence in four sets. At the Olympics he had taken India to the third round before a hard-fought five-set loss to the American, Vincent (Vinnie) Richards. Richards, perhaps the greatest volleyer of that decade, deprived him of the chances of a medal, and would go on to claim the gold in both the singles and doubles events that summer, adding the mixed doubles silver for good measure. Over a career spanning twenty-seven years, Richards would win seven Grand Slam doubles titles, four US Professional singles titles and reach five Grand Slam singles semi-finals. Mohammed Sleem's dreams of an Olympic medal could not have been denied by a more capable opponent.

The Illustrated Sporting and Dramatic News would write a glowing tribute to Sleem's craft, that mirrored Ramaswami's account:

That inexhaustible student of tactics, Mohammed Sleem, continues to win singles in this country. After capturing the Deauville Cup, he pocketed the singles at Torquay with consummate ease, then dived into Wales and swept a seaside town of prizes, going on to Worthing to beat that other patient product of India, Leighton Crawford. But make no mistake. Sleem may not have the speed of stroke which smashes an ordinary defence; his service may be a mere trickle compared with the torrent of Patterson, yet he can put the ball almost every time into a spot which is more embarrassing to his opponent than any other. His mind-reading is as quick and as faultless as any player I know, he is quite a master in the art of paralysing enterprise by offering soft stuff and then covering the point of reply. He took two sets from Vincent Richards at the Olympic tournament after that young man had beaten Alonso and Lacoste. To despise him as an opponent is to court disaster.[20]

Sleem ended the year with eight championship titles from nine finals in 1924. But with his career as a barrister taking off, never again would he regain the form that defined him these years at the peak of his sport.

Tennis and Law—A Life Worth Living

Between 1924 and 1928 Mohammed Sleem took a break from his tennis career to concentrate on his profession as a lawyer, and set up his law practice in Lahore. The only tournament he is recorded to have played during this period is the Punjab Championships in 1927, where he lost in a close four-set final encounter to Denis O'Callaghan, an Irish army officer then attached to the 2nd Punjab Regiment.

In 1928, Sleem once again found himself at Wimbledon. By winning the Wimbledon Plate (held at that time between players who had lost in the first and second rounds), defeating J.B. Gilbert of Britain in straight sets, Sleem became the first Indian tennis player to have won any title (albeit minor) at Wimbledon. It would be another twenty-six years before Ramanathan Krishnan's junior Wimbledon victory in 1954 would top that effort.

This run into the finals of the Lahore tournament combined with the Wimbledon plate victory appears to have spurred Mohammed Sleem to make a comeback on the circuit. He would go on to win three championships at Lahore over the next four years, reach the finals of the All India in 1930 and appear again at Wimbledon before reaching the fourth round at Roland Garros in 1934.

By this time Sleem was forty-two. But he doesn't appear to have slowed down. There is a wonderful snippet this author discovered in the archives of the *Portsmouth Evening News* well worth reproducing here. On 6 July 1934, talking about a local tournament held right after Wimbledon, the Lawn Tennis Review section of the newspaper would report:

> The tournament will be improved in standard bv the visit of the two Indian Davis Cup players, Dr A.H. Fyzee and Mohammed Sleem. These two famous exponents of the game have been competing at Wimbledon and will add pleasant element of uncertainty into the tournament. Whether or not either of them can wrest the title from E.C. Peters a matter upon which I cannot comment, as I have seen neither of them play.[21]

The reporter with the amusing pen name 'No Mad', went on: 'Sleem has probably a bigger reputation than his compatriot, and at the beginning of the season was considered something of a menace to the British Wimbledon brigade. Although he did not visit England until 1921, he is forty-two years of age, but still seems to be in the limelight of first-class tennis. Among his triumphs have been the South of England Championships 1924, the All-England Plate at Wimbledon 1928, and Punjab Championships thirteen times.'

There is no doubt that Sleem had lost none of his skill. *The Belfast Telegraph*, less than two weeks later, would write: 'Mohammed Sleem, the Indian Davis Cup player, is world renowned for his court craft, his subtle 'Sleeming'. To see him exploit this technique is an object lesson in what a first-rate eye and brain for ball games can accomplish against any kind of handicap.'[22]

Sleem would continue playing the circuit off and on, and it was only in 1940, at the age of forty-eight, when he lost in the quarter-finals of the All India Championships that he stepped away from competitive tennis. It was time to concentrate on his profession, and on living the full life.

Even before he had retired from tennis, however, Sleem was very much entrenched in his profession and a well-respected figure in Lahore legal circles. The evidence of his pre-eminence exists in several archived newspaper reports of the time of a famous trial in Punjab where Sleem was one of the judges.

The Yorkshire Post and Leeds Intelligencer reported in 1933:

Considerable importance is attached to the successful prosecution of the 'Punjab conspiracy case', which closes an ugly chapter in anarchist crime. The special tribunal for the case consisted of Mr Justice Blacker, a European, a Hindu, Rai Sahib Gangaram Soni, and a Moslem, Mohammed Sleem, the Indian Davis player. The case, which lasted three and a half years, involved 419 prosecution and 202 defense witnesses.

Twenty-one Hindu youths, being members of the Hindustan Republican Army, were charged with various offences including an attempt to blow up the Viceroy's train in 1929. The first clue to the case came with an explosion in a trunk carried by a young man in June 1930. The man bolted, but the contents of the trunk gave the police valuable information. The three judges, in an unanimous judgment covering 500 foolscap pages, traced the history of the terrorist conspiracy.

Hansraj, one of the chief organisers, had an inventive mind and evolved a scheme in which a number of houses were rented in different towns of the Punjab. Small decoy bombs were placed in them and were to be exploded by candle fuses at approximately the same time. On the police going to the scene of the explosion they would find a small box with handles and revolutionary literature on top. These boxes were declared to be 'booby traps' containing dangerous bombs, which would explode as soon as the box was lifted. The scheme succeeded, and resulted in the death of two police officers in Lyallpur and Gujranwalla respectively. The defence argued that the magistrates and witnesses were under the thumb of the police, gave false statements, and altered their original statements, but the tribunal remarked that a large number of defence witnesses were relations and friends of the police and were antagonistic to the police.

The judges differentiated between those accused who merely agreed to join the revolutionary party, and were not liable for acts to which they had not definitely agreed, and those accused who, having agreed generally, to the murder of persons, were responsible for the murders committed in pursuance of that agreement. They accordingly sentenced to death the brothers Amar Singh and Gulab Singh. Three men, Rupchand, Jehangirlal and Kundanlal, were sentenced to transportation, eleven were sentenced to varying terms from two to seven years' imprisonment and five were acquitted. All the accused, because of their social status, were placed as class one prisoners.[23]

Khushwant Singh, who knew Sleem well, wrote about his friend's life in Lahore: 'It was common knowledge that he had turned down the offer of being elevated to the Bench and had refused to accept a knighthood. He did not talk about them. He never talked about himself. His only pre-occupations were law, tennis and gourmet food. After spending his mornings and afternoons at the court, he drove to the Gymkhana Club and played tennis for a couple of hours. He had been India's number one player longer than anyone else and captained the Indian Davis Cup team for many years. After tennis, he joined his friends and their wives for tea. On his way back he stopped at Stiffles restaurant on the mall and discussed the menu for his dinner. He examined birds he was to be served—pheasant, grouse, partridge, quails or duck. He chose the appropriate French wine to go with his food. He proceeded homewards, had a bath and got into his dinner jacket. He ate his dinners alone, savouring his food and wine. After a cup of black coffee and cognac, he smoked a Havana cigar and went back for the night.'[24]

Sleem remained a bachelor throughout his life, but continued to enjoy playing the sport he had excelled in. Khushwant Singh talks about the last time he met Sleem at Piccadilly Circus tube station in London, a couple of years before the latter passed on in 1980. It's a fascinating account notwithstanding Singh's recall of his own age at the time (he would have been in his sixties) of the encounter being off by about two decades. Singh's account sums up best the life and times of Mohammed Sleem, India's first tennis superstar:

> But for his greying hair, he had not aged. The same aquiline features—hawk-nosed, grey-eyed, athletic slim. We walked out together. I invited him to my home. We talked of our days in Lahore. I discovered he kept up his old schedule minus the law: he played tennis and enjoyed his special dinners. 'Aren't you too old to play tennis?' I asked him. 'I play only doubles, two sets. But I think I can take you on for a singles match.' He was in his 80s and I still in my 40s. 'Dinner's on the winner,' he said. We shook hands to confirm

the bet. He was a member of the Queen's Club, which had covered courts with wooden floors. He had no difficulty in beating me 6-1, 6-3. He had chosen a gourmet eatery in Soho. He ordered dinner for three with vintage French wine. It was a memorable feast.

SYDNEY MONTAGUE JACOB
CIVIL SERVANT TO GRAND SLAM
SEMI-FINALIST

JALLIANWALA BAGH, 13 APRIL 1919

It was the festival of Baisakhi and ten thousand men, women and children from in and around Amritsar had gathered at Jallianwala Bagh in the city. Most were there to celebrate the festival and a few had come to protest.

The First World War had ended the previous year, but the draconian Rowlatt Act that gave the government emergency powers to combat subversive activities had been extended. It was an act that aimed to snuff out any nationalistic activities. Mahatma Gandhi had called for a general strike in protest, and the British reacted by arresting prominent leaders. Amritsar had erupted in protest, and parts of the city were not fully under British control. Anticipating problems on the holiday, a ban on public gatherings in Amritsar had been passed, but the message was not widely dispersed.

As the people gathered were joyously celebrating the onset of the harvest season, Brigadier General Reginald Edward

Harry Dyer, tasked with maintaining peace by District Commissioner Miles Irving, walked in leading fifty soldiers armed with .303 Lee–Enfield bolt-action rifles, part of the troops he had moved the previous day from his regimental headquarters in nearby Jalandhar.

Jallianwala Bagh was a garden only in name. In reality, it was a plot of barren land, an irregular quadrangle surrounded by houses. It was, at the time, a private property whose main entrance was a narrow passage, and there were four other very small exit points. Dyer sealed off the exits, and marched in with his troops through the entrance. Then, without any warning, he ordered his troops to open fire on the crowd until all their ammunition was spent.

Between 379 to 1,000 men, women and children died from the indiscriminate firing. Dyer was to say in his testimony to the Hunter Committee a year later that his intention was to make a 'wide impression' and strike terror in the region.

Barely an hour after the massacre, blissfully unaware of what had transpired, Sydney Montague Jacob, director of agriculture in Amritsar, dropped into Miles Irving's office before leaving on a tour of the districts. While there, they received a call from Brigadier General Dyer's headquarters where they heard about what had happened.

Dyer confirmed that he had already wired lieutenant governor of the Punjab, Sir Michael O'Dwyer, on whose instructions he had brought his troops to Amritsar, and O'Dwyer had endorsed the action of the man he had sent (with Irving's consent) to manage the situation on the ground. The conversation shocked and incensed Jacob.

Sydney Jacob in 1921. Sydney Jacob's personal album, courtesy of Philip Jacob.

Sydney Jacob was a man whose approach to managing tense situations was vastly different from his colleagues. When he had been asked to accompany troops on a punitive action in a village near Lahore, he had pulled rank on the major and left him and his troops outside the village. Entering the village with two officers, he had amicably dealt with the little matter of some rebellious villagers having cut the telegraph wires. Dialogue and some reassurances had been sufficient to calm things down.

In his autobiography titled *Favour for Fools in a Decadent Empire*, Jacob speaks about how his view that it was the duty of the British government to develop the Indian people did not go down well. An account written by Donald Lehmann, a grand-nephew of Jacob's, takes this further:

> He joined the Indian Club which met with disapproval. Responsible for judging disputes at a magisterial level, he hit upon the novel idea of visiting the village where a dispute between two litigants had originated. After a talk in the presence of the village elders, the guilty party usually readily admitted his fault. Again, this did not go down well with those in higher authority.[25]

It was hardly surprising, therefore, that Brigadier General Dyer's actions at Jallianwala Bagh, and its obvious long-term ramifications, had shaken Sydney Jacob to the core.

Donald Lehmann's account, reconstructed from conversations he had with Sydney Jacob (then in his nineties), talks about what happened next:

> Though Dyer had wired the Lieutenant Governor of the Punjab, Sir Michael O'Dwyer, Jacob insisted that Irving should write out a full report. He eventually prevailed over both Dyer's and Irving's opposition and drove to Lahore to deliver the report, with a Sikh friend, Wathen, the principal of the Khalsa College for the sons of Indian princes. They arrived at 3 a.m. and awoke Sir Michael, who read the report and responded frostily to their comments.[26]

Sydney Jacob had done his best, but sadly, as history would prove, it had not been enough. He resigned his position in protest at the massacre, and was appointed superintendent of census operations, a job where he would enjoy interacting with the common man.

Brigadier General Dyer was censured and removed from service after he returned to England, and British troops forbidden from firing on civilians henceforth. Three decades later when partition riots erupted across the country, the British troops stood by with the Jallianwala Bagh sword hanging over their necks, their guns silenced.

THE EARLY DAYS

Born in Dalhousie in 1879, Sydney Montague Jacob was the eldest child of Lieutenant Colonel Sydney Long Jacob (born in Ahmedabad) and Elizabeth Petronella (born in Ceylon). In his autobiography he talks about his early childhood:

> The first ten years of my life were spent mostly on the banks of the Punjab canals, on which my father worked, firstly as Executive, then as Superintendent and finally, as Chief Engineer. The only schooling was that handed out by my eldest sister, Eveline, seven years older than myself, and that in rare sessions during the summer. In the winter, that is from October to May, we were travelling from place to place along the banks of the Chenab and Bari Doab canals.

Jacob was homeschooled until the age of eleven and then sent to a religious school in England, the Channel View School in Clevedon, Somerset, which he hated, particularly Sundays which were spent largely in hymns and prayer. 'The deadly monotony of those Sundays was a crime against a child's natural desire for physical and mental development,' he writes in his account. Eventually, like all things, this torture too ended, and he got a prestigious Mathematics scholarship to University College London. Jacob then joined the Indian Civil Service at the age of twenty-three and returned to India, where his heart was.

Unlike most Indian-born Englishmen of his day, Jacob truly believed he was Indian and tried to help his people from within the system. In his first posting to the Jalandhar Division, he suggested to the deputy commissioner, Sir Michael Fenton, that it was the duty of the British government to develop the Indian people. Neither that, nor his action of joining the Indian Club, went down particularly well with his boss.

What the latter move did, however, was increase his interaction with the Indian tennis fraternity as he indulged in the sport he had honed his talents at while in England.

A GLORIOUS TENNIS CAREER

While the ultra-religious school did not give much opportunity to indulge in sports, Jacob's first forays into tennis came at a friend's house at the age of sixteen and over the next seven years, the only games he could get were against his brother in the summer.

A decade later when Jacob moved back to India in 1903, he had access to the tennis courts at the clubs and the Army Cantonments in Punjab, and with the Punjab Championships in full swing, he had no shortage of high quality partners to practise with. However, given his assignments in the Agriculture Department, much of his time was spent outside Lahore, where the championship was held.

By 1907, encouraged by his ability to beat celebrated local players back in India in a non-competitive environment,

Jacob decided to enter his first competitions that summer. At the South of England Championships that September, Jacob came out of a field of fifty-six players to make the quarter-finals of the grass court event at Eastbourne. George Hillyard, who beat Jacob, would go on to win the tournament.

A month later, on the indoor wooden courts of the London Queen's Club Covered Court Championships at Eastbourne, he bowed out in four sets in the second round, and success would be hard to come by the next two years. In 1912, appearing at the All India Championships for the first time, Jacob made it to the semi-final where he lost to eventual winner H.W. Davies. Davies had also won the All-England Badminton Championships a decade earlier, the world's premier badminton event.

For much of the decade Jacob's appearances continued to be sporadic, based on how often he could get away from his administrative duties, and it was not until 1917, when he was thirty-eight, that he would come into his own as a serious tennis player at the highest levels. That year, he made it to the final of the Punjab Championships, beating Lewis Deane in the semi-finals. But in the finals he came up against a rampaging Mohammed Sleem, who brushed aside Sydney's challenge on the way to his third successive victory at Lahore.

It was not, however, the end of the road at Lahore for Jacob that year. An equivalent of the All England Plate at Wimbledon had, over the years, been added to the Punjab Championships. The Raja of Chamba (a kingdom in today's Himachal Pradesh that traces its royal lineage back to 550 CE), Shri Bhuri Singh, a serious tennis tragic and patron of the sport and indeed of the arts in general, had instituted the Challenge Cup. Unlike the All England Plate, which was meant for losers in the first two rounds at Wimbledon, the Challenge Cup at Lahore was to be played by only those players who had lost to the eventual winner that year on their way to the Championship title.

Jacob not only won that year, but went on to lift the trophy a total of three times until 1919, and as per the rules of the competitions, being a three-time winner, he had the privilege of taking home the trophy permanently.

Sadly, Raja Bhuri Singh passed away in 1919, soon after he had handed the trophy for permanent safekeeping to Jacob. The (still) glittering silver trophy continues to remain in the Jacob family over a hundred years on.

The Challenge Cup trophy. Sydney Jacob's personal album, courtesy of Philip Jacob.

In fact, it was his tennis that eventually led to Jacob becoming an unwitting but intriguing side player of that momentous event in Indian history—the Jallianwala Bagh Massacre. As Jacob self-deprecatingly admits in his book, 'That I was posted to Lahore at that time [1918] could not be attributed to any desire of Sir Michael O'Dwyer, the lieutenant governor of the Punjab to be 'consequent' (in the German sense) to his assertion that I was one of his best officers, but rather to the fact that I had some capacity as a tennis player and Sir Michael was very fond of the game.'

After Jallianwala Bagh, Sydney Jacob was moved to the Census Department, where, while his skills would be well utilised, it was perhaps accompanied by the vain hope that here, he would fade into oblivion and not publicly highlight and demand consequences for the injustice that was endemic to how the country was governed.

The period from 1921 to 1923 was a very interesting time to be involved in the work of this department. The 1921 Census of India was being conducted, and Jacob immersed himself in this task. Between 1923 and 1924 the reports on the 1921 Census were published. While J.T. Marten, another Indian Civil Service (ICS) official was in charge of the main report, Sydney Jacob's ICS contribution to this historical document is recorded for posterity as the co-author of Volume XV. Jacob co-authored the main report as well as the volume that contains all the statistical tables that form the core of the census report on Punjab and Delhi, two of the most important areas included in the survey, with his colleague, L. Middleton. Copies of these volumes are available with India's Census Office as well as on the Census Digital Library of the Government of India.

During his time at the Census Department, Jacob spent far more time appearing on the international tennis circuit.

By this time, Jacob was well entrenched among the top Indian players of his time and was meeting with remarkable success, notwithstanding his age.

Census of India, 1921. Sydney Jacob's personal album, courtesy of Philip Jacob.

In 1921, Jacob made it to his first Wimbledon. The fourth round of the Gentleman's Singles boasted two Indians that year—Sleem and Jacob. Like Sleem, this was about as far as Jacob would get that year, losing in straight sets to Brian Norton of South Africa, who went on to win the Tournament that year, eventually losing the Challenge Round in five sets to Bill Tilden. But when Jacob paired up with Lewis Deane for the doubles that year, they would make history becoming the first Indian pair to make the semi-finals of a Grand Slam event.

Later that year Sydney Jacob was part of the first Indian Davis Cup team that would, against all odds and expectations, make it to the semi-finals with a famous victory over France.

All India Davis Cup team, 1921. Sydney Jacob's personal album, courtesy of Philip Jacob.

THE FIRST INDIAN GRAND SLAM SINGLES SEMI-FINALIST

In 1923, Jacob was appointed captain of the Indian Davis Cup team that played Ireland at Dublin. Ireland won the close encounter at home 3-2, and one of India's two victories was in the opening singles when Jacob beat Cecil Campbell, Ireland's top player. An Irish newspaper, reporting on the match, would write the next morning about Jacob: 'This opponent was a model of accuracy. He rarely attempted anything out of the ordinary, but was content to play a sound, steady game, waiting for Campbell's mistakes. And the policy paid. At no stage of the three sets did he (Campbell) look as if he could reduce S.M. Jacob's lead.'

That year, among the many tournaments that Jacob appeared at (and won) in England, the East of England Championships at Felixstowe deserves a special mention. The *Lawn Tennis and Badminton*, a periodical of the time, says in its 21 July issue: 'Described as the finest entry that had ever been received for the East of England Championships at Felixstowe, the play brought forth in the later stages some really great contents and more than one astonishing result.'

It then goes on to add about the semi-final (where Jacob once again came up against Cecil Campbell of Ireland) and the final: 'Campbell had to oppose Jacob in the semi-final round. All were much intrigued about the match, for Jacob had put an amazing score across the Irishman in the Davis Cup tie. Personally, I had fancied Campbell equal to taking his revenge. Throughout the second and third sets—knowing what Campbell was capable of—I waited and waited for his last-lap burst. And it never came. Jacob's steadiness and accuracy opposed to [D.M.] Grieg's (one of England's leading players at the time and a member of the Davis Cup team) brilliancy and over-eagerness just tipped the scale in favour of India's Davis Cup captain in the final. In a thrilling five-set match Jacob got home in the fifth set at 6–3 after three-all had been called, repeating his victory in the final of the grass court tournament last July.'

The following year Jacob led India once again at the Davis Cup, where in the Europe Zone, the team traveled to beautiful Arnhem in the Netherlands to battle the Dutch on clay. But at Paris in the quarter-finals that year, the Four Musketeers had their revenge, blowing away the Indians 4–0. That year France would go all the way to the Davis Cup Inter-Zonal final before losing 2–3 to Australia.

All India Davis Cup team, 1924. Sydney Jacob's personal album, courtesy of Philip Jacob.

In 1924, Jacob again made it to the fourth round at Wimbledon, and representing India at the Paris Olympics a few weeks later, he battled through some of the best competition he had ever faced, into the quarter-finals, going further than any other Indian at the summer games. He was forty-four at the time.

In the quarter-finals, Jacob ran into Jean Borotra, one of the all-time greats of French tennis. In a singles and doubles career that spanned an incredible thirty years, Jean Borotra would win nine French Championships, six Wimbledon titles and one US Championships besides nineteen other tournament titles. He also helped France lift the Davis Cup between 1927 and 1932.

Although there was an air of inevitability to Jacob's quarter-final loss at the Olympics to Borotra, Paris would prove to be the city where he would achieve the greatest heights of his career.

In 1925, at the age of forty-five, given his successes at the Olympics and the circuit in recent years, Sydney Jacob found himself invited to play at Roland Garros at the French Championships. For good measure, he was seeded eighth. Besides the strong field of younger and better-ranked players than Jacob, Roland Garros at the time was the exclusive domain of France's 'Four Musketeers'. Besides Borotra, there were Rene Lacoste, Jacques Brugnon and Henri Cochet. Together, the four dominated world tennis in the 1920s.

In the third round at Roland Garros that year, Jacob played Jacques (Toto) Brugnon. Brugnon was an accomplished singles player, but better known for his doubles prowess. In doubles, Brugnon had won the Olympic silver partnering Henri Crochet the previous year, and would go on to win four Davis Cup titles, seven French Championships, four Wimbledon titles and one Australasian Championships.

Jacob got past Brugnon in four captivating sets of tennis. He then defeated Andre Gobert, a former Olympic silver medalist and Wimbledon finalist, once again in four sets, in the quarter-finals, becoming the first Indian player to reach the semi-finals of a Grand Slam.

In the semi-finals, Jacob ran into the second of the Four Musketeers, Rene Lacoste. While Lacoste may be better known today for the brand with the 'crocodile' logo founded by him and his partner Andre Gillier in 1933, in the mid-1920s it was Lacoste's tennis that was all the rage of the tennis world.

Jacob and Lacoste battled on the Roland Garros' clay for over three hours before Lacoste prevailed in four hard-fought sets, 6-2, 6-1, 4-6, 7-5. In the finals, Lacoste prevailed over Borotra in straight sets to win the first of the ten Grand Slam titles and one runner-up cup he would eventually add to his trophy cabinet over the next four years.

For Stanley Jacob, this was the closest he would get to a Grand Slam singles title. Indeed, it would be another thirty-five years before another Indian, Ramanathan Krishnan, would make a Grand Slam singles semi-final appearance.

A month later, Jacob was back on the Wimbledon lawns, playing with renewed confidence. In the fourth round he came up against Belgium's Jean Washer who had been the other semi-finalist at Roland Garros. At twenty-nine, Washer was at the top of his game, winning several tournaments at the time. In a bruising five-setter stretching almost four hours, coming from two sets behind, Jacob defeated Washer, fifteen years his junior, 2-6, 1-6, 10-8, 6-4, 7-5.

Exhausted but determined, less than twenty-four hours later he once against faced Lacoste in the quarter-finals. It took all of Lacoste's guile, skill and energy to overwhelm Jacob, 6-3, 6-8, 6-0, 6-4. The Frenchman would go on to win the Championships.

For Jacob, this was his last hurrah at the top. While he would go on to win the British Covered Court Championship that year, defeating South Africa's Patrick Spence, and become a multiple Mixed Doubles Grand Slam winner in a hard fought five-setter, never again would Jacob ascend to the dizzying heights of Grand Slam success as he had done in 1925. In the first recorded instance of an Indian tennis player coming up against the administrative machinations of the AILTA (something that will be a recurring theme in this book), Jacob was suspended for a year on what proved later to be trumped-up minor charges, that as captain and manager of the Indian Davis Cup team of 1925 at Brussels, two items of personal expenses, one being a taxi bill, had been deducted from the money handed over to the association. This was apparently based on an accusation by Sleem, which in a letter to Jacob (reproduced by Jacob in his autobiography), Sleem disclaimed he had ever made. Nonetheless, the damage was done just at the point where Jacob appeared to be touching a late career peak.

Jacob's parting words in the chapter that talks about his tennis career are reflective of the deep pain that he felt even years later when he penned the account, 'Hitherto there has been no competent [Indian] writer on the game. Maybe the scientific writer of the future will be able to pierce the shadows and pretence of the public record and reach a fair assessment of potential achievement.'

While he made two more appearances at Wimbledon, the last at the age of forty-nine in 1928, it had been a glorious run at the highest level of the game, and it was time to give up the sport that had been such an important part of his life for over four decades, to concentrate fully on the last few years of his career as a civil servant.

A Fighter to the End

In 1928 Sydney Montague Jacob was sent on deputation to Nigeria where he was tasked with managing the 1931 Census. He stayed on to work on and release a Report on Taxation and Economics in Nigeria in 1934. This report was never, however, officially published as the British government did not appreciate the fact that Jacob pointed out the adverse impact of colonial exploitation of Nigerian resources to fund the aftermath of the Great Depression that had swept the world since 1929. Jacob published it anyway at his own expense, and the document has become an important part of any study of the Nigerian economy of the period and impact of the colonial rule of Britain's largest African colony. After the publication of the report, Jacob was asked to leave Nigeria, and went to Austria.

This was a crucial period before the Second World War and large sections of the British government were in denial about German intentions. In his book, Jacob talks about how he understood what many in Britain did not, that the newly resurgent Germany posed a real threat to world peace. He had previously been in Dresden, where he had got to know a number of SA and SS men. One of these men, who he refers to as S.S. Jansen, was someone he came to know particularly well, thus gaining good insight into Germany's real intentions. Jacob's warnings to the British authorities fell on deaf ears, but by the time he came back to Britain in 1939, German intentions had become absolutely clear.

When war broke out, the ministry of food had advertised for a statistician. Sixty at the time, Jacob had retired from the service, but when he applied, he got the job. He found that food rationing was going to be applied, but the ministry had absolutely no details about the British population, and hence no way to effectively implement it. Registrar General Sir S. Vivian had refused to supply the data to the food ministry when they went through the official channels, so Jacob charmed him into releasing it. Once he got the data, he realised it had to also include potential recruitment numbers into the armed forces. He called his cousin Colonel Ian Jacob who was directly reporting to Churchill in the war ministry, and obtained the data.

Sadly, using one's initiative to get information through back channels was anathema to the staid British bureaucracy, and seeing him go over their heads was neither palatable nor acceptable to Jacob's bosses in the ministry. He was dismissed from service for his efforts. Jacob spent the war years doing home guard duties, and after the war he settled down to a quiet life in the beautiful Surrey countryside.

India's first Grand Slam semi-finalist, a man who loved the country of his birth to the core, and always dealt with life with a straight bat, Sydney Montague Jacob passed away peacefully in 1977, just before his ninety-eighth birthday. The *Woldingham Parish Magazine*'s obituary, published a month after his passing, was a fitting tribute to a most remarkable man: 'Not only has our village lost what must be its oldest inhabitant, but also a very exceptional character—a fine chess player, a mathematician, a philosopher, a man of letters, and an international tennis player. Many a budding Borotra will be grateful for the coaching he gave them.'

GHAUS MOHAMMAD KHAN

THE PRE-INDEPENDENCE GIANT OF INDIAN TENNIS

My God, he is dynamite, what can I do with him?

—Bobby Riggs at Wimbledon 1939

WIMBLEDON, 26 JUNE 1939

The capacity crowd at Centre Court in Wimbledon could hardly have known that this would be one of the last three times they would gather around the hallowed patch of grass for six long years. Neville Chamberlain's 3 September declaration of war against Germany after its annexation of Poland was two months and a lifetime away. Many of those seated in the stands that day to witness the men's singles quarter-finals would not be alive when the next edition of the tournament took place.

But as the second-seeded Bobby Riggs took the court against the unfancied Indian, Ghaus Mohammed Khan, the only thoughts of war in the minds of the spectators were purely sporting in nature, the weapons—two wooden racquets and a semi-hard, furry ball. The anticipated result—a walk in the park for Riggs.

This was only the second time that twenty-four-year-old Ghaus Mohammed, India's national champion for the past three years, was making an appearance at Wimbledon. The first time he had made it to the last sixteen. This time, he was in the quarter-finals, becoming the first man of Indian ethnic origin to reach this stage.

But there was no sign of nerves as the first ace left his racquet to start the match. Three more followed in quick succession to wrap up the game. Riggs, a big server himself, held his serve, and at 1-1, Ghaus delivered his fifth ace in a row. Then the sixth, the seventh, and finally, the eighth.

After two service games of increasing frustration at his inability to put his racquet on a serve, Bobby Riggs famously threw his racquet in the air and exclaimed: 'My God, he is dynamite, what can I do with him?'[27]

At the changeover, calming himself down, Riggs would indeed find a way.

There was no way to avoid Ghaus' magnificent fast serve, which swerved away from Riggs' outstretched racquet when it fell true. But those who had followed the Indian's game knew that his real weapon was the powerful one-handed backhand, unleashing down the line returns with awesome power. If you neutralised this, the job became easier. This is what Riggs proceeded to do.

Every return was targeted to Ghaus' relatively weaker forehand. Broken twice in the first set, the Indian champion lost the set 2-6. His confidence fast evaporating against the onslaught from Riggs, Ghaus Mohammed ended up losing the biggest match of his life 2-6, 2-6, 2-6.

Speaking to Rima Kashyap of *Sportsweek* three decades later, he would lament: 'I lost through sheer nervousness ... the atmosphere and the tension were too much for me.'[28]

At twenty-four, Ghaus Mohammad was just coming into his own at the highest level of the sport, and he could have been forgiven for supposing that this was just the first of many shots he would have at the title. Sadly, the next six years of devastating war would deprive him and thousands of sportspersons at the peak of their athletic prowess the chance at sporting glory.

By the time he came back to Wimbledon in 1947, Ghaus was thirty-two, a shadow of his former self, the war and the consequent lack of top-level competition having arrested his growth as a tennis player. He would return that summer to an independent India, but his ultimate aim, watching the tricolour being waved at Centre Court, was to remain a dream.

It would be a full two decades after Ghaus Mohammad's match against Riggs before another Indian, Ramanathan Krishnan, just one year old at the time of the Riggs-Ghaus encounter, would go past the quarter-final hurdle at Wimbledon.

The Man from Malihabad

Malihabad near Lucknow is today known more for its mangoes than its tennis, for it is the Dussehri mango that put the village on the world map. The Malihabadi Dussehri was granted Geographical Indication (GI) registration in 2009. It now enjoys the same exalted status as Darjeeling tea.

But almost a century before its mangoes wooed the world, Malihabad was getting ready to make its presence felt internationally when Ghaus Mohammed Khan was born into a Talukdar family of Pathans (the family originally came from Afridi, Khyber Pakhtunkhwa, with the Mughal armies) in 1915.

Football was his preferred sport and cricket a close second as young Ghaus was growing up among the clusters of mango orchards in Malihabad. But the twin influences of his father who built a tennis court at home, and Professor Hyder at the Aligarh Muslim University where Ghaus was enrolled, were to move him away from the distraction of other sports, and get him to concentrate on tennis.

In 1936, Ghaus won his first national title and would continue to remain India's no. 1 player until 1940. Immediately after his 1936 victory, for the first time ever, he received formal coaching under the United Provinces Coaching Scheme. The Austrian coach, Weis, helped him develop what would become his trademark weapon in the years to come—the one-handed backhand, played while on the run. So much so, that as Ghaus would later tell *Sportsweek*, 'Before the coaching camp, I had only two strokes, the serve and the forehand. (Afterwards) I didn't have a forehand because it became a purely defensive stroke.'[29]

A Very Special Talent

He might have been self-deprecating about the variety of his strokes, but the fact that Ghaus Mohammed earned the respect of his formidable peers in one of the most competitive eras in tennis certainly says a lot about the quality of his game.

Bobby Riggs, Fred Perry, Baron Gottfried von Cramm and Don Budge were four of the greatest tennis players the world has known. This was the field that Ghaus faced and often successfully overwhelmed in his brief pre-war international career.

Just the week before Wimbledon that year, Ghaus had made it to the final of the London Championships at the Queen's Club, the traditional precursor to Wimbledon. There he met Gottfried von Cramm, who had blown away Bobby Riggs 6-0, 6-1 in a scintillating display of complete tennis in the semi-final.

Von Cramm was the greatest tennis player Germany had produced before the arrival of Boris Becker in the 1980s. His down the line elongated strokes on both sides and a formidable serve earned him seven Grand Slam singles final appearances and two French Championships in 1934 and 1936.

Six feet tall, with blonde hair, green eyes and a sleek, athletic build, von Cramm had the type of magnetism and persona that drew a legion of admirers. His global appeal was reflected in him featuring on the 13 September 1937 cover of *Time Magazine*. His sportsmanship was legendary.

Von Cramm's gesture in the 1935 Davis Cup inter-zonal final against the US in conceding a point, and consequently the championship, because unnoticed by officials the ball had grazed his racquet before his partner smacked home a winner, is still considered one of the greatest sporting moments in the Cup's history. When castigated by his captain for letting

Germany lose the Davis Cup by his gesture, von Cramm replied, 'Do you think that I would sleep tonight knowing that the ball had touched my racquet without my saying so? Never, because I would be violating every principle I think this game stands for. On the contrary, I don't think I am letting the German people down. As a matter of fact, I think I am doing them credit.' A poll taken at the time suggested that his countrymen agreed with him.

His looks and his popularity made him the perfect face of Nazi Germany, or so Adolf Hitler believed. Unfortunately for Hitler, von Cramm refused to be poster boy for the fascist regime. He was imprisoned for a year by the Gestapo in 1938 on trumped up charges of homosexuality. He returned to tennis in 1939, and promptly decimated Riggs at Queens Club.

Sadly, because he had also been stripped of his German nationality after his conviction, he was not allowed to participate in that year's Wimbledon. It is very likely that Riggs would have struggled to lift the Championships if von Cramm had played in the kind of form he had displayed at Queen's.

This then was the man Ghaus Mohammed faced in the final. Gottfried von Cramm, on a high after the semi-final against Riggs, sent down ten aces in the match. Ghaus countered with fifteen, aces accounting for all but one point that he won. But it was not enough against a man out to prove himself again to the world. Von Cramm made sure Ghaus' deadly backhand was neutered, and won 6-1, 6-3.

There was, however, more to Ghaus Mohammed than the serve and the backhand. A report in *The Scotsman* of his pre-quarter-final match at Wimbledon in 1939 gives us a flavour of his multi-faceted game:

> The most remarkable match of the championships so far was in progress on an outside court, where Ghaus Mohammed (India) was playing O. Szigeti, a Hungarian left-hander. They battled for two hours and twenty minutes, and Mohammed won after losing a second set of thirty games, 6-4, 14-16, 2-6, 6-3, 6-4.[30]

It goes on: 'Mohammed showed himself to be a fine volleyer, and it says much for his stamina that he was able to win after being two sets to one down. Szigeti, of much heavier physique, was frequently caught unawares by a "donkey drop" service of Mohammed's. Instead of the Indian delivering the ball with the usual punch, he would send it over the net in pat-like fashion, leaving his opponent standing well beaten at the baseline. Mohammed looked a beaten man when he lost the third set, but he proved himself to be a great little fighter.'

The year before, Ghaus Mohammed, appearing at a Grand Slam event for the first time, had faced another giant of the time, top-seeded Don Budge, in the third round of the French Championships. Budge that year would become the first man to ever win the Grand Slam.* The match was epic.

Coming out of a hard-fought five-set victory over France's George Glasser, Ghaus took time to find his feet against Budge, the best player in the world by far that year. The Indian was blown away in the first two sets, the 1-6, 1-6

---

*The term 'Grand Slam', when used correctly, refers to a player winning all four Majors, or Grand Slam events, in a single calendar year. Don Budge was the first person in the world to do so. Rod Laver achieved the feat twice—in 1962 and 1969. No one has done it since.

scoreline doing nothing to hide Budge's total domination. In Budge, Ghaus had met his match as far as the backhand was concerned, although, at the time, their two deadliest backhands in world tennis were very different. The match would help improve the game of both players, in different ways.

All of five feet six inches in height, left-handed Budge, then not yet eighteen years old and yet to grow to his full height, had no choice but to adapt his game to his moderate size and attempt to keep the ball in play. Starting off with his first love, baseball, Budge applied the same smooth low-to-high swing technique to his tennis backhand. This was much more effective than the traditional chopped return from high to low with under-spin on the ball so that it would loft over the net. 'Taking the ball on the rise' would become the mantra for the men who followed him, and while Budge didn't know it at the time, he had created a motion that would revolutionise tennis. As he grew seven inches over the course of the next year to finally emerge at his impressive six feet one inch frame, this weapon would complement the big serve and power that came with size.

At the French Championships, by the time the third set came around, Ghaus had got the measure of Budge's game. On the slow clay, he turned Budge's backhand weapon against the American. Staying back at the baseline, Budge's backhands were returned cross-court, with the speed taken off the ball, to his less deadly forehand. This gave Ghaus the ball on his own backhand, allowing him to send stunning down the line winners past the American. Breaking Budge in the eleventh game, Ghaus served out the set with a brace of aces.

It was too little too late however, against the world's no. 1 player. Budge, learning quickly from the loss of the set, changed his game around, getting to the net faster on Ghaus' return and putting those away with his own blistering winners. He won the fourth set 6-0 and would go on to win the Championships that year, the second leg of his Grand Slam journey.

His greatness attributable to how he was always learning, Budge would pick up on the stunning flat backhand down the line return from Ghaus to make his own returns even more deadly. At Wimbledon and the US Championships later that year, this stroke would often be the tipping point in close matches. In his typically modest way, batting away the suggestion that his own backhand had contributed to Budge's game, Ghaus would tell *Sportsweek*: 'My backhand was a child's compared to his.'

Sadly, Don Budge's statement to the press that Ghaus Mohammed could one day well become the best tennis player in the world, did not get a chance to be proved true, as Germany invaded Poland two months after Wimbledon 1939. The era of Perry, Riggs, Budge, von Cramm and Ghaus was at an end.

A CAREER LOST IN THE WAR YEARS

By the time the Second World War ended, while Ghaus Mohammed Khan was still one of the best players on the national circuit, the lack of international competition had dulled the edges of his once formidable game. In 1947, he did go to Wimbledon one last time, but was unlucky to run into

Hungarian Jozsef Asboth in the second round. Fresh from his French Championships title a few weeks before, Asboth beat the Indian 6-3, 6-2, 6-4. In the doubles, Ghaus was a tad bit more successful in reaching the third round with compatriot Iftikar Ahmed.

On his return from Wimbledon, Ghaus was appointed a revenue officer with the erstwhile Baroda State. Kashyap remarks in her feature in *Sportsweek*, 'Lack of competition, marriage ('God save tennis from wives,' he said wryly) and a dull job deteriorated his game. He was still no. 1, but he wasn't improving. In 1947, he led the Davis Cup team and that was his au revoir gesture to tennis.'

After independence, Ghaus Mohammed moved to Hyderabad from where his wife hailed. Short of funds, he sold almost all of the 200 to 300 trophies he had won over the course of his career, each weighing 2 to 3 seers.* Finally, he obtained a government job there which he held until retirement in the mid-1970s, travelling to and fro from home on his trusted motorbike.

The only tennis he played by then was social. Former Test cricketer Abbas Ali Baig, no mean tennis player himself in his youth, played a couple of sets against Ghaus at the famous Asif Club located in the Hyderabad Public Gardens. Ghaus had at the time been retired from the sport for well over a decade. Baig tells me how good the great man was even then, 'I could not return any of his backhand strokes, and barely

---

*A seer was a traditional unit of mass and volume used in large parts of Asia prior to the middle of the twentieth century. In India, the seer (government seer) was defined by the Standards of Weights and Measures Act (no. 89 of 1956, amended in 1960 and 1964) as being exactly equal to 1.25 kg (2.755778 lb).

took points off him given how good his reach was to anything that I sent across the net.'[31]

Imran Mirza, father and coach to Sania Mirza, tells me about an exchange between his father and his close friend Ghaus Muhammad: 'I remember my dad pulling Ghaus Saab's leg and telling him "You were lucky Krishnan came a few years after you. Otherwise you would have had no chance of winning any tournaments in India!" And Ghaus Saab would laugh and say "It was Krishnan who was lucky!"' By the 1970s, behind Ghaus' office desk hung the only memento from his playing days—a framed collage of photos from his playing days, one of his famed backhand stroke and several of him holding up the National Championships trophies. His personal collection of photos had long been dispensed with as his wife hadn't approved of them.

'Girls,' he had said to Kashyap explaining away with a mischievous gleam in his eyes the absence of photos. 'There are all those girls at tennis matches. Yes—even in those days. And tennis was always a game for me. I kept late hours, went to parties, had a great time—and played the next day. Today, tennis is a job. To play it well and make it earn you have to sleep eight hours a day, no smoking, no drinking, no fun. Tennis was fun in those days, it's too commercial now.' A statement that one suspects would make Novak Djokovic cringe in his cryogenic sleep chamber.

Ghaus Mohammed passed on in 1982 at the age of sixty-seven, his short but impactful war-interrupted career a beacon of hope for the coming generations who would carry the baton forward.

INDIAN TENNIS COMES OF AGE

THE BIG THREE

INDEPENDENT INDIA'S FIRST MEN OF TENNIS—DILIP BOSE, SUMANT MISRA AND NARESH KUMAR

In my opinion, Sumant Misra had the best serve among all Indian tennis players past and present. His second serve was deep and penetrating. A good server is gauged by the quality of the second serve.

—Ramanathan Krishnan

For six long years, as the Second World War wrought death and destruction across the world, tennis, like every other sport, was consigned to the ranks of leisure that the world could ill-afford. But as the world emerged from chaos and destruction in 1945, it was time once again for sport to take its rightful place in society.

Britain, which had emerged victorious, was devastated. London's bombed buildings were unrepaired, hundreds of thousands of youth were dead, rationing was still in place and the economy was in ruins. The country needed an injection of normalcy, and sport, the government felt, would provide it. So, in 1945, the 'Victory Tests' led the way, and in 1946, the West Indies and Indian teams were invited to revive Test cricket.[32] Alongside, Wimbledon opened its courts that summer to host its sixtieth, and the first post-war Championships.[33]

Sports in India had been less affected by the war than Europe and the Far East, so notwithstanding the fact that international competition had been hard to find for India's tennis players, they had continued to hone their skills at home.

Domestic tournaments in India benefited from the continued presence of international players serving in the Indian Army. Between 1943 and until the end of the war two years later, as the hostilities dragged on, and on the eastern front the Japanese advanced on India, the lesser competitions ceased. The All India Championships, India's premier competition of the time, continued to be held. In 1943, it was Ghaus Mohammed, still a cut above anyone else in the country, who emerged victorious, but the following year he lost in the finals to Hal Surface Jr of the US.

In 1946, the All India Tennis Association (now AITA) decided to henceforth conduct two national championships, to give the Indian players the opportunity to excel across surfaces. In 1940, the All-India Championship at Allahabad had been merged with the East India Championship of Calcutta and renamed the All-India and East India Championship with its venue shifted from Allahabad to Calcutta. In 1946, this tournament would be renamed the National Championships and become the premier grass court competition in the country, played at the South Club in Calcutta. The Championships were also thrown open to foreigners. Simultaneously, the All India Hard Court Championships also kicked off.

It was time for the sport to be revived in India, and business as usual status to be restored on the grass and hard courts across the country. While the international career of the supremely talented Ghaus Mohammed had sadly been cut off in its prime with the outbreak of war, a new breed of Indian players was emerging. They would reach for their rightful place in the firmament as the post-war sun rose to reveal a new dawn.

DILIP BOSE

Born in the industrial city of Jamshedpur in 1922, Dilip Kumar Bose was the first of the post-war generation of Indian tennis players to make his mark on the international stage.

Moving to Calcutta at an early age, Dilip Bose honed his skills on the beautifully maintained grass courts of the South Club. It was but natural that it would turn out to be his favourite surface. At fourteen, he became the Bengal junior singles champion, and two years later, in 1938, Bose would win his first senior tournament, at the Calcutta North Club.

In 1939, alongside Ghaus Mohammed, the precocious seventeen-year-old talent of Dilip Bose had appeared on the greatest stage of world tennis—Wimbledon. While he didn't set the world of tennis on fire, his first round display against Swiss Davis Cup player Henri Pfaff gave every indication that a special talent had been unearthed. Fighting hard and showing delectable net play, Bose would take the Swiss to five sets before his inexperience finally showed, losing

2-6, 6-4, 1-6, 6-1, 2-6. The valuable lessons from that loss would, however, stand him in good stead in the years to come.

The following year, Dilip Bose won three successive tournaments in Calcutta—the Ordnance Club Tournament, the Cossipore Club Tournament and the Shyambazar Tournament, defeating Sir Walter Harold Strachan Michelmore, twice winner of the Bengal Lawn Tennis Championships, both in straight sets. Bose finished the year as Bengal's no. 1 player.

Between 1941 and 1943, Dilip Bose reached the semi-finals and finals of most major tournaments in India. On almost every occasion, he lost to Ghaus Mohammed, then at the peak of his prowess. Finally, at the East India Championships in 1943, Bose broke the jinx, defeating Mohammed in the semi-finals, but lost to Hal Surface Jr in the final in straight sets. He would have to wait until after the Second World War for his first major title. Ghaus Mohammed would be back in Bose's nightmares one last time in 1946, defeating him in four sets, 7-5, 3-6, 6-3, 6-3, in the finals of the All-India Championships.

Dilip Bose's time in the sun would finally come in the winter of 1948-49 on grass, at the Indian International Championships at Calcutta. With Ghaus Mohammed having laid down his racquet, the stockily built Bose had a new rival, the tall strapping young Sumant Misra, who was coming rapidly up the ranks at the same South Club courts. In this instance, Bose's experience would prove too much for young Misra. But the four-set hard-fought victory would be a warning to Bose that life after Ghaus Mohammed was not about to become easier.

The Asian Championships, 1949—A Landmark Event

The biggest triumph of Dilip Bose's career was to come exactly a year later, once again in Calcutta.

Between 22 December 1949 and 1 January 1950, the South Club organised India's first official international tennis tournament, the Asian Championships. The event was a landmark in the annals of Indian tennis in its organisation and importance. An incredible sixty-three players from twelve countries around the world took part, which explains why eleven days were needed to complete the tournament. Some of the leading players of the time from France, Belgium, England, Scotland, Yugoslavia, Czechoslovakia, Spain, Poland, Argentina, Philippines and Pakistan joined the top Indian players in the draw.

Among the players who deserve more than a passing mention were Felicisimo Hermoso of the Philippines, twice quarter-finalist at Roland Garros and winner of the Pan American Championships later that year in Mexico City who would fight his way into the semi-finals at Calcutta; Dragutin Mitic of Yugoslavia and Paul Remy of France who would make the quarter-finals at Roland Garros a few months later; Robert Abdesselem of France who had achieved the same feat earlier in 1949 and Philippe Wasker of Belgium who would go on to win two Wimbledon Plate Championships subsequently besides making the quarter-finals of the French Championships.

It was against this glittering field that the leading Indian players—Dilip Bose, Sumant Misra and Narendranath—strode out to do battle on the South Club courts. A bit more than a week later, in a remarkable turn of events, given the level of competition, the three Indians found themselves in the semi-finals.

Looking at the draw, it is perhaps fair to say that Dilip Bose had the easier path to the semi-finals. Over the past seventy years, there has been some speculation about how that draw was exactly made and the schedule of matches determined, and the players I spoke to were unwilling to discuss it other than mentioning that Sumant Misra perhaps received the short end of the stick.

Be that as it may, Bose was in the form of his life on those last few fateful winter days of 1949. Ramanathan Krishnan, who started his career as Bose was peaking and then winding up, talked me through Dilip Bose's game, 'He was an intelligent player who would use clever tactics against different opponents. He had an extremely good overhead smash, in spite of the fact that he was not tall.'[34]

Using every bit of this skill and tactical superiority, Bose defeated Narendranath in the semi-finals, moved into the final, and on New Year's Day 1950, brushed aside Misra's challenge in an imperious manner, winning 6-1, 6-2, 8-6. Bose was champion of Asia.

The Asian Championships would remain Dilip Bose's greatest triumph on a tennis court, although he had one more first to add to his already impressive resume.

Wimbledon 1950—The Last Hurrah

The real impact of the Asian Championships title would be clear to Bose when he arrived to play what would turn out to be his last Wimbledon Championships in June 1950. That year, the Championships realised that the level of competition from across the world was going up, and for the first time, instead of eight players being seeded at Wimbledon, the field was increased to sixteen. Much to the chagrin of the British newspapers of the time, Dilip Bose found himself seeded fifteenth, ahead of Britain's Tony Mottram who had beaten Bose in a Davis Cup encounter not so long ago.

While the announcement of the rankings made Dilip Bose the first Indian to be seeded at Wimbledon, there was drama to be played out yet on the issue. For as soon as the announcement had been made, Bose wrote to the organisers requesting that his name be removed from the rankings. No such request had ever been received in the history of the Championships, and unsurprisingly, the request was denied.

It has been a matter of much speculation over the years as to why exactly Bose took this unusual step. There have been unkind suggestions that perhaps he wanted to get the pressure off himself. But a report in the *Illustrated London News* on 8 July 1950 gives the reason: '(On Day 1) all the seeded players won their first round matches. On the second day, the Indian, Dilip Bose, champion of Asia and seeded fifteenth, collapsed with stomach cramp. He had previously requested his seeding to be cancelled because he feared the after-effects of malarial fever.'

That would turn out to be the last time Dilip Bose put in an appearance at Wimbledon. He retired from active tennis the next year.

Talent Spotter and Coach Extraordinaire

Notwithstanding his achievements on the court, perhaps the greatest contribution of Dilip Bose to Indian tennis came off it. Knowing his career was on its last legs, Bose had turned to coaching at a relatively young age.

Ramanathan Krishnan calls him 'an excellent coach'.[35] Coming out of his stable, among many others, would be two of India's greatest tennis players of the 'Golden Age' that was about to arrive—Jaidip Mukherjea and Premjit Lall.

Bose was the first of the great coaches at the South Club courts. He would be followed by Australian coach Stan Edwards and India's Akhtar Ali, who continued the rich tradition kicked off by Bose. Besides coaching, Bose also

Dilip Bose and Sumant Misra

remained in touch with the sport as an administrator and was the first Indian to be nominated to the managing committee of the International Tennis Federation.

Dilip Bose passed on in 1996 at the age of seventy-five. The end, perhaps fittingly for a man who had lived for sport every moment of his life, came on a sporting arena—he suffered a fatal heart attack while playing golf with his friend Byomkesh Bose, former Indian footballer.

SUMANT MISRA

Sumant Chandra Misra, one of India's post-independence greats, was born in Faizabad in 1923. Introduced to tennis at an early age by his father L.P. Misra, a former chief commissioner of Indian Railways, young Sumant, like his contemporary Dilip Bose, honed his skills on the South Club courts at Calcutta.

As he moved into his twenties, Sumant Misra had grown substantially in stature, both physically and as a player, earning the ironic nickname of 'Tiny' because of his height (he was one of the few players who, at well above six feet, towered over his contemporaries). Along the way he had also earned the reputation of being one of the most dangerous players on the circuit with his power-packed game.

Ramanathan Krishnan, who would go on to play against Misra over the next several years and partner him on the Davis Cup team, tells me, 'In my opinion, he had the best serve among all Indian tennis players past and present. His second serve was deep and penetrating. A good server is gauged by the quality of the second serve. He was an excellent partner in doubles because he would always take the blame! He never complained about his partner and was a good-hearted person. He was my first Davis Cup captain and gave me an important piece of advice—never pat the ball, always hit it.'[36]

At the age of twenty-two, Misra won his first National Championship in 1945 beating K.R. Kapanipathy in the final, and for good measure picked up the All-India Championships the same year, besting the same opponent. In 1947 he defended his national title, beating Sohan Lal. With the second national title under his belt, Misra proceeded to England in 1947 as the European tennis season began, the first to be held after the Second World War.

He started off with a title at the West of England Championships at the expense of contemporary Atri Madan Mohan in the final, then followed up with semi-final appearances at the British Hard Court Championships and the Queens Club tournament. At the Hard Court Championships, Misra had lost to a player who had first emerged on the circuit before the war, at Wimbledon in 1933—Ignacy Tloczynski from Poland.

A back story on Misra's opponent is well worth telling. In 1939, Tloczynski had gone underground in Warsaw as German troops crossed into Poland. During the war, he was a member of the Polish Resistance and took part in the Warsaw Uprising of 1944, fought for sixty-three days with little outside support. The Uprising was the single largest military effort undertaken by any European resistance movement during the Second World War.

In the first few days of the uprising, along with his brother Ksawery and several prominent sportsmen, Tloczynski stormed an SS barrack and occupied it. They took seventy-two SS soldiers prisoner and seized a handful of ammunition and an armoured car. The brothers and another Polish tennis player, Czeslaw Spychała, were wounded as a result of the fight.

This, then, was the remarkable man young Sumant Misra ran into in the semi-finals. It is safe to assume that the legend of the man may have played as big a role in Misra's defeat as much as his prowess on the tennis court. The following year, back at the West of England tournament, in what must count as a remarkable coincidence, Misra would progress to the final with a victory in the semis over the other man who had been involved in the takeover of the SS barracks, Czeslaw Spychala.

While his attempts at making the higher rounds at Roland Garros and Wimbledon in singles would be largely unsuccessful, Misra had more luck in the doubles format. Partnering contemporary Jimmy Mehta, he reached the quarter-finals at Wimbledon both in 1947 and in 1948.

In 1952, Misra would win the National Championships for the second time. This time he beat Naresh Kumar in five hard-fought sets coming back from two sets down, the scoreline of 6-8, 2-6, 6-3, 9-7 showing the epic battle that had ensued. On the national circuit, this would be his last major success, bowing out to the new kid on the block, Ramanathan Krishnan, in straight sets in the semi-finals the following year at the All-India Championships.

Two decades later, in 1972, his son Gaurav Misra would make history, winning the National Championships. This would make the two Misras the first father-son duo to be crowned national champions. Gaurav Misra's vanquished opponent in the final, quite remarkably, was the man who had beaten his father two decades before at the All-India Championships—Ramanathan Krishnan. Life, as it often does, had come full circle.

In the period before Ramanathan Krishnan arrived to dominate the Indian Davis Cup scene, Sumant Misra was the mainstay of the team alongside Naresh Kumar between 1947 and 1953, and part of some significant campaigns. He also captained the side in the final year of his Davis Cup appearance.

Sumant Misra's commitment to the Indian flag in the most trying circumstances was legendary, and nothing demonstrates this better than what happened at the inter-zonal semi-final encounter between Italy and India played at Brisbane, Australia, in December 1952.

Misra had been suffering from a pain in the right lower abdomen going into the tie. But with Naresh Kumar and himself being the two key players, he was desperate to play. After Kumar lost the opening match in four sets, Misra braved the pain and brought parity to the tie with a straight sets win.

The *Sydney Morning Herald* with its headline, 'Indian Plays on in Doubles Despite Rupture', tells us what happened the next day as Misra joined Kumar in a quest to win the doubles and give India a crucial 2-1 lead in the tie, with a possible inter-zonal final berth against the US at stake:

Indian tennis player Sumant Misra played on after suffering a right inguinal hernia in the Davis Cup tie against Italy today. Misra suffered the injury in the third set and almost collapsed when he entered the dressing room for the interval. Queensland Lawn Tennis Association officials hurriedly strapped the injury, and Misra went out and played for another hour with the pain.

Despite his heroic efforts, the Italians managed to scrape past by the skin of their teeth, 1-6, 1-6, 6-2, 6-2, 13-11, saving three match points in the final set, to go 2-1 up in the tie.

The report continues: 'It was an exciting match only in the fifth set. The Italians looked like novices in the first two sets, and won less than twenty points. Misra, despite his injury, was the best player in today's doubles. (Sadly) Misra's fall and injury contributed to a fall in the stars of the Indians' play.'

The *Herald* wraps up the narrative with this: 'At 7.30 tonight Misra said he intended to play, if possible, in the singles against Fausto Gardini tomorrow. A special truss is being made for him. Misra pleaded with Dr Eric Yates for permission to play. The doctor agreed reluctantly but he warned Misra of the possible consequences. Misra said: 'I feel I must play, as we Indians believe we have a chance to defeat Italy.' After consultation and argument, permission was given for Misra to play tomorrow.'

In a separate interview with the Italian team who were oblivious to Misra's injury, since he had gritted his teeth and not shown it on court, the *Herald* reports that a seemingly relieved Gardini had remarked, 'It's bad luck for Misra, but maybe it's my good luck. He would have been hard to beat.'

Misra would indeed play the first singles against Gardini the next day, but the injury severely hampered his booming serve and movement on the court. He came back from two sets down, 6-8, 6-8, to take the third against a rattled Gardini. But a single break of serve in the fourth enabled the Italian to take the set 6-4 and take his nation into the final against the US. Naresh Kumar won the dead rubber in four sets to provide a final scoreline of 2-3 for India.

Continuing to appear at tournaments sporadically until 1960, after retirement Sumant Misra served as the secretary of the All-India Tennis Association between 1963 and 1967 while balancing a full-time job at the Calcutta Port Trust and then at Indian Aluminium Company.

Sumant Misra in 1953 at the Royal Kings Park Tennis Club, Australia

He continued to play tennis socially at the Delhi Gymkhana Club well into his eighties. Former Wimbledon and US Championships finalist Tom Brown tells an amusing story about meeting Misra there in his book, *As Tom Goes By*: 'Rarely do I travel without my racquet, even if it's a trip solely for sightseeing. In New Delhi, India, in my seventies, I was invited for a game of doubles at the elegant Gymkhana Club. We were all about the same age, grey-haired, and strangers, or so I thought. Sitting around over cups of tea afterwards, one of the Indians casually said to me, "I understand you played at Wimbledon."[37]

'"Well, yes, I did," I replied. "So did I," he countered. "Oh, really? What year?" "In 1946 and 1948," he answered. Hmmm. I was intrigued. "That's interesting," I said. "I was there those years." "I know," he smiled. "And how far did you get?" I asked. "The round of sixteen," he answered.

'Gee, I thought to myself, he must have been pretty good to get that far. Aloud, I ventured, "And who did you lose to?" "Why, to you, of course, both times." I was taken aback. He roared with laughter. It was Sumant Misra.'

Sumant 'Tiny' Misra passed on in 2011 at the age of eighty-eight. Quite appropriately, he continues to be referred to as the 'Grandfather of Indian Tennis'.

NARESH KUMAR

Like many Indians before and after him, Naresh Kumar was born at his maternal grandparents' house where his mother had gone for her childbirth from her usual abode in Calcutta. Her parents happened to live in Lahore, and one can only wonder if the rich tennis history of the Punjab city rubbed off on young Naresh.

If it did not at the time, it certainly influenced him when he was sent to Lahore during the Japanese bombing of Calcutta. It was in Lahore that he completed his Matriculation and joined Government College, which, he tells me '... was a fantastic place, the grounds had place for every sport, our hockey team had five Olympic players, they had tennis courts, a swimming pool. It was a wonderful place for sports.'[38]

Young Naresh had started playing tennis at the age of twelve at the Bengal Lawn Tennis Association (BLTA) courts, as a part of their free coaching scheme. But he was asked to leave after a while because he was not deemed good enough. 'They did what they had to do,' he muses, shaking his head. At Government College, Lahore, with six courts and a 'marker'* available for students, Kumar quickly showed promise and won the Punjab Lawn Tennis Championship junior title. 'I still have the ten rupee voucher that I won as a prize that day,' he says with a happy smile.

Despite the title, when Kumar returned to Calcutta after the war, neither would the BLTA admit him back into the free coaching scheme nor would South Club give him a club membership, without which he had no courts to practise on. 'It hardened my resolve,' Kumar tells me.

Fortunately, nearby was the Punjab Club where Kumar's brother was a member, and he arranged for a marker called Nur Muhammad, a Pathan with an excellent game, to practise with his brother. Muhammad soon taught Kumar all he knew, and at the age of eighteen, Kumar won his first National Championships at the South Club courts, beating all the graduates of the BLTA scheme on the way to his title. South Club, in a mea culpa gesture, gracefully extended him a membership.

---

*The term used in India in clubs even today for players who are employed to play with members. They are usually former competitive players who serve a dual role by giving tips and informally coaching the young players or beginners seeking to improve their game at the Club.

The most difficult battle, however, was yet to be fought. Kumar would soon discover that the move from the junior to senior level was a deceptively difficult one. Two years of struggle followed, and then came the break.

In 1948, somehow arranging the money and a family stay, Kumar travelled to Delhi to play at the Championships there. He found when he got there that the industrialist who had agreed to take him in had given him a bed in the outhouse among the domestic helpers.

Nonetheless, he progressed through the early rounds of the Championship, coming up against the no. 1 player in the country, Narendranath, in the quarter-finals. Kumar talks me through the encounter: 'I was due to play at 3 p.m. and Narendranath arrived late, and instead of being hauled up, he was given a very warm welcome. He used to work for KLM, had a big car, and (I shouldn't say Romeo) he was a "lad about town". There were a bunch of teenage girls (fans of his) sitting behind the umpire's chair, and he turned to them and said, "I am hungry, will someone fetch me some tea and cakes?" Then while sipping the tea he proceeded to chat with the girls. As this went on, it added more fuel to my fire, and I got more and more annoyed. This spurred me on when we eventually started and I won the first set. That was a jolt to the champion. He came back to take the second set. In the decider he got a bit nervous because I was attacking the net all the time, and under this intense pressure, he succumbed.'

Narendranath was a name that came up often as I spoke to the early players of independent India. He seemed to be a popular figure about whom there isn't much written other than the fact that he was a Punjab University graduate from

Lahore who reached the third round of Wimbledon in 1948 and 1950 and was a mixed doubles quarter-finalist in 1951. He captained the Davis Cup team in 1954-55 and played the two doubles matches in those couple of ties, winning one and losing the other.

I asked Kumar to describe Narendranath's game, and this is what he told me: 'Narendranath was a base liner, good ground strokes, not very stylish, but a tough player to beat as he didn't miss much.'

Ramanathan Krishnan concurred. 'Narendranath beat me in the earlier years. Later on, I scored over him. He was an attacking base liner from Delhi. I played under his captaincy in Davis Cup.'

Kumar went on to eventually win the tournament. He would never look back. That match against Narendranath, and the confidence it gave him, would be the turning point in his career.

The next stop was the Bengal Lawn Tennis Championships at the Eden Gardens. This was the real deal, a tournament where all the big guns of Indian tennis showed up. 'They used to make twelve tennis courts around the pitch at Eden Gardens and hold the tournament there,' Kumar recalls.

In the best of five sets final, Kumar met India's top player at the time, Sumant Misra. Down 1-2, Kumar developed cramps and took a medical break. His friends brought back news that Sumant Misra was busy on court with a skipping rope, keeping warm (this was winter in Calcutta) waiting to finish the match. Back on court, a refreshed Kumar levelled the match, and then went on to beat an exhausted Misra 6-0 in the final set to pick up the Championship.

Kumar tells me a poignant back story on the victory, an incident that he says stole one of the lovelier moments of his young life from him. The story opens the morning after his victory over Misra.

'I was waiting anxiously for the morning paper—*The Statesman*, for this was special—a major victory at home. The newspaperwallah* pressed the bell, and the whole family rushed up to the door. We picked up the paper, turned to the sports page and read to our utter disbelief that Misra had beaten me easily in five sets. It went even further and gave descriptions of the fourth and fifth sets that had no relation to the actual match. I had to show my dad my trophy yet again to prove I had actually won! The laziness and insincerity of the reporter in not staying back and instead filing a fake account of the final after asking for the final score, and even neglecting to ask who had won, assuming it was Misra, staggered me. He stole a wonderful day of my life from me.'

His career had, however, just started, and his serve-and-volley game, suited to the South Club grass, brought Kumar famous victories against some of the greatest players in the world, including the likes of Sven Davidson, who would remain the only Swede to win a Grand Slam title until Bjorn Borg came on the scene in the 1970s.

A Long International Career

It is every Indian tennis player's dream to play at Wimbledon. Naresh Kumar would live this dream for an incredible two decades, stepping onto the hallowed courts for the first time

---

*Newspaper delivery person

in 1949. In 1969, when he played his last match at SW19, he had been a part of a staggering 101 matches across formats.

'When I first played as a youngster on Centre Court, I was overawed. I felt afraid that I was perhaps not good enough to play there, but then I found that all the crowd wanted were two things—your best, and good behaviour. When I played in 1949, I could hear the tinkling of the tea cups, not any more of course. The Centre Court hasn't changed, but the crowd outside has changed,' he tells me.

That first year he had a good winter circuit, reaching the final of the Queen's Club Covered Court Championship and doing well in a few tournaments in the US. But the best results at Wimbledon would come in 1955 when he reached the quarter-finals of the doubles event with Ramanathan Krishnan. This was right after storming into the fourth round of the singles the same year before bowing out 4-6, 2-6, 2-6 to the eventual champion and winner of five Grand Slam titles, world no. 1, Tony Trabert of the US.

In the Davis Cup Kumar would be a part of one of the best Indian outfits of all time, playing alongside Sumant Misra at the start and then with Ramanathan Krishnan, Jaidip Mukherjea and Premjit Lall.

Making his Davis Cup debut in 1952, Kumar played forty-six matches over seventeen ties for India. His 12-5 doubles record compares favourably with the best Indian players in the history of the competition. Ramanathan Krishnan, his Davis Cup teammate for many years, tells me about Kumar:

> Naresh and I played a lot of matches together, had good doubles results internationally and were one of the top doubles teams of that era. Although he was a few years

older, we enjoyed some lovely times together. We shared rooms at Wimbledon and during Davis Cup ties and became good friends, as we remain till this day. As a player, he was very hard-working and ran for everything. He was very knowledgeable too. His one weakness was that he was largely a defensive player in crisis situations. It was a pity he was eight years older than me, with the result that when he was at his peak, I was coming up and when I reached my peak, he was retiring.

In 1959, just over a decade since he first played at Wimbledon, Naresh Kumar's father passed away. Earning a living became a priority, and while he would go on to build a formidable multi-million-dollar business in the years to come with his natural acumen, it severely impinged on his ability to devote time to tennis.

That year, when he dropped out of the Davis Cup team after his father's passing, a young Premjit Lall stepped up to take his place. While Kumar would come back into the team and continue playing for his country and at Wimbledon for another decade, the peak of his career had come and gone. It was time to concentrate on family and business while he kept his ties with tennis alive through television commentary, and his would become a familiar face to millions of Indians over the next two or three decades.

The French Finale

Despite his frequent run-ins with the administrators of the sport in India (during the course of writing this book, I did not meet many players across generations who had a positive word to say about them), in 1993 it was to Naresh Kumar that the administrators turned with a request to captain the Indian Davis Cup team, explaining, as Kumar tells me with a wry smile, that 'everyone else had already turned them down'.

When Leander Paes and Ramesh Krishnan pulled off the miracle at Frejus under the guidance of Naresh Kumar and coach Enrico Piperno, the wheel had turned full circle. The journey of a twelve-year-old boy that had started on the grass courts at Calcutta in Undivided India had culminated six decades later in his team beating the mighty French at home on their favoured red clay. No career could have had a more fitting finale.

It is immensely appropriate that in 2020, the Government of India conferred on him, for his lifetime contribution to the cause of Indian tennis, the Dronacharya Award, given to outstanding coaches in sports and games.

Naresh Kumar, now in his nineties, mind as sharp as ever, memories vivid, always full of stories to tell, resides with his lovely wife Sunita at their home in Central Kolkata, surrounded by a stunning collection of art, much of it from the genius brush of their late friend M.F. Husain.

THE 'GOLDEN AGE' OF DOMESTIC TENNIS

The presence of the giants of the sport in their own backyard did help players such as Premjit Lall and Jaidip Mukherjea, the men who bridged the gap between the two great eras— the Krishnan era and the Amritraj era—in India tennis.[39]

—Nirmal Shekhar

When Rajkumari Amrit Kaur, herself an accomplished tennis player in the pre-independence era, and the first Health Minister of independent India, took over the running of the All-India Lawn Tennis Association in 1954, she kicked off what would turn out to be the 'Golden Age' of domestic tennis in India.

There were two things that worked as game changers during the period—the Rajkumari Amrit Kaur Coaching Scheme, and the establishment of the Indian winter domestic tennis circuit.

The coaching scheme was inaugurated in 1953 and would continue for the next four years. It was a scheme that fundamentally changed sports in India and this was the first instance in the history of Indian sports that coaching had been accepted as an inevitable necessity.

During 1953-54 the scheme engaged the services of four Indians and one foreign coach to cover athletics, hockey, tennis, cricket and table tennis. Two years later the scheme was bringing not only coaches of international repute but also international sportsmen of the calibre of Jesse Owens and Emil Zatopek to participate in domestic competitions and help raise the standards of Indian sports. All the money was not spent only on coaches, but was also used to conduct coaching camps across disciplines and throughout the country. Tennis would be a major beneficiary of this effort.

Simultaneously, over the next decade and a half, the Indian domestic tennis circuit, one of the longest in the world at the time, extending from the middle of October to the middle of March, attracted some of the best players in the world. The credit goes not merely to the administrators of the sport, but also the circumstances that weighed in their favour. As Ramanathan Krishnan says in *A Touch of Tennis*, 'In the 1950s, there were very few indoor tournaments in the world and several top players found it convenient to play in India during the European winter, just before they reached Australia for the summer events Down Under.'[40]

Naresh Kumar tells me, 'The sole builders of Indian tennis during the time were three men—Ganesh Dey, Akshay Dey and Anadi Mukherjee who used to run South Club. They were instrumental in getting some of the greatest players in the world to play in Calcutta, and this competition improved the quality of the Indian tennis players as nothing else could have.'

Jaidip Mukherjea provides more colour on how it all started: 'It was 1918 or 1919 when two Bengalis were cycling past the Woodburn Park when they saw a game of tennis. They inquired if they could play. They were told they couldn't because the matches were being organised by the Punjab Club. These gentlemen were Ganesh Dey and Anadi Mukherjee, two of the founders of the South Club; Aukhoy Dey was the third. Ganesh Dey and Mukherjee spoke to J.M. Sengupta, later mayor of Calcutta and club vice-president, who helped lease land for two courts in the same park. That is how it started. Soon, the British started coming here.'[41]

About the South Club, the great Bill Tilden, one of the early legends to play on the club courts, wrote in his book *Aces, Places and Faults*, 'The centre court at the South Club in Calcutta is one of the best grass courts of my experience.'[42] This from a man who had won ten Grand Slam titles on grass at Wimbledon and the US Championships.

The presence of top global talent playing across the length and breadth of the country not only helped raise the profile of the sport in India, but was to immeasurably improve the quality of Indian tennis.

Benefitting from the coaching scheme and the competition provided by the circuit were three men who would define the Golden Age of Indian tennis—Ramanathan Krishnan, Jaidip Mukherjea and Premjit Lall.

While this section of the book will delve deeper into the lives and careers of this fascinating trio, it is worth reflecting first on the extraordinary period that saw the Indian tennis circuit benefit from the embarrassment of riches that descended upon it in the form of quality players at the apogee of their game. It is at the same time an opportunity to consider what playing the sport was like for the players during this long forgotten amateur era, as India embarked on its early journey as an independent nation.

TRAVELLING THE CIRCUIT

The early years of tennis in India had seen the growth of the sport around the army cantonments of the North and the East. But very quickly, it had spread west from Punjab, through Sindh into Bombay. Gradually, it had then taken root in the south, particularly Madras, spilling over into what is currently Kerala. By the mid-1950s, tennis as a sport was popular in pockets across the length and breadth of the country. So much so that in his fascinating book, *Down the Line*, Premjit Lall would describe the Indian circuit thus:

> It covers almost every corner of the country; from Amritsar in the north to Trivandrum in the south. The list of centres could read as a tourist tour. Many a foreign player came with that in mind and tennis thrown in as the passport![43]

While the weather was perfect during that time of the year, the living and travelling conditions were far from ideal. The accounts that one hears from the Indian players of the time who played the circuit provide a fascinating imagery of the times and their travels and travails. Access to the tournaments outside the major cities was one of the major challenges.

Lall continues, 'I have played at places I had never heard of, having to locate them on the map when the invitation arrived. Jai (Jaidip Mukherjea) and I have travelled to tournaments by almost every possible mode of transport except maybe on horseback. Many a time a plane was delayed or cancelled causing us to hire a car and drive hundreds of miles, but we always reached in time! This happened when El Shafei, the Egyptian, was playing the circuit.* We got stranded at Bhubaneshwar airport. We hired a car and drove all night to arrive at Rajamandir to find the crowd waiting and the organising committee running around in circles.'

Krishnan recounts an amusing anecdote about the time when he and Barry Mackay from the US played exhibition matches in several Indian cities in 1959, before proceeding to the Asian Championship at Calcutta. That year Mackay was a semi-finalist at the Australian Championships and Wimbledon and would also reach the quarters of the US Championships.

'For our match at Vijayawada, we travelled by an early morning train from Madras. Taking in the scenes as the steam-engine driven train chugged along, Barry saw people squatting in a neat row along the tracks. Bewildered, he turned to me and asked: "Krish, are they praying?" I explained to him that many Indians, particularly those living in rural areas, did not have toilet facilities at home and relieved themselves out in the open. He was surprised but he understood.'[44]

Interesting as this cultural enlightenment might have been, Mackay was in store for an experience that would be far more first-hand. Krishnan continues: 'At Vijaywada, we were put up in the Railway Retiring Room for an overnight stay. It was a basic sort of place but rather uncomfortable. The

---

*Ismael El Shafei would be a quarterfinalist at Wimbledon a few years on and later become the president of the Egyptian Tennis Federation.

only problem was, it had only an Indian toilet—something
that is a greater threat to a white man's personal freedom
than anything he might encounter in India. Barry said
nothing about his problems and we found ourselves on court
a few hours later. But, in the middle of the match, a railway
employee, accompanied by two police constables, stormed
on the court and grabbed Barry by his shirt collar. The
crowd booed, unable to comprehend what was happening.
But I knew what was going on. The railway employee was
demanding damages. Obviously, Barry had been up to his old
trick in the morning. He had carved a hole into one of the
cane chairs in the retiring room with a breakfast knife and
used it as his own improvised Western toilet!'

Premjit Lall has a toilet story of his own to relate when
he talks about him and his wife Georgina staying at the best
hotel of a small town while on the circuit, 'The room was a
bare whitewashed one with a hard bed and a table. It cost the
princely sum of Rs 5 a day. That was fine, but the toilet was a
shack at the end of a dark garden and to reach it one had to
get past a fence dog.'

It was true that for the leading players, the travel was a tad
more comfortable (relatively speaking) than for the stragglers.
Lall talked about the disparity. 'The top eight players receive
excellent treatment and hospitality but the mediocre and the
junior really have to go through the grind ... On one occasion
in Amritsar during the winter the juniors, having travelled
there in third class compartments, arrived to find that they
had to live in tents and eat almost inedible food after having
paid extremely high entrance fees.'

A decade and a half on, clearly things had not changed.
Ramesh Krishnan, describing his junior days travelling the

Indian circuit, recounted: 'Although the railway network in the country had improved since my father's days as a teenager, it was not necessarily more comfortable. For one thing, the number of people travelling by rail had increased too and the pressure on space was all too apparent in the third class compartments by which we did most of the travelling. Of all the journeys by train, I can never forget the night I spent in an unreserved third class coach, coming from Vijayanagaram in Andhra Pradesh to Madras. You couldn't move so much as an inch in a compartment packed with four times as many people as there were seats. It was quite an experience that long night when the whiff of burning coal mingled with sweat and exhaled warm air to produce an aroma my nostrils were not quite familiar with!'[45]

Nirupama Vaidyanathan, former women's national champion, describes in her autobiography, *Moonballer*, her journeys as a junior, made in the 1990s, more than three decades after Krishnan and Lall. The narrative is startlingly familiar: 'We always travelled second class on the train. Trains to Bombay, now Mumbai, took about twenty-four hours while trains to New Delhi took about forty hours. Each trip was a huge process starting from packing food packets to actually packing tennis stuff. Trains were quite unclean and the food available in the stations would ensure a stomach upset.'

She goes on to narrate an incident that gives a flavour of the challenges of travelling on Indian trains: 'The weirdest incident I remember was when my father and I were on an overnight train to Chennai. I was sleeping on the lower berth and woke up in the middle of the night to go to the washroom. When I got back, I found some guy on my berth, under my blanket, snoring! At first, I thought, maybe I was in the wrong compartment but then I spotted my father. So I woke him up. He immediately switched on the light and woke up the man on my berth. Soon everyone in our coupe woke up. Another gentleman cried, 'That's my shirt you have on!' It turned out that the man had been suffering from dementia and had wandered from one compartment to the next till he saw my berth and decided to occupy it! He was asked to get off at the next station.'

As Krishnan and Lall both concede, however, these problems disappeared when you went up the ranks as a senior and were eligible to travel by air, paid for by the organisers. But travel by air in the first decades after independence was nothing like it is today when it is more the norm (at least between large cities and towns) than the exception.

Krishnan's description of a typical journey will sound quaint to today's Indian traveller, spoilt for choice in terms of connectivity: 'A flight from Madras to New Delhi—the fare was Rs 100!—in 1955 meant spending a whole day in an aeroplane. One left Madras at 6 a.m. by a Dakota flight, stopped at Hyderabad for breakfast, took in lunch at Nagpur, then landed at Bhopal for evening tea before finally walking out of the Delhi terminal looking forward to dinner in the hotel room, a good twelve hours after leaving Madras.* I also

---

*The DC-3 light transport aircrafts used during the Second World War were converted to post-war passenger airlines use. It retained the popular name 'Dakota' that the Royal Air Force gave it. When Indian Airlines was formed in 1953 after merging several small airlines, it inherited 74 Dakotas.

recall that almost all the passengers on an aircraft those days wore jackets and ties ... it was almost as if it was occasion for one to dress up!'

But travel and stay challenges aside, those were simpler times. The nation had been independent for a short time, and the joy and freedom of seeing one's own country and meeting the people was more valued than it is today.

Krishnan speaks for the players of the time when he talks about this in *A Touch of Tennis*: 'But playing in the cities and town of India had its own rewards—as much for someone like me as for visiting players ... Playing in the small towns brought me closer to the real India. After a tough day's tennis I would often sit out in a hotel balcony or on the terrace of the house where I'd be staying and take in the scenes of everyday life, such as a marketplace quarrel or womenfolk standing in line for a pot of water from a public tap on the road.'

It was not only the pleasures of simplicity that was special about the times, but the fact that the sport of tennis was actually watched, understood and appreciated by a surprisingly wide spectrum of society given the lack of media and social media that can today spread the word far and wide.

Krishnan goes on: 'One of the most emotionally gratifying aspects of my own career was the fact that I played quite often in some of the remotest parts of the country. I have played exhibition matches in small villages with a solitary tennis court. Once we even played a match watched by inmates of a jail in North India. But then, sports awareness in rural India in the 1950s was astounding. You'd find rustic village folk brushing their teeth with slender sticks of neem-tree branches, watching the morning matches at tournaments.* If you are playing for the first time in such an ambience, you'd think it would make no difference to them whether you played tennis in front of them or ran an impromptu mini-circus with tightrope walking, et al. Yet, no sooner had you played a delicate drop shot than there would be spontaneous applause. These people knew the game, and followed the scores perfectly too.'

Premjit Lall talks about playing matches in a remote part of Andhra Pradesh where 'a tonga would be sent through the main streets of the surrounding villages, announcing the day's play over a loudspeaker'.

The playing arrangements were often less than ideal, but the heart of the organisers and fans were always in the right place. Lall continues, 'Jai (Jaidip Mukherjea) and I were invited to a small town to play a flood-lit exhibition match. We arrived to find a large crowd waiting anxiously around the court. The organising committee proudly walked us to the court. To our amazement we found that the only light on the court was from a large bulb hanging over the net.'[46]

Jaidip Mukherjea tells me in a recent conversation about another experience with flood-lit tennis courts. 'We had just finished playing a Davis Cup tie against the Australians and went to play a series of exhibition matches. One such match was in Premjit's home town of Bhagalpur. He had been assured that we would enjoy playing under lights. When we arrived, there was the court with twenty bulbs lining on one side and twenty on the other. That was their flood-lit tennis

---

*Neem is an evergreen tree of the Mahogany family with scientific name Azadrichta Indica, a native to the Indian subcontinent. Its twigs are traditionally used for cleaning teeth and in recent years, its extract has been used to make toothpaste.

court!' However, the fact that matches were played in such rural areas in difficult conditions didn't deter the foreigners playing the circuit. Krishnan again, 'It gave me immense pleasure playing before a rural audience, whether it was in Srikakulam in Andhra Pradesh, Nagercoil in Tamil Nadu, Raichur in Karnataka or Digboi in Assam. I was touched by their enthusiasm. Very often, some of the most recognisable names in the sport from Australia or America followed me to these remote corners of India. This made the whole thing even more satisfying for me.'

THE BEST IN THE WORLD ARRIVE

Given the fact that tennis in India owes its origins to the British civil servants and defence personnel, it is hardly surprising that foreigners won most of the early tournaments and played widely across the length and breadth of India. What was different about the foreign players who appeared in Indian tournaments from the 1950s was that they came to play the Indian Circuit as a part of their annual routine and made it the time when they could combine some much-needed off-season practice with fairly exotic tourism paid for by the organisers.

What this achieved was that some of the greatest players in the world to grace a tennis court appeared at regular tournaments and exhibition matches in the most unlikely corners of India, over the course of a decade and more. Two of Australia's seemingly neverending stream of tennis geniuses to emerge in the last century, Neale Fraser and Roy Emerson, were regulars on the Indian Circuit.

Left-handed Neale Fraser was one of the three all-time greats that Australia produced in the decades that followed the Second World War. Beginning his Grand Slam winning journey in 1959 with his first US Championships trophy, Fraser, in a twenty-five-year career (from 1950 to 1975) would go on to win nineteen Grand Slams—three singles (one Wimbledon and another US Championship in 1960), eleven doubles and six mixed doubles titles in the course of a glittering career. By doing what he did in 1959 and 1960 at the US Championships, Fraser remains the last person to win the singles, doubles and mixed doubles titles in a calendar year at a Grand Slam tournament on two consecutive occasions.

And yet, making Fraser look almost ordinary in comparison and converting world tennis titles into an Australian monopoly during the period was contemporary Roy Emerson, a man who, just incidentally, was clocked at 10.2 seconds during a 100-metre sprint.

Over the course of a staggering thirty-year tennis career, from 1953 to 1983, Emerson would hoard twelve Grand Slam singles titles (six Australian, and two each of the others) and sixteen Grand Slam doubles titles. During this period, Emerson was also a part of the Australian Davis Cup team that for the most part held an embarrassing plethora of riches—Emerson, Fraser and the third (and perhaps greatest) musketeer—Rod Laver (before he turned professional), together picking up eight Davis Cup titles over a nine-year period between 1959 and 1967.

The only break in Australia's Davis Cup run during that period came in 1963. That year, moving into the inter-zonal final were two teams, one that was fully expected to be there—

the US—and the other that wasn't—India. The winner would play Australia in the Challenge Round. Having overcome Japan in the Eastern Zone finals, India found the Americans too much to handle, losing 0-5 despite the best efforts of Krishnan and Lall. The Americans then went on to upset Australia 3-2 and pick up the Cup.

In 1959, American Barry Mackay, ranked no. 2 in the US and a mainstay of their strong Davis Cup side, came to India. He lost to Premjit Lall in the semi-finals of the Indian National Championships and then went on to play a series of matches across the country. Joining him was Swede Ulf Schmidt, winner of the Wimbledon doubles title that year, and a singles semi-finalist the previous year.

A few years later, Ion Tiriac (nicknamed 'Count Dracula' in reference to Transylvania, his place of birth) and Illie Nastase (appropriately nicknamed 'Nasty' for his temper tantrums on the court) of Romania came to play on the circuit, this time sent by their government on a 'goodwill' tour. The agreement between the governments was that they would play for the token sum of Rs 7.50 per day. They were relatively unknown at the time, but both would rise to become world-renowned players in the very near future. Nastase would, in fact, make a permanent place for himself in the record books, becoming the first official world no. 1 in 1973 under the computer ranking system introduced by the Association of Tennis Professionals (ATP).

Georgina Lall (Premjit Lall's wife) recounts a couple of stories from the circuit that year: 'Nastase, a great natural player, was shy, with a somewhat childish sense of humour. He'd spend hours chasing Tiriac around the club holding a cockroach (of which the massive Tiriac, rumoured to be a member of the Romanian Secret Police, was mortally scared). He (Nastase) too had temper tantrums that are known throughout the world. He was also headstrong. Prem was once to play him in an exhibition match in Hyderabad. Prem was to receive Rs 1000 and he the official 750. Since the organisers were charging for tickets and sold out, Nastase asked for some more money. The committee refused. Nastase went on court and in front of the capacity crowd did not hit a single ball over the net and in court. Prem won 6-0, 6-1.'

Such, then, was the quality of the players who competed on the Indian circuit. It was therefore hardly surprising that Indian tennis would be elevated to a different level as the extremely talented group of domestic players that came through the system at this time, foremost among them Premjit Lall and Jaidip Mukherjea, honed their skills against the best in home conditions.

Between Ramanathan Krishnan, Premjit Lall and Jaidip Mukerjea, Indian tennis rose to unimagined heights, even surpassing the achievements of the early pioneers like Mohammad Sleem and Sydney Jacobs. They would come to be referred to as the 'Three Musketeers' of Indian tennis.

Krishnan reached the highest world ranking ever achieved by an Indian tennis player—world no. 3, and given a bit of luck could well have been India's first Wimbledon champion, at least on one of the two occasions that he made the semi-finals. There was no champion of the time who remained unconquered by this genius from Madras.

Premjit Lall, while not rising to these dizzying heights, was a player of extraordinary talent. Up two sets to love and

3-2 against defending champion Rod Laver at Wimbledon in 1969, he let the greatest opportunity of his life slip from his grasp. Laver went on to complete his second Grand Slam that year.

Jaidip Mukherjea completed the count of the Three Musketeers. Without the supremely talented Mukherjea, an exceptional doubles player and a force to be reckoned with in singles on his day, the achievements of Indian tennis during the period would not have been possible.

The Three Musketeers (later joined by Vijay Amritraj) would convert India into a force to reckon with at the Davis Cup, taking their nation to the inter-zonal finals for three years from 1960 to 1963, and again in 1968. The musketeers also steered India to its first-ever Davis Cup final against Australia in 1966. Rarely, in the ensuing decades, would tennis in the country reach such dizzying heights. It would not, therefore, be remiss to term the decade of the 1960s as the true 'Golden Age' of Indian tennis.

RAMANATHAN KRISHNAN
THE KING OF INDIAN TENNIS

Krish is, without doubt, the greatest player India has ever produced till date.[47]

—Premjit Lall

On 10 March 1954, the *Coventry Evening Telegraph* in England carried a report from the erstwhile colonial capital of Calcutta about the exploits of a young Indian boy. The headline announced: *India Has a Lawn Tennis Hope at the Age of 16.*[48]

The report went on to say: 'India thinks it has a new tennis player who will soon be challenging Lewis Hoad and Ken Rosewall, the young Australian champions. He is Krishnan Ramanathan—known in tennis circles as R. Krishnan—at sixteen, the new national champion of India. After two seasons of top-flight tennis, Krishnan beat the experienced Australian Jack Arkinstall in straight sets at Calcutta to win the title. He stormed his way through the championship without losing a set and he is regarded as India's best hope for international honours for many years.'

The reporter who filed the piece could not have imagined quite how prescient that would turn out to be. That sixteen-year-old would go on to become his country's greatest-ever tennis player, so much so that seven decades on, as I wrote this book, no Indian had come even remotely near touching the heights scaled by Ramanathan Krishnan. This is the story of that remarkable man, the undisputed 'King of Indian Tennis'.

A WIMBLEDON TITLE

Two years before the *Coventry Evening Telegraph* took notice of the talents of young Krishnan, he had already been making waves on the tennis circuit.

At the South India Championships in 1952, Ramanathan Krishnan, aged fourteen, stormed into the finals, defeating a strong field of senior players before losing narrowly 6-8, 6-8, 2-6 to Tony Mottram, Britain's no. 1 player, a doubles finalist and singles quarter-finalist at Wimbledon.

The AILTA sent in the names of Krishnan for the Boys' Singles and Rita Davar for the Girls' Singles events at Wimbledon that year. A grand sum of Rs 2,500 was offered to Krishnan's father T.K. Ramanathan for the trip to England. The sum, while princely for the times, was not enough, and Vishweshwar Gajapati Raju, or Vishy, Rajkumar of Vijayanagaram, stepped in to help. Krishnan was on his way.

Very often in life, a journey is as memorable as the final destination. For the fourteen-year-old Krishnan, it certainly was. The money raised was enough to get him to England, but not by air.

Father and son boarded a Boat Mail from Madras to Dhanushkodi. That connected to a ferry that took the duo to Thailaimannar in Sri Lanka and onward by train to Colombo. Two days of exhibition matches against Sri Lanka's top players followed, and then they were on board the *SS Orantis* from Colombo to London.

On that long journey, food was an issue for the vegetarian duo, and the lack of understanding of fellow passengers added to the problems.

Krishnan recalls, 'We had to make do with breads, salads, fruits and ice cream for the most part. The first few days on the ship we managed to pick up two apples each when fruits were served, although we were expected to take just one each. One day, as I reached out and grabbed two apples, a Frenchman sitting at our table caught me by my wrist and said, "One for each, son." I was flushed.'

Hunger found its own solution. Krishnan goes on, 'Two weeks later, Father would need all his skills in winning friends and convincing people when he had to speak to an Indian student in the UK whose mother had sent a jar of pickles and a box of sweets with us for her son—for, when the ship reached Marseilles, both the jar and the box were empty!'[49]

At Wimbledon that year, Krishnan's age and inexperience would work against him as he faced up to the bigger and older players in the event. But his obvious talent got him a Fred Perry clothes contract, allowing him to shed the baggy shorts and round neck t-shirts favoured by his father. More importantly, it gave him the opportunity to watch the men's final at Wimbledon between Jaroslav Drobny and Frank Sedgeman. Sitting courtside, his father would give him a lesson that would turn out to be one of the most important of his career.

Krishnan explains, 'I didn't take my eyes off their faces during the match until Father tapped me out of my reverie and said, "Look at Sedgeman's feet, not his face." As I watched Sedgeman's dancing feet and remained in awe of his speed about court, it turned out to be a big tennis lesson for me—it is the feet that play tennis.'

The lessons of 1952 would hold Krishnan in good stead the following year when he reached the first round of the men's event before losing to the no. 3 seed Mervyn Rose of Australia, but not before taking a set off him. In the Boys' event, Krishnan reached the final before losing to W. Knight

Krishnan and Misra in 1953

of England. He was still only fifteen, and improving by the day.

In 1954, two years after first travelling out of the country, Krishnan ventured out alone as a sixteen-year-old on the circuit. Full of confidence from his first national title against Arkinstall, the young Indian stormed through the field to lift the junior Wimbledon title, beating Ashley Cooper of Australia in the final.

Cooper would go on to occupy the world no. 1 ranking later that decade, beating Neale Fraser and bagging his first Australian Championship title in 1957. In 1958, Cooper would come close to achieving a Grand Slam, winning the Australian, US and Wimbledon titles before losing a tight semi-final at Roland Garros.

The thigh-slapping celebration after the win against Cooper at Wimbledon by the normally taciturn Krishnan showed the world how much it meant to him. Five decades after the first Indian had walked on the Wimbledon grass, the nation had its maiden title at the home of tennis. As importantly, it was the first Grand Slam title in any category for an Asian player.

A week later, Krishnan beat Tony Mottram at Sunderland to register his first overseas tournament victory in senior tennis, defending the title successfully in 1955. That year he also reached the third round at Wimbledon.

Rising to the Top—1956 to 1959

Perhaps the reason why Krishnan would go on to have a long and successful career was that he never stopped enjoying his game. Back from his triumph at Wimbledon, he was soon on the tennis courts playing for Loyola College in Madras. He tells this story of a teenage boy far removed momentarily from the pressures of international tennis:

> I remember an inter-collegiate match, played over the best of nineteen games, in which I was leading my opponent 7-0. While we were changing sides, my opponent whispered into my ears: 'Please give me a couple of games. My girlfriend is watching.' I obliged. But when the score was 8-3 in my favour, the young man edged close to me during the changeover and whispered, 'Please finish the match. My girlfriend and I are planning to go for a movie.'

Enjoyment aside, the serious business of building a career on the challenging men's circuit was upon him as expectations soared. In 1956, soon after helping India record a victory over Japan in the Davis Cup, Krishnan travelled from Tokyo to join the start of the English tennis season.

Just when Wimbledon was round the corner, while playing in a tournament at Bristol, Krishnan sprained his right ankle and had to be carried off the field. Fortunately, age was on his side and recovery was remarkably quick as he prepared to face off in the first round on the Centre Court of Wimbledon against a man he had hero-worshipped as a junior—Jaroslav Drobny.

Drobny was a man whose life and career would have fascinated any youngster. He was a World Championship winner and Olympic silver medalist in Ice Hockey, multiple Grand Slam tournament winning tennis champion, and a Top Ten ranked player continuously from 1946 to 1955. Starting his tennis career in his native Czechoslovakia a year before the outbreak of the Second World War, Drobny would end up representing four different countries at Wimbledon during the course of his career—Czechoslovakia, the Protectorate of Bohemia and Moravia (after the German invasion of Czechoslovakia), Egypt (he remains the only Egyptian Grand Slam title holder) and Great Britain.

The evening before the match against Drobny, after practice, seeing Krishnan's ankle still strapped, compatriot Akhtar Ali asked him, 'Krish, are you going to play?'

The answer came, 'Certainly. I'll leave my ankle near the baseline if it hurts, and go to the net. But play I will.'

Krishnan needed a left-hander to practice against for his big match. Rod Laver walked up to him as he prepared to hit on Court no. 17. 'Krish, I know who you are looking for. I'll hit with you,' said Laver. Then after the practice session Laver added, 'Krish, you go ahead and change. I will return the practice balls.' The preparation would be invaluable, and the friendship between the two men formed at the time endures decades later.

Stepping onto the court against Drobny with confidence, Krishnan went in all guns blazing. He was going in behind each shot, volleying, playing wonderful down the line passing shots. Two hours later, Jaroslav Drobny, a big name on the European circuit even then, lay vanquished 6-1, 4-6, 6-1, 6-4.

Congratulations flowed in, newspaper headlines announced his arrival, and it was capped by a personal invitation from Prime Minister Jawaharlal Nehru and daughter Indira to a South Indian breakfast the next morning in London.

That year Krishnan lost in the third round to Australian Malcolm Anderson, who, the following year, would win the

US Championships. But the journey had found its legs. He was still only eighteen, and Krishnan knew success was around the corner. This was the long haul, and he was in it for keeps.

With a college degree in hand by 1957, there were no distractions. Over the next two years, from April to October, Krishnan played the European circuit. In 1957, a victory over Italy's Nicola Pietrangeli on clay propelled Krishnan, thus far known as a good grass-court player, into instant limelight across Europe.

Before Rafael Nadal arrived on the scene four decades later, there had been few clay court players better than Pietrangeli. His forty-three career titles included two singles titles at Roland Garros and a doubles and mixed doubles title to boot. His 120 victories in the Davis Cup is a record that is yet to be bettered. Late in 2019, Leander Paes went past Pietrangeli's forty-two doubles wins, but the accompanying seventy-eight singles victories makes Pietrangeli a class apart when playing for his country.

The win over Pietrangeli brought Krishnan a contract to play the US circuit in 1957, an experience that would hold him in good stead as he marched towards his destiny. With some significant victories on the European circuit the following year and eight successive doubles titles partnering Jaroslav Drobny, by the time 1959 came around, Krishnan was ranked among the top ten in the world.

Despite the ranking, the ultimate prize—glory at Wimbledon, would prove elusive. In the third round, Krishnan ran into no. 1 ranked Alex Olmedo from Peru. A valiant four-set effort was not enough and the Indian lost 4-6, 6-3, 4-6, 5-7. A line in Olmedo's speech at the Champion's

Ball—'Once I beat Krish in the tough match, I knew I was going to win the title,' may have assuaged Krishnan's ego, but only heightened the sense of an opportunity lost.

Travelling to the US for the fall circuit, Krishnan justified his billing by winning the 1959 US Hard Court title at Denver, Colorado. But success at the US National Championships on grass, despite that being his favoured surface, would elude Krishnan for the entirety of his career.

This has often foxed his admirers, but as he explains, 'Because the Davis Cup matches were not scheduled as thoughtfully as they are now, playing in the inter-zone finals meant you could not make the trip to Forest Hills. I only played there three times in my career, in 1957, 1959 and then in 1968. (Besides) I never did enjoy playing there. The grass was not even and unless you served extremely well, you did not have much of a chance there. In fact, the centre court at Forest Hills sloped to one side and many a big server did well there.'[50]

Krishnan may not have done well at Forest Hills, but he got to the finals of a bunch of other tournaments in the US that year. Unbeknown to him, he had caught the attention of Jack Kramer, the man who was creating a breed of professional tennis players.

Just before taking a flight from Los Angeles, Krishnan was met at the airport by one of Kramer's agents with an incredible offer for the time. The offer guaranteed a minimum of $150,000 and much more if he stayed healthy and played often enough over a three-year period.

If one were to make the conversion to 2020 terms, this would put the minimum guaranteed amount at $1.3 million, roughly what the current world no. 10 (which is what Krishnan's ranking was when the Kramer offer was made) David Goffin has earned annually over the course of his career.

To add further perspective for modern fans of the game, an amateur like Krishnan, making the semi-finals of Wimbledon, would at the time receive, besides actual expenses, merely a £30 voucher that stated clearly: 'According to the rules and regulations of tennis, the voucher could be used only to buy sports goods.'

Krishnan told the agent he would discuss the Kramer offer with his father when back in Madras, and revert. The decision that father and son took was a brave one for a middle-class Indian family.

Krishnan talks us through it. 'We decided not to take up the offer. Nothing in the world was worth staying away from Wimbledon and Davis Cup (both of which did not allow professionals at the time). We wrote a polite letter and informed Kramer that we were not ready to take the offer at that point of time. Kramer was livid. He called me on the telephone and told me that I was letting go of a goldmine. I said I was making "enough" (pocket money) as an amateur. He laughed and said, "You call that money!"'

Reflecting on the decision years later, Krishnan would say, 'Was I stupid to throw away such an opportunity to get rich? No, I don't think so. It was a rational rather than an emotional decision. If the Open Era had dawned then, rather than in 1968, I would certainly have become a professional. But, pride in performance on the traditional stages of the game, and a place in history, outweighed all the money Kramer could often then.'

The next two seasons would vindicate his stand.

The Peak Years

Ramanathan Krishnan started 1960 ranked no. 3 in the world. Since Olmeda announced that he was turning professional after the rankings were released, Krishnan was technically world no. 2. Never before, nor since, has an Indian reached such heights in the men's singles rankings.

It would not, however, be smooth sailing. In April, Krishnan contracted chicken pox and was quarantined. His marriage had been fixed many months before for 2 May. So by the time he was back on the court, Wimbledon was upon him, and he was sorely short of match practice.

As he confesses with dry humour in his book, *A Touch of Tennis*, 'When my teenaged wife Lalitha and I arrived in London, her diamond nose stud drew more attention than did my tennis, for a start.'

Once he had played a couple of doubles matches and got past Andres Gimeno in the second round after being down 2-6, 1-3, the form and the confidence came rushing back. In the quarter-finals, Krishnan took out Luis Ayala of Chile, a man he had never beaten before, in straight sets. Ayala had been a two-time finalist at the French Championships, including earlier that year.

In the semi-finals, waiting for Krishnan was his friend, Neale Fraser. The Australian's opponent had forfeited the match because of cramps, so Krishnan privately felt Fraser was lucky to be there.

Neale Fraser was a man who would go on to win three singles and sixteen doubles and mixed doubles titles at Grand Slams during the course of his long career. In the semi-final against Krishnan that year at Wimbledon, he would demonstrate exactly why luck had little role to play in his being where he was.

Krishnan talks us through the match which saw him step on Centre Court as the first Indian to play the singles semi-finals at Wimbledon:

> Neale decimated me with a masterly display of left-handed serving. It was a windy day and I struggled to come to terms with the serve that broke into my body or spun past my outstretched racquet. On the other hand, on my serve, Neale turned a weakness into a strength as he hit out freely on his weak backhand and broke me at crucial moments. I ended my career with an impressive 5-2 record against Neale but he beat me at Wimbledon and in a crucial Davis Cup rubber. That made all the difference.

Fraser would go on to win Wimbledon that year.

Beaten, but with his head held justifiably high, Krishnan was back the following year at his favourite Grand Slam after a series of impressive performances on the circuit. He was now ranked no. 6 in the world.

With straight sets victories in the first two rounds, Krishnan ran into Italy's Orlando Sirola in the third. At 6 feet 8 inches, Sirola was largely a clay court player and a semi-finalist at the French Championships that year. Krishnan decided that he couldn't out-hit or get past the long reach of Sirola, and adopted a tactic no one had ever tried against the tall Sirola. He drew Sirola to the net, and incredibly, given the fact that he was facing an extremely tall man, lobbed over his head consistently to win in four sets. It was tennis mastery at its best.

In the quarter-finals Krishnan played one of the finest matches of his career. Against fourth-seeded Australian Roy Emerson, who would eventually end a glorious career with twelve Grand Slam singles titles, including the Australian and US Championships that year (1961), Krishnan, displaying magnificent grass court skills, prevailed 6-1, 6-4, 6-4.

For the second year in a row, Ramanathan Krishnan was in the semi-finals of Wimbledon. Waiting for him there was another Aussie, left-handed Rod Laver. Krishnan had a 3-0 record against Laver at that stage and so he had reason to feel confident. Unfortunately for him, this was a new and improved Laver, the one the world would greet with awe even six decades later when he put in appearances in special boxes at Grand Slams around the world.

Rod Laver's backhand return until then had always been a slice, which Krishnan had dealt with adequately in the past. At this meeting, Laver revealed a weapon he would forever come to be feared for—the topspin backhand. Krishnan writes, 'My racquet often wobbled in the face of the spin onslaught mounted by the young redhead who would go on to become the greatest player of all time.'

Laver won 6-2, 8-6, 6-2. He would hold aloft the Wimbledon trophy that year, the first of eleven Grand Slam singles, six doubles and three mixed doubles titles that eventually found their place on his mantelpiece.

1962 could well have turned out to be Krishnan's glory year. He was arguably in the best form of his life, and all his major rivals had lost in the early rounds of the tournament. Seeded fourth and waiting for his third-round singles match, Krishnan stepped on court to play the first round of a doubles encounter partnering Bob Howe. Playing a doubles match had for long been Krishnan's preferred way of getting into top form for crucial singles encounters. So, for him, this was routine.

Sadly, this time it would turn out to be a bad decision. He twisted his ankle during the match, and although he stepped out on court against John Fraser, Neale's brother, Krishnan had to forfeit the match after a while. His best chance at a Grand Slam title had been snatched from his grasp by a freak injury.

Three years in the wilderness followed as Krishnan dealt with a mid-career mental let-down. Acutely conscious now of the lack of financial security, he set about building his new business—running an LPG gas agency in Madras to provide for his and his family's future, the tennis circuit temporarily forgotten.

In early 1965 Krishnan felt mentally ready to make a comeback and chose to launch his efforts on the winter circuit at the indoor courts in the US. The only practice time the organisers at Maryland would grant him was at 3 a.m. in the morning. So, at temperatures well below freezing, Krishnan would wake up at 2.30 a.m., hit for an hour and a half and go back to sleep as dawn broke. He lost to Arthur Ashe at Maryland, but would go on to make seven tour finals, winning three of them.

The biggest of these wins was at Houston where Krishnan had an interesting encounter. He recounts:

A certain George Bush, a prominent member of the River Oaks Country Club, the venue of the tournament, 'bought' me in a Calcutta pool auction for $3500. Calcutta pool, I believe, had its origins in the capital of West Bengal among racing aficionados there. This Mr Bush would promptly arrive at my practice and watch all my matches and remind me constantly that I should do my very best to win. I told him I would. As it turned out, I beat Rafael Osuna (US Championships winner and world no. 1 the previous year) in the quarter-final, Emerson in the semi-final and young Cliff Richie in the final. Mr Bush—the very man who would become president of the United States two decades on—was the first to leap into the arena to hug and congratulate me. By then we had become good friends. His son (the future President George Bush Jr) was a ball boy in the final that I won.[51]

By the end of 1965, Krishnan was ranked no. 9 in the world and on the way back to the top. Unfortunately, he developed a cyst in his playing wrist on top of a tendon and had to sit out for seven long months. He was now twenty-nine and recovery from injuries was taking longer and longer.

Davis Cup 1966—The Almost Year

'Davis Cup is pure magic—there is nothing quite like it. The joy of representing your country, the goose pimples that freeze you when the national anthem is played and the flag goes up, the camaraderie in the dressing room and most of all, the crowds ... the feeling is very, very special. Take away Davis Cup, and tennis itself will be a lesser sport, much less attractive.'[52]

It is hardly surprising that these words come from a man who turned down not once, but three times, at the age of twenty-two, the Jack Kramer offer of financial security for life.

From his debut in 1953, Krishnan would go on to represent India in the Davis Cup for seventeen long years. During this period he played ninety-seven matches for the country, winning sixty-nine of them, including fifty singles. Krishnan's list of memorable wins in Davis Cup ties is long. But a few deserve special mention, often for the back stories associated with them.

1959 was a year when Krishnan was moving towards his peak as a tennis player. But so was his eventual nemesis at Wimbledon, Rod Laver, who would go on to be a finalist that year before winning the Championship at the next attempt.

When India came up against an Australian team boasting of Rod Laver, Roy Emerson and Neale Fraser in the interzonal final, it was a foregone conclusion which side would prevail. So it was said, and so it would be, but not before Krishnan provided a little twist to the tale.

The venue of the tie was iconic—the Longwood Cricket Club on the outskirts of Boston in the US. The club had the distinction of hosting the first ever Davis Cup competition.*

---

*The first Davis Cup took place in 1900 and saw the US take on Great Britain, then playing under the name of the British Isles. The US won 3-0. It was held at the Longwood Cricket Club in Boston. The tournament was conceived in 1899 by four members of the Harvard University tennis team who came up with the idea of challenging the British to a tennis competition. Dwight Davis of the Harvard University team led the US side, designed the tournament format and spent money from his own pocket to purchase an appropriate sterling silver trophy from Shreve, Crump & Low. The tournament was originally known as the International Lawn Tennis Challenge, but soon became known as Davis Cup after Dwight Davis's trophy.

As it so happens, I spent two years residing a few hundred metres away from the iconic Club. The Club had seen its last serious cricket match played in 1933, but I knew its rich Davis Cup history, and its beautiful grass courts had always held enormous fascination for me.

It is on one of these courts that Krishnan played Laver in the opening match of the tie, an encounter Krishnan tells me was 'my best ever Davis Cup match'.[53]

Krishnan took the first two sets from a dazed Laver, 6-1, 6-4. Serving beautifully, with his volleys and drop shots in full flow, Krishnan faltered only once, in the seventeenth game of the third set, to lose 6-8. But in the fourth he pulled away and one break was sufficient to leave him victorious at 6-4. Sadly, India lost the rest of the matches including Krishnan's reverse singles against Neale Fraser, the Indian unable to handle Fraser's serves, as would be the case the following year at the Wimbledon semi-finals. Australia won the tie 4-1.

In 1961, Krishnan played the fifth match, a dead rubber, against Chuck McKinley of the United States, after the tie had already been won by the visitors. Rarely has New Delhi seen a better five-setter.

McKinley was to reach the Wimbledon finals against Laver and go on and win the US Open on grass that year, one of the four Slams he would bag on his way to becoming world no. 1. But on this day, with the two men ranked in the world's top five battling it out, no quarters would be asked for and none given. Their own, and national pride, was at stake. In a match that was spoken of with much nostalgia for decades afterwards, Krishnan won 6-3, 4-6, 1-6, 6-3, 6-4, making the final tie scoreline a close 2-3.

Later that evening, the teams were invited to Rashtrapati Bhavan by Dr S. Radhakrishnan. Stumped by the erudite Indian president who asked him for the origins of the tennis terms 'love' and 'deuce', Krishnan was inadvertently rescued by McKinley trying to convince Dr Radhakrishnan that visiting players should be better compensated at Indian tournaments. It was only later in the evening that the well-meaning McKinley understood to his embarrassment that he had been talking to the president of India and not the president of the AILTA!

But Krishnan's greatest Davis Cup match was to come in 1966, a year when he had not played on the circuit and was woefully short of match practice. To compensate, Krishnan arrived at the South Club courts in Calcutta two weeks before the tie and started intense practice days playing six sets every day with teammates Premjit Lall and Jaidip Mukherjea.

Leading Brazil in the inter-zonal final was left-handed Thomaz Koch, an accomplished grass court player then ranked no. 12 in the world. Koch blew away Mukherjea in the first match, Krishnan restoring parity against Jose Mandarino in four sets. Krishnan and Mukherjea then prevailed over Koch and Mandarino in five extremely hard-fought sets to take India up 2-1 into the final day. By midday, and leading into the final session of play on Sunday, the teams were back level at 2-2, Mukherjea losing a heartbreaking five-setter to Mandarino.

When twenty-nine-year-old Krishnan stepped onto the court for the tie finale, he had already played nine hard-fought sets in less than forty-eight hours. After losing the first set 3-6, Krishnan came back to win the next 6-4. Then, with three set points in the third set in his favour, in Krishnan's own wistful words, he 'contrived to lose it 10-12'.

At 1-2 down in the match, onset of darkness meant the match would go on to the fourth morning. Krishnan talks about what went on in his mind that evening: 'It's funny how your body and mind complain a lot louder when you are trailing in a match. The mind plays its dirty games when you least want to deal with them. But as a sportsman, you have to learn how to tackle them. Sitting in my bed that evening, I said to myself: "All is not lost. I just have to win a best of three sets match in two straight sets on the morrow."'[54]

Krishnan's mind may have taken the decision, but execution by the body the next morning would be a tad more difficult. With their idol trailing 3-6, 6-4, 10-12, 2-5 and 0-30, the stands were beginning to empty with embarrassing rapidity. With two points separating Krishnan from defeat, only a few scattered eternal optimists remained.

And then it happened.

Krishnan clawed his way back to 30-30 and hit a stunning forehand crosscourt past a flat-footed Koch. He took the game, but was still down 3-5. Then the years of experience kicked in and at the changeover, snatches of a conversation Krishnan had had two years before at Wimbledon with Dennis Ralston came back to him. Ralston had beaten Koch multiple times, and on being asked for his secret, had pointed out a weakness in Koch's game that he had exploited every time they met. The Brazilian, a brilliant baseliner, was sluggish on his forward movement.

As Koch began serving for the match, Krishnan did something that Leander Paes would emulate at a crucial Davis

Cup match decades later—he started playing clever drop shots, drawing Koch forwards, and in forcing that unnatural movement for the Brazilian, leaving him stranded time and again. The remarkable bit was that while Paes would have the advantage of a slow clay court in implementing this strategy, Krishnan was doing it on the fast grass court of the South Club.

From 2-5 down in the fourth set, Krishnan won 7-5 and raced to 4-0 in the fifth. While this remarkable turnaround was happening, the radios were still on, the word had spread, and the fans were racing back from the exits. At 4-0, the temporary stands were once more packed, as were the rooftops of every highrise building around South Club. There was barely space to move beyond the court lines. Clearly, fans had brought some friends back as well.

Krishnan remembers, 'Koch was shell-shocked and a bundle of nerves. I could see him trembling.'

Scripting one of the greatest comeback victories in the history of Davis Cup, Krishnan would go on to win 'the most famous victory of my Davis Cup career', 3-6, 6-4, 10-12, 7-5, 6-2.[55] More importantly, almost five decades since the nation had sent its first Davis Cup team to the competition in 1921, against all odds, with no player ranked in the top 100 in the world, India was in the final.

It would sadly not be a fairy tale ending to the story as the strong Australian side won the Davis Cup that year, 4-1, with Krishnan and Mukherjea pulling off a stunning doubles victory over John Newcombe and Tony Roche, handing the Aussie pair the only defeat they had had to suffer the entire year in competitive tennis.

A couple of years and a few more Davis Cup victories later, including a famous one against West Germany at Munich in 1968, Ramanathan Krishnan laid down his racquet at the age of thirty-two. He would come back as the non-playing Davis Cup captain over the course of the next decade and guide India to its second Davis Cup final in 1974, with Vijay Amritraj now taking up his place as the nation's leading player. When his son Ramesh came into the team, Krishnan stepped back from the captaincy to avoid any conflict of interest while picking the team for future Davis Cup ties.

Krishnan continued to be associated for many years with his son Ramesh's tennis academy in Chennai. As I found to my delight while researching and writing this book, the sharp mind and keen intellect of India's 'King of Tennis' continues to provide valuable insights from his home in Chennai to those who care to seek it.

THE GREATEST PLAYER

'Krish is, without doubt, the greatest player India has ever produced till date,' Premjit Lall had written just a few years after Krishnan's retirement. He was Krishnan's contemporary, and could perhaps be accused of some bias as a result, but how have the future generations judged him?

Fast-forward five decades. During a conversation that I had with Leander Paes in the course of writing this book, we spoke about the generations of great tennis players India has been blessed to have, from Mohammed Sleem to the present.

'The greatest of all? Ramanathan Krishnan, without a doubt,' the winner of eighteen Grand Slam titles and

India's only Olympic medal winner in tennis told me with undisguised admiration in his voice. 'Getting to two Wimbledon semi-finals and world no. 3, how can you possibly beat that?' Paes added.[56]

I asked Krishnan himself how he looks back on his career. He talks me through it and adds to what he mentions in his book:

> I did not win a Grand Slam because of the lack of a good serve. This was my handicap. But the truth is also that I did not win it because I lost a big serve. I did have it as a sixteen-year-old when I beat Arkinstall to win the national title. I used to average an ace a game at that time. I had a beautiful toss and a perfect transfer of body weight. But towards the end of 1954, I had a minor shoulder injury and when I came back I found to my dismay that my service action was gone. I never got it back.[57]

He goes on: 'That apart, I never learnt the art of peaking. It's a quality all great champions have. In my days Fraser, Laver and Emerson did. Another reason, as I see it now, was in the mind: I felt too satisfied too soon for my own good. I looked back and said, "Ah, good, I have won five matches." Instead, I should have motivated myself saying, "Go out and win two more." In sport at the highest levels, contentment is suicidal. It's a dangerous feeling. (Sadly.) Indian players get contented quickly.'

Ramanathan Krishnan is perhaps his own harshest critic, as great sportsmen are wont to be. But the fact of the matter is that Krishnan plied his craft at a time when the original 'Big Three' of tennis, Rod Laver, Roy Emerson and Neale Fraser, with twenty-six Grand Slam singles titles between them, dominated world tennis, much as Roger Federer, Rafael Nadal and Novak Djokovic have done over the past decade and a half. To have competed with them at the highest level, beaten each of them multiple times at Slams as well as Davis Cup encounters and other big tournaments was no mean feat.

Five decades after he retired, Krishnan continues to be treated with awe and respect both by the tennis community at large, as well as future generations of players and fans. Until India produces its first Grand Slam singles champion, the mantle of the 'greatest tennis player India has ever produced', will continue to rest easily on the broad shoulders of Ramanathan Krishnan.

THE 'BENGAL TWINS'
PREMJIT LALL AND JAIDIP MUKHERJEA

A tennis player's life besides the glamour is a very lonely one; so if your travelling partner is someone you don't get along with, it can be miserable. Luckily, Premjit and I get along exceptionally well which has helped our tennis a great deal.[58]

—Jaidip Mukherjea

As Ramanathan Krishnan rapidly moved up the ranks to emerge as India's great tennis hope on the world stage, the stalwarts who had dominated the stage until then were on the last legs of their career. With the tennis pipeline seemingly bare, emerging from the iconic courts of South Club in Calcutta were two young men who came to be referred to as the 'Bengal Twins'.

Together with Krishnan, Premjit Lall and Jaidip Mukherjea, both proteges of Dilip Bose, would make the most formidable Davis Cup side in the history of Indian tennis, and raise the standard of the sport in India to levels never seen before.

PREMJIT LALL

The Premjit Lall story, like Naresh Kumar's before him, almost didn't get off the ground thanks to a coach who failed to recognise the talent before him. At the age of fourteen, when a doting elder brother, Ranjit, convinced there was something special about the raw ability of his sibling, took him to a coach at the South Club, the disappointing advice he received was, 'Take him home, he'll never make a tennis player.'[59]

Left to young Premjit, whose first love was cricket (at the age of thirteen, on a holiday in London with the family, he queued up all night to buy a ticket to Lord's, but had to be dragged to Wimbledon to watch Narendranath play the great Lew Hoad on Centre Court), he would never again have walked on a tennis court. Fortunately, the determined Ranjit Lall would not accept no for an answer, and took Premjit to meet Dilip Bose, who was then in charge of the Rajkumar Amrit Kaur Coaching Scheme at the club.

Dilip Bose would later say, 'Premjit was a handsome young boy and appeared to be keen. I asked him to hit a few balls and he gave me the impression that he had talent which properly developed would take him places. I had no hesitation in enlisting him on the spot.'[60]

There were forty-two young hopefuls who trained under the watchful eyes and firm discipline of Dilip Bose, but within a year, with some correction to his service action to give it more power, and a lot of exercise to get his slow moving legs up to speed, there emerged one clear outstanding talent among them—Premjit Lall, by now irreversibly smitten and head over heels in love with the sport.

In 1955, Dilip Bose made fifteen-year-old Premjit Lall enter every event of every tournament he could find. Within a year of that, Lall was junior National Champion, and for good measure partnered fellow South Club trainee Akhtar Ali to pick up the doubles crown as well.

In 1957, having won all the junior titles on offer in the country, Premjit Lall, at the age of seventeen, was fast tracked into the Davis Cup team to play Philippines at Manila. The same year he would have his first experience of playing at Wimbledon, a competition he would return to a further seventeen times in the course of his career, appearing in sixty-two matches across formats.

Serendipitously, Lall's doubles partner that first time was Narendranath, the very man whose centre court match against Lew Hoad a thirteen-year-old cricket-obsessed Lall had reluctantly witnessed. The Narendranath-Lall duo lost in the first round, but by then the romantic bug of Wimbledon had claimed yet another victim in the younger man.

In 1958, Lall played the singles at the Boys' event, fighting his way into the final before losing to Butch Buchholz of the United States. Buchholz won three Grand Slam junior titles between 1957 and 1958 and would go on to be ranked world no. 5 in 1960.

Between 1957 and 1975, Lall would win thirty-one of the sixty-two matches he played at Wimbledon, twice making it to the quarter-finals of the doubles event partnering Jaidip Mukherjea. In 1973, the second time they reached the last eight, the 1-6, 2-6, 7-5, 2-6 loss against eventual champions Jimmy Connors and Ilie Nastase was the closest they would come to making a Grand Slam semi-final.

In singles, the fourth round of the 1962 Australian Championships was Lall's best Grand Slam result. Seven years on, at Wimbledon, would however come one of those opportunities that life throws up but rarely. It was a match that could potentially have placed Premjit Lall in a different league altogether.

Premjit Lall

Wimbledon, 25 June 1969

It was not expected to be much of a challenge, which probably explains why there was not a single spectator on Court 4 where the defending Wimbledon champion and winner of both the Australian and the French Open earlier that year, Rod Laver, was taking on Premjit Lall of India in a second-round encounter.

The expectations were so low that Lall's wife Georgina and doubles partner Jaidip Mukherjea, instead of being by the court side as they normally would be, were shooting a home movie of Wimbledon from their vantage point up on the players' terrace.

Lall writes about his preparation for the match: 'I was pretty relaxed though rather tired after my marathon three-and-a-half-hour match with the American, Steele, the evening before. Play goes on till 10 p.m. due to extended daylight. I had made up my mind that since I had nothing to lose, I would hit out and really go for my strokes.'

The first sign fans had that something unexpected was happening at SW19 was when the late edition of the *Belfast Telegraph* that day carried this report on the match at the time of going to press. The headline screamed: *Lall Has Laver on the Run.*

'The first major upset of the Wimbledon Championships loomed up this afternoon when, in the comparative obscurity of court no. 4, the reigning men's singles title-holder Rod Laver (Australia) dropped the first two sets to the twenty-nine-year-old Premjit Lall. Lall took the first two sets 6-3, 6-4, leaving the champion fighting for his life.'

Lall's wife Georgina talks about the rest of the match in her account, 'Concentrating on my filming, I happened to turn the camera on to Prem's scoreboard and got the shock of my life. Two sets to Prem! The news spread like wildfire. People and the press rushed to the court, and within minutes, the whole area was jammed. Prem was hitting the ball like a man possessed.'

Sadly, it was too good to last. Georgina continues, 'Then down 3-4 and serving in the third set, he suddenly seemed to crack up and missed two easy smashes. This was the beginning of the end. He told me later that at that stage he realised the situation and the possibility of beating the great Laver. He got tense and his enemy, cramp, attacked.'

Once reprieved, Laver used all his experience and superior mental strength and went for the kill in the last two sets, winning the encounter 3-6, 4-6, 6-3, 6-0, 6-0. In his book, *The Education of a Tennis Player*, Rod Laver would later write with characteristic wit:

Premjit Lall and I go back a long way together. He is a nice looking, tall fellow, soft spoken, a University man from Calcutta where he sometimes works as a cement salesman. I had never lost to him, but he was clearly outplaying me as he won the first two sets. Prem was the kind of player who always made a good showing but hardly ever could sustain good play long enough to swing a really big win or take a tournament. I kept waiting for something to go wrong with his game, and when it didn't, I began to worry. He held for 3-2 and I won my serve for 3-3. It was right here that I restated a very important truth about tennis to myself: You can only lose a tennis match. That's all. If I was going to lose to Premjit Lall, I was going to go out with everything blazing. Up to that moment, I had been gripped by a certain fear of losing, but after I'd gotten myself straight on that, the fear disappeared. I began hitting the ball better and stayed close to Prem in that game, 30-30. I felt I'd get him there for the break, but he hit a good forehand down the line that sent me into the corner on the enclosure and I had to lob. I'd been lobbing short all through the match, and I didn't alter my pattern here. Fortunately for me, some of his better cement lodged in his right elbow at that critical stage of the third set. He knocked the ball past me and beyond the baseline.

Lall sums it all up when he writes wistfully, 'I have cursed myself, my nerves, my luck. It was a once-in-a-lifetime chance and I missed it.'

Laver would go on to win Wimbledon that year, beating compatriot John Newcombe in the final, and also complete his second Grand Slam later that year. He remains the only player in the history of the sport to achieve the feat.

Beyond the Slams

It is unfortunate but understandable that posterity tends to judge tennis players mainly on the basis of results in the Grand Slam events. Seen in that light, Premjit Lall's career could well be consigned to the back pages of an account such as this. But that would be a travesty indeed, given the crucial role Lall plays in the story of Indian tennis.

During the course of a long career, on his day, Lall prevailed over the best players in world.

In 1967, Premjit Lall became the national champion, defeating Thomaz Koch of Brazil, the world no. 12 in the quarter-final, defending Asian champion Jaidip Mukherjea in the semi-final and Ramanathan Krishnan in the final. The following year, braving severe thigh cramps, Lall defended his title beating world no. 8, Romania's Ion Tiriac, who had prevailed over Ilie Nastase in the semi-final, 6-0, 2-6, 9-7, 6-3.

Three years later, Lall's final national title would come in his hometown of Calcutta, at the expense of Soviet Union's world no. 9, Alex Metrevelli, who had just beaten the Indian in the Asian Championships the week before.

Playing for the Tricolour—A Davis Cup Giant

The greatest exploits of Premjit Lall would be reserved, in the tradition of all legendary Indian players, for the Davis Cup. Playing ninety matches across forty-one ties, Premjit Lall's Davis Cup record of 63 per cent of singles matches won vies with the best that Indian tennis has thrown at the world. To put this in the historical context, this win-loss ratio ranks third after Ramanathan Krishnan and Leander Paes.

Lall's doubles record of 67 per cent of all Davis Cup matches won is as impressive. To put it in perspective, among those with thirty or more doubles matches played in the Davis Cup, Premjit Lall stacks up in third place behind Mahesh Bhupathi and Leander Paes among India's all-time greats.

But it wasn't only about the numbers, but about the quality of matches won under pressure, and what they meant for Indian tennis.

In 1963 in the Eastern Zone final, India took on a strong Japanese side in Tokyo. At stake was the inter-zonal final against the United States. On the second day, with the teams tied at 1-1, Lall stepped onto the court for the all-important doubles match. Partnering Lall was Jaidip Mukherjea, facing up to a formidable Japanese duo led by Atsushi Miyagi. The Japanese would later go on to win the Grand Slam doubles title at the US Championships. The Indian pair's brilliant 4-6, 6-3, 6-2, 7-5 victory paved the way for Ramanathan Krishnan to win the tie for India 3-2, with a characteristically classy display in the final reverse singles.

In the inter-zonal final, the formidable Americans, with reigning Wimbledon champion and world no. 1 Chuck McKinley in devastating form, outclassed the Indians 5-0. But it was not before Krishnan in the singles and the Lall-Mukherjea combine in the doubles gave McKinley some very anxious moments.

It is perhaps worth pausing this narrative for a moment to talk about the Lall-Mukherjea combine. The reason for their success as a doubles pair went much deeper than mere understanding or chemistry on court. As Mukherjee tells me: 'Prem and I were very close friends. We were rivals, we were from the same city, we grew up in the same coaching camp, we had the same coach—Dilip Bose. Both of us traveled together, lodged together, shared rooms, shared a flat. He was a very good friend.'

In 1966, India would reach for the Davis Cup firmament and touch it, marching into the final for the first time. The 'Three Musketeers'—Krishnan, Mukherjea and Lall, had united the whole country in a campaign that changed the face of Indian Tennis.

In the Eastern inter-zonal final, India once again faced Japan at Tokyo. After Krishnan had got past that year's

Asian Games gold medalist Osamu Ishiguro in four sets, Koji Watanabe levelled the tie beating Lall. Then Lall and Krishnan teamed up to give India a straight sets doubles victory over the Japanese pair. In the reverse singles, two sets to one up, Lall raised his game, as he was wont to do in crucial Cup matches, prevailing over his much fancied opponent, Ishiguro, 2-6, 8-6, 7-5, 10-8, and leading India into the next round. Krishnan then wrapped up the inconsequential dead rubber for a 4-1 Indian victory.

In the inter-zonal semi-final at Delhi, India met powerful West Germany. Leading the German side was Wilhelm Bungert, ranked no. 4 in the world, twice semi-finalist at Wimbledon, and fated, just a few months later, to become the first German finalist at Wimbledon in thirty years since Gottfried von Cramm last achieved that feat.

India won that tie 3-2, but it was a disappointing outing for Lall who lost the doubles in straight sets partnering Mukherjea, and the final dead rubber to Bungert in five hard-fought sets.

India's next tie, the inter-zonal final at the South Club courts against much-fancied Brazil, would cement its place in Davis Cup history as one of the classic ties of all time. Perhaps it was with Lall's failing against the Germans in the crucial match in mind that at the South Club against the Brazilians, Krishnan kept Lall on the sidelines and all the five crucial matches involved only Mukherjea and the captain himself, as India won the tie and moved into the final of the Davis Cup for the first time in its history.

Krishnan talks about what happened behind the scenes, in an interview with Dhiman Sarkar of the *Hindustan Times*:

> After the first day, Akhtar (our coach), Jaidip and I were in my room at the (Oberoi) Grand Hotel when Akhtar came up with the idea of ditching the regular pairing of Premjit and me for Jaidip and me. Akhtar said Jaidip could play beautifully on the right court because they had played once. In a tense situation, we felt Jaidip was a better bet than Premjit. We didn't even tell Premjit. The rules said, one hour before the match you could change doubles pairings. Premjit had come in tennis clothes but took the decision really well. And Jaidip rose to the occasion.[61]

The pattern would be repeated at Melbourne two weeks later when Australia blew away India 4-1 on grass. On his favourite surface, Premjit Lall, who, a month later, would become India's national champion defeating his two teammates, kept the bench warm. It was something he would never fully forgive Krishnan for, despite how close they remained as friends.

Lall would pen poignantly in *Down the Line*: 'Krish was and still is a great player and person but I feel he falls short as a captain. We are good friends and will always be but I still wonder why these incidents took place. Maybe he just didn't have enough confidence in me.'

Two years later, India's progress in the Davis Cup followed a now familiar pattern. In the 4-1 victory against Japan at Tokyo, Premjit Lall, now the country's top player, won the opening singles in straight sets. In the semi-finals against Germany, this time in Munich, Lall again gave India a 1-0 lead in the opening match of the tie to help take his team through 3-2 to the inter-zonal final against the United States at Puerto Rico.

But this time, the Americans led by the legendary Arthur

Ashe, reigning no. 1 in the world and fresh from his US Open victory less than two months before, were too strong for the Indians. To Lall's credit, he took the fight to Ashe in the opening match of the tie before bowing out 2-6, 7-5, 2-6, 4-6 in four sets, while Krishnan lost to Ashe tamely in three. The United States took the tie 4-1.

A Sad Ending to the Story

Premjit Lall continued playing into the late 1970s and then retired to run his own business of a printing press. Sadly, this was an age when issues of mental health were not taken seriously in most parts of the world, let alone India. The fact that Lall had gone into depression after two troubled marriages and other personal issues would not be obvious to those around him until it was too late.

In 1992, a shocked Calcutta and nation woke up to the news that one of its most beloved sporting sons, Premjit Lall, had reportedly made a suicide bid that failed. The incident, rarely referred to thereafter, would confine Lall to a wheelchair existence. A brain stroke that followed would only make matters worse.

In 2008, when Premjit Lall passed away, Naresh Kumar would poignantly say to *DNA India*: 'He was just like his game, ramrod straight and classical ... A terrific fellow ... Perhaps he failed to cope up with the spin and turn of his two failed marriages. (In the end) he seemed trapped in a body which limited his mind. I hope wherever he is now, he is happy.'[62]

But perhaps the best way to remember Premjit Lall is in

the words of a young Japanese lady who wrote to him after his multiple Davis Cup successes in Tokyo. 'Dear Lall,' she said, 'you are as marvellous as Mount Fuji.'[63]

JAIDIP MUKHERJEA

The story of Jaidip Mukherjea, the second of the Bengal Twins, couldn't be more of a contrast with Lall's. He was born into a remarkable family that breathed sport and exuded nationalism in equal measure.

Great-grandfather Chittaranjan Das, fondly referred to as Deshbandhu (friend of the nation) is one of India's best-known figures from the independence movement. Born into a family of lawyers, C.R. Das went to England after graduating from Presidency College in Calcutta. Failing in his attempt to clear the ICS, and falling back on a legal career, Das practised law in London.

In 1917 Das joined the Congress Party, and had a fallout with Mahatma Gandhi when the latter abandoned the Non-Cooperation Movement in 1922. He was then elected Congress president, but resigned and formed the Swaraj Party with Motilal Nehru. Soon after, he decided to quit politics and use his legal training to help Indian revolutionaries, successfully getting Aurobindo Ghosh acquitted in the famous Alipore Bomb case. He also defended other freedom fighters charged with sedition.

Jaidip Mukherjea's father Adip Mukherjea was a Cambridge Blue in Hockey. Maternal grandfather J.C. Mukherjea had helped found the Calcutta South Club. It was but natural that young Jaidip would take to the sport he had grown up with on the beautiful lawns.

But it was not a natural transition. Like Lall before him, tennis was not the sport of choice. But fate intervened, as it is wont to do. Breaking a collar bone playing his favoured rugby, Mukherjea was firmly told that it was the end of playing contact sports.

In 1954, two years after the accident, Mukherjea was hitting the tennis ball with visible talent on the South Club courts. Once again it was the legendary Dilip Bose and the Amrit Kaur Coaching Scheme that would play a crucial role in shaping Jaidip Mukherjea into the player he would become.

In 1959, Mukherjea won the junior National Championships, and in 1960, two years after his friend Lall had shown the way, Mukherjea made his way into the final of the Wimbledon junior championships. But like Lall, he stumbled at the final hurdle, losing to Rod Mandelstam of South Africa, 6-1, 6-8, 4-6.

A Sterling Career

Just as for his friend Premjit Lall, it would be a travesty to look at Jaidip Mukherjea's career purely in terms of his success at Grand Slam events. Which is not to say that he was not consistent or impactful at the Majors. Far from it.

In a career that spanned over a decade and a half, and remarkably for a man whose highest career singles ranking never approached the top 25, Mukherjea reached the last 16 of the men's singles at Wimbledon no less than four times—in 1963, '64, '66 and '73. He also made the last 16 at Roland Garros in 1965 and '66, as well as the US Championships and the Australian Championships, both in 1962.

Picking up his first National Championships in 1966 and the second in 1970, he would also win the Asian Championships three times during the course of his career. The first time, when he won in 1966, he also became the first Indian to ever defeat Ramanathan Krishnan at that tournament.

But what made Mukherjea such an effective player?

Premjit Lall tells us: 'Jai was a natural player, a born sportsman. His greatest advantage was his speed and quick reflexes. In tennis, his strong point was his forehand which, together with his speed, enabled him to put away beautiful volleys and smashes. He was a player with guts—taking chances on his weak backhand.'[64]

Given his own failing in buckling under pressure, it is both natural and big-hearted of Lall to acknowledge that for Mukherjea, it was a strength. Ramanathan Krishnan concurs when he talks to me about Mukherjea, 'Jaideep was an aggressive forecourt player. He was bold and took his chances. I enjoyed playing (doubles) with him the most because in times of crisis, he was bold and fearless.'[65]

As always, Krishnan nails it. It was these very strengths that made Mukherjea such an impactful doubles player. Combining his speed and forecourt advantage with the stronger serve and superior backhand of Premjit Lall, Mukherjea would forge a formidable partnership with his childhood friend. Alongside Lall, he made the doubles quarterfinals at Wimbledon multiple times. Two occasions merit a special mention.

In 1966, the Mukherjea-Lall combine beat the team anchored by the greatest Davis Cup player of all time, Italian legend, Nicola Pietrangeli, to move into the quarter-finals.

There, they raised their level a notch and took the Australian duo of Ken Fletcher and John Newcombe to four hard-fought sets before bowing out. Fletcher-Newcombe would go on to eventually win the Wimbledon title that year.

In 1973, with both their careers winding down, the Bengal Twins had one last hurrah left for their fans. In the quarter-finals they met the top seeds Jimmy Connors and Ilie Nastase.

Lall had just come out of a marathon match against a seventeen-year-old Swedish sensation who was the rockstar of Wimbledon that year, and was to become one of the greatest tennis players of all time over the course of the next decade. His name was Bjorn Borg. While Lall lost that match 3-6, 4-6, 8-9, he would forever put himself alongside Borg in the record books for the longest recorded Wimbledon tiebreak of all time.[66] The third set tiebreak went to an incredible 38 points before Borg prevailed 20-18.

Nastase, in the meantime, had come into the tournament with a severe kidney pain and played through the fortnight popping painkillers. He would eventually lose in the semi-finals of the singles event.

But none of this could stop the quarter-final encounter between the two pairs rising to great heights before the top seeds prevailed 6-1, 6-2, 5-7, 6-2. Once again, Mukherjea–Lall had been taken out at the last eight stage by the eventual championship winners.

Davis Cup Glory

Jaidip Mukherjea undoubtedly had his moments of glory on the amateur and then the professional circuit once the Open

Era dawned. But he reserved his best, like the other two musketeers, when he played for the flag.

Along with Krishnan and Lall, Mukherjea took India to the Davis Cup inter-zonal finals for three years from 1960 to 1963 and then again in 1965 and 1968. And Mukherjea's contribution at important stages of all these ties, including a rousing five-set comeback victory in the final inter-zonal match against Spain in 1965, in the process taking down top-25 player Juan Gisbert, was central to India's success. The musketeers also steered India to its first-ever Davis Cup Final in 1966.

In 1966, India's path to the final was past two of the most formidable teams in the world—Germany, led by Wilhelm Bungert who would emerge Wimbledon champion later that year, and Brazil that had just beaten the much-fancied United States.

Against Germany, Mukherjea played two of the greatest singles matches of his career. In the second singles he got past Ingo Budding to give his nation a crucial 2-0 lead. On Day Three, after losing the doubles with Lall, Mukherjea exhibited brilliant tennis, elevating his game several notches, stunning Bungert 4-6, 8-6, 8-6, 6-3 in front of an adoring and vociferous South Club crowd, ensuring an unassailable 3-1 lead and a place in the inter-zonal final against Brazil. There, he would combine with Krishnan to win the doubles and help India move into the Davis Cup final against Australia.

Ramanathan Krishnan tells me why, at crucial moments, despite having the hugely talented but mercurial Lall in the team, he would put Mukherjea forward in singles, and on a couple of occasions, himself join the doubles despite the high work load from playing both singles matches in a tie. 'Jaideep was an aggressive forecourt player. He was bold and took his chances. He performed his best in Davis Cup tennis. We defeated the formidable team of Newcombe and Roche in the Davis Cup Challenge round. He was the most aggressive of the four (that day).'[67]

The match that Krishnan refers to is often forgotten because of the 1-4 scoreline in that largely one-sided 1966 Davis Cup final encounter. But the story merits re-telling because it was no ordinary victory.

The Australian team that the Indians ran into in December 1966 was perhaps the most formidable Davis Cup side of all time.

There was world no. 1 Ray Emerson who would win nine Grand Slam singles and doubles titles in the twelve-month period before and six-month period after this encounter (four at the Australian Championships, two at the French Open and three at the US Open). Playing the other singles matches was world no. 2 Fred Stolle, who, during the same period as his compatriot, had picked up six Grand Slam titles, and reached the finals of two more.

But in the most enthralling encounter of the tie, Krishnan and Mukherjea, in the doubles, met the World's no. 1 doubles pair and one of the greatest combines of all time, Tony Roche and John Newcombe. The Aussie pair had been unbeaten in competitive tennis for the preceding twelve months.

Krishnan talks us through the match: 'Jai played a superb match, especially at the net, and I hit a few forehand topspin lobs to perfection. When we found the break in the seventh game of the fourth set (we were leading two sets to one) to go up 4-3, we shared a few words during the changeover.'

'Krish, we just have to hold one serve each. How are you going to serve?' Jai asked me. 'You can be sure I won't serve any aces. Nor will I serve double faults. I am just going to put in my "Ye Bhagwan" (Oh Lord!) serve,' I said. We all knew what a Ye Bhagwan serve was—a safe spin serve well over the tape into the backhand. And you followed it to the net, leaving the rest to God! That exchange relaxed us, eased the tension.'[68]

The *Birmingham Daily Post* match report takes over from where Krishnan leaves his narrative: 'It was Newcombe's service that gave the Indians the breakthrough in the fourth set. The Indian pair were tense as Mukerjea held service on 5-4 for the match. They did not crack when the Australians, contesting every point fiercely, had Mukerjea and then an advantage to break. First Krishnan hit a magnificent volley down the sideline and Mukerjea, following in (to the net on) his service, smashed a forehand volley past Roche. Mukerjea then forced the Australians into return service errors to win the set 6-4, and the match.'[69]

The Indian pair's stunning 4-6, 7-5, 6-4, 6-4 victory briefly put life back into the tie. Emerson came back the next morning to put the result beyond doubt. In the final match of the tie, refusing to bow out, Mukherjea took Stolle to a thrilling five-setter before standing down 5-7, 8-6, 3-6, 7-5, 3-6.

As Krishnan would modestly put it later, 'In the Challenge Round, the Aussies were far too strong for us but we were not really humiliated.'

Beyond the Court

After retiring from tennis, Mukherjea followed in the footsteps of his mentor Dilip Bose and set up two training academies, the Jaidip Mukherjea Tennis Academy in Kolkata and the Himalayan Tennis Academy in Siliguri. He has also had long stints as non-playing captain and coach of the Indian Davis Cup team. He led the administration at South Club for many years and continues to be involved with the club and the sport, leading the efforts to celebrate the centenary of the club in early 2020.

VIJAY AMRITRAJ
THE 'A' OF TENNIS

After watching him play here at Forest Hills I feel he has the least amount of shots to improve among the young players. Borg and Connors, for example, still have weaknesses they need to work on, but Vijay gets to the ball very early with his long strides and good reach.[70]

—John Newcombe, the US Open champion in 1973

THE ABC OF TENNIS

It was the year the Vietnam War ended, the Watergate scandal broke out, the Yom Kippur war started and ended, and Aerosmith released their debut album.

But 1973 would be a watershed year in other ways as well. It was to be the year *Sports Illustrated* famously carried a cover story announcing the new ABC of world tennis, the trio that was going to dominate the sport in the coming decade—Vijay Amritraj, Bjorn Borg and Jimmy Connors.

In his *Sports Illustrated* column, Kent Hannon would write: 'Vijay Amritraj, the nineteen-year-old from Madras, India who reached the quarter-finals at both Wimbledon and Forest Hills this summer, has a relish for the game and a regard for the people involved in it that has not only impressed players and officials but has endeared him to the fans as well. Smiling broadly at opponents and clapping his racket strings overhead in appreciation of their winning shots, Amritraj has hit enough winners of his own to make a name for himself and for India, which has had little stature in world tennis since the prime of another Madras native, Ramanathan Krishnan.'

At Wimbledon, Amritraj had lost in the quarter-finals to Jan Kodes, the eventual champion. At the US Open, he had been a tiebreak point away from a place in the semi-finals.[71] But what catapulted Amritraj into global limelight was his third round match against Rod Laver at Forest Hills.

Amritraj had already met Laver, the four-time Wimbledon champion and the only living man to have won the Grand Slam five weeks earlier on clay at the Grand Prix event in Bretton Woods. There, from being down 6-7, 5-6, 0-40 on Laver's serve, the young Indian had pulled out from his hat what appeared to be the 'Great Indian Rope Trick', and won the match 6-7, 7-6, 7-5. He had then packed away Jimmy Connors in the final.

But that was Bretton Woods, back of beyond for many, and the surface, clay. Five weeks later when fourth-seeded Laver and unseeded Amritraj walked out on court, it was on Laver's favoured grass and on prime time television. CBS was broadcasting it live across the United States.

Pancho Gonzales, Amritraj's childhood hero and then coach, had played Laver extensively over the years on the circuit. His advice to the young man was to get down low for the volley when the ball went to the backhand of the left-handed Laver. Laver's favourite shot was the top spin just over the net, dipping into the opponent's forehand court.

Amritraj was too young to remember it, but it was the very shot that had denied Ramanathan Krishnan a place in the finals of Wimbledon a decade and a bit earlier.

It would prove to be sage advice. After almost three hours, the two were level at two sets apiece, 6-7, 6-2, 4-6, 6-2, and 3-3 in the fifth set. Then Laver broke the Amritraj serve to take what appeared to be a decisive lead. Amritraj remembers thinking, 'The packed Stadium Court sensed the knockout blows had been delivered. Good match kid, but it's all over.'

As Laver tossed up the ball to serve, it started raining. The rain was not heavy enough to stop play, but it made the grass slippery. Laver called for the match referee and asked for permission to wear spikes. Then, much to the nineteen-year-old's surprise, the veteran took a pair of spikes out of his kit bag and put them on. Amritraj, of course, didn't have a pair, and had to, with some embarrassment, turn down the match referee's offer for him to put on his spikes as well. 'Well, I can't help you then, can I?' was the response from the referee when Amritraj explained why he wasn't changing into spikes.

Amritraj talks us through what happened next: 'As soon as play started again, I was right back into it and took to wiping the soles of my shoes with a handkerchief after every point. Laver, meanwhile, did not look too comfortable in his spikes which have such a different feel about them, and when he served for a 5-3 lead I came up with two passes on the run which broke his serve and then won the next two games to wrap it up 6-4 in the fifth.'[72]

Having beaten arguably the greatest player the world has ever seen, at a venue that Laver had made his own over the years, Amritraj would eventually lose to the fifth-seeded Ken Rosewall in the quarter-finals. The fault would be entirely the young Indian's, refusing to listen to his coach's series of reminders not to serve to Rosewall's backhand.

'Whatever you do, don't serve to his backhand,' Gonzales said the previous night. 'Don't serve to his backhand,' was the reminder in the morning as they walked back from practice. 'Remember, don't serve to his backhand,' was the final word from the coach as his ward walked onto the court.

Ken Rosewall won the toss, and much to Amritraj's surprise, asked his opponent to serve. He remembers: 'Strange, I thought. It was a blistering hot day, I had been serving brilliantly against Laver and Stone. Pretty cocky move.'

Amritraj continues, 'There was Rosewall, this small figure with limited reach, standing so far over to the forehand side that both his feet were in the alley. You could drive a tank down the backhand side. "This is ridiculous," I thought. "This is an extremely fast court, I've got a big serve and if I get it in there's no way he can even reach it from where he's standing. No need to blast it. Just a decent pace first serve will do it." So I served it to the backhand. Took three paces towards the net and watched the ball fly past me for a winner.

'"Fluke," I thought. At nineteen, you think things like that. You think when a great player hits a superlative backhand service return winner off a first serve that's a fluke. At least that's what you tell yourself. So I served three more times to the backhand, never missed my first serve and never touched a volley. They were all past me before I could blink. It was absolutely unbelievable. Sitting down in my chair, I picked up my towel and looked over to Gonzales. He wasn't there. "Hmm, must have gone to get a drink," I thought.'[73]

Gonzales had not gone to get a drink. He had walked out of the stadium, packed his bags and left for the airport before Rosewall had finished lathering the Amritraj ego onto the Stadium Court grass. The final score read 4-6, 3-6, 3-6.

It was days before Gonzales would answer the Indian's panicked calls. When he finally did, his opening line, laced with sarcasm, was, 'Can you speak English?'

It had been an expensive lesson in humility and discipline. Vijay Amritraj didn't know it then, but he had thrown away one of only two shots he would have during his entire career at entering the semi-finals of the US Open.

That US Open, Connors lost to the eventual winner, tenth-seeded John Newcombe in another quarter-final, and Borg was taken out in the third round by third-seeded Arthur Ashe. The reign of the 'ABC of Tennis' would have to wait.

THE GREATEST YEAR

When 1974 came around, India found itself facing Neale Fraser's Australia for the second time running in the Davis Cup, this time in the quarter-finals. Since Australia was not designated as a part of the Asian Group at the time, all its matches against Asian opponents had to be played away. As Fraser would tell journalist Richard Evans years later, 'We seemed to spend our lives playing in India in those days.'[74]

In 1973, at the Eastern zonal finals in Madras, the first Davis Cup tie to be played there since 1962, the result had been an unmitigated disaster for the hosts. Going into the tie with misplaced confidence of upsetting the Aussies, the Indians had whimpered off the courts with their tails between their legs, beaten 5-0.

The venue this time was the South Club in Calcutta, the surface—grass. The opening rubber, in the absence of John Newcombe, found the two lesser singles players of either team, Bob Giltinan playing Jaz (Jasjit) Singh.

Amritraj describes the match. 'In front of a typically huge Calcutta crowd, the pair of them did their best to produce a tennis match, given that both were suffering from the handicap of virtual rigor mortis. In tennis parlance, they were choking so badly it was amazing the ball ever got over the net, but in the end Jaz got himself together quicker than the moustachioed Aussie and won in four sets.'

Jaz Singh would have the last laugh when four hours later Amritraj came off the court having lost 15-17, 14-16, 6-4, 7-9 to the powerful John Alexander. Rigor mortis or not, Jaz Singh's victory had given India a respectable 1-1 end to the first day.

On the second day the Amritraj brothers won the doubles after a hard-fought five-setter, and despite Alexander drawing the visitors level with a victory against Jaz Singh the third morning, Vijay Amritraj took India past the Aussies with a straight sets win over Giltinan. India was through to the semi-finals of the Davis Cup against the Soviet Union at Poona.

The *Liverpool Echo* reported on the match with a headline that screamed, *Its Oh! Calcutta for the Aussies*, and went on to say, 'Australia's defeat, coupled with the elimination of the United States by Colombia, since beaten by South Africa, means the end of a monopoly by these two nations stretching back to 1937. During this period Australia won the cup seventeen times.'[75]

In India's decisive Davis Cup victories over the years, there has almost always been one outstanding performance, often unexpected, that has tilted the scales in the team's favour. At Poona in 1974 against the Soviet Union, that performance came from an unlikely source—Anand Amritraj, the older sibling—in singles.

In the opening rubber the older Amritraj had expectedly been blown away by Alex Metreveli, finalist at Wimbledon the previous year. His younger sibling had restored parity with a win over the less-fancied Teimuraz Kakulia. In the doubles, the intimidatory tactics of Sergei Likhachev, trying to hit the Amritraj brothers on the head with close range volleys, had backfired. Not only were the brothers too good and quick for this to succeed, but an incensed Metreveli had come down heavily on his partner, which rattled him. India won in four sets.

With India 2-1 up in the tie and a chance to seal the win, Anand Amritraj found himself down two sets to one and 2-5 in the fourth to Kakulia. Vijay was now bracing himself for a very difficult fifth rubber against Metreveli, although neither Ramanathan Krishnan, the captain, nor Vijay wanted the tie to go there.

But as Amritraj recalls, 'Anand clawed his way back from the very brink of defeat and finally clinched a truly heroic victory, 6-3, in the fifth. It was a superb fighting performance that ensured India a place in the Davis Cup final for only the second time since the inception of the competition in 1900.'

As the team celebrated their entry into the finals, they were blissfully unaware of what was about to unfold away from tennis. *The New York Times* would describe that year's Davis Cup finals as 'the most important tennis matches never to be played'.[76] At the heart of the issue was South Africa's policy of apartheid.

Apartheid ('apartness' in the Afrikaans language) was the system of legislation implemented and enforced by the all-white government of South Africa when they came to power in 1948. The country's majority population, who were non-white, were forced to live in separate areas from whites and use separate public facilities. Marriages and relations between whites and other races were banned. More than 80 per cent of the country's land was reserved for the white minority. Between 1961 and 1994, more than 3.5 million black South Africans were forcibly removed from rural areas designated as 'white' and their land sold at throwaway prices to white farmers. The displaced were reduced to a life of poverty. The leader of the African National Congress, Nelson Mandela, had been thrown into prison, where he would remain, largely in solitary confinement, for twenty-seven years.

India, led by Prime Minister Indira Gandhi, was at the forefront of the opposition to apartheid. This included a ban against all interactions with South Africa, including sporting encounters. India had led the fight that had been adopted by most countries around the world. It therefore immediately became a political issue, when, against all odds, laying tennis history by the wayside, India and South Africa unexpectedly marched into the finals of the Davis Cup.

A few weeks after the semi-final victory against the Soviet Union, on perhaps the saddest day in the history of Indian tennis, R.K. Khanna, acting on behalf of the Indian Tennis Federation, defaulted India and allowed South Africa to win the Davis Cup. The allegation would always be that this was done without a concerted effort to explore other possibilities with the Indian government, and indeed before the Government of India had issued any edict on the matter. The reality was that the decision in all likelihood came directly from the prime minister's office. Khanna's was merely the voice that broke the news.

Perhaps it was for the best. Even if the tie had gone on, as Sy Lerman who covered the Davis Cup that year for *The Daily Mail* explained in the same article in *The New York Times*, 'The crowd at Ellis Park would have been segregated with just a very small section near the top reserved for non-whites.' The relatives of Indian players, officials and fans alike would have been relegated to that segregated section while their team played the biggest tennis tie in the nation's history. 'That would have been a ludicrous chance for us to take,' Vijay Amritraj would admit. His brother did not necessarily agree, and still doesn't.

Anand Amritraj, playing in Paris at the time with Vijay, read about AITF's decision in the *Herald Tribune* and had a heated exchange on the telephone with Khanna that was carried around the world. Unknown to the incensed elder Amritraj brother, and as alleged by his younger sibling in his book, the Reuters correspondent had been listening in from outside the room where the telephone was located.[77] It's unclear, however, whether the quotes from the brothers at the end of the report were given by them, or also made up from the overheard conversation.

The New York Times the next morning carried the headline: *Amritraj Brothers Quit India's Tennis Cup Team.* The article reproduced the Reuters story from Paris:

> Anand and Vijay Amritraj said today they would not represent their country again in the Davis Cup competition following India's refusal to play South Africa in the 1974 final. The Amritraj brothers told R.K. Khanna, the secretary of the All-India Tennis Federation, who is in New Delhi, of their decision in a telephone conversation. The Indians are playing here in the Jean Becker tournament. 'We asked him whether the decision had been taken by the AITF or the government. He said it was his decision. So we told him we would not play for India again,' Anand, the elder brother, said. 'If the decision had been taken by the government, it would have been different. We would have had nothing to say,' Vijay added.[78]

In the end, the two brothers would have to do damage control with press conferences across India that explained their outburst which had been against Khanna's unilateral decision rather than the government's anti-apartheid stance. The Davis Cup team would stay unchanged.

As we discussed this again almost five decades later, Vijay Amritraj was unequivocal that India's decision to not play in South Africa was consistent with the anti-apartheid stance the nation had rightfully taken and was 'correct from the point of view of humanity' as he put it. He did point out though, that the offer made to move the final to a neutral venue had never been taken up seriously by India. Wistfully, he answered my question with his opinion about the result if the final had gone ahead: 'While either team could have won, we felt we had a very good chance to lift the Davis Cup given we would have played at a neutral venue.'

Away from the Davis Cup, young Amritraj was making strides on the circuit as he crisscrossed his way across the global tennis circuit in 1974. While Wimbledon 1974 was a disappointment after the heroics of the previous year, the high point on the circuit for the Indian would come once again at the US Open where all eyes were on the *ABC* of tennis.

In a mouth-watering second round clash at Forest Hills, twenty-year-old Vijay Amritraj faced the eighteen-year-old no. 4 seed Bjorn Borg, the defending French Open champion. The encounter reignited talks of the beginning of the reign of the new crop of future superstars. Connors was, of course, the confirmed leader of the pack, having won two titles on the Grand Slam stage, including that year's Wimbledon.

A bit more than an hour into the match, it was already obvious why Amritraj was being touted as one of the best grass court players of his generation. The first set was a blow out, Vijay taking it 6-1. The second was closer, but a 7-6 verdict meant the Indian had a 2-0 lead and a serious chance at an upset early in the tournament. But Borg stayed calm, displaying the resilience that would eventually make him one of the greatest tennis players of all time, and pulled back the next two sets 6-3, 6-1 with his trademark backhand returns passing Amritraj time and again, both down the line and cross court.

Saving his energy towards the end of the fourth set, Amritraj came back guns blazing in the fifth. He changed his tactics, concentrating all his serves on the Borg forehand and avoiding the two-handed backhand to the extent possible. The tactic paid off. While Borg stayed with him for the first four games, once Vijay broke him and mounted the pressure, Borg wilted. Amritraj went past the no. 4 seed 6-1, 7-6, 3-6, 1-6, 6-2.

'A' had prevailed over 'B'.

In the quarter-finals, Vijay Amritraj ran into his nemesis Ken Rosewall again for the second time in two years. Remembering to not serve to Rosewall's backhand, he was up 6-2 after the first set. But Rosewall brought all his experience to bear thereafter, pulling through in four sets. It would need a breathtakingly brilliant Jimmy Connors to decimate Rosewall in the shortest ever Grand Slam singles final 6-1, 6-0, 6-1, the former prevailing in an hour and eighteen minutes.

The Indian Open 1975 and the Next Five Years

The $50,000 Indian Open, then a part of the Grand Prix circuit, moved to Calcutta in 1975. The tournament, played outdoors on clay, garnered widespread interest, for leading the draw was the reigning US Open champion, Manuel Orantes, who had just defeated Jimmy Connors in the final.

Even for the tennis fans of Calcutta, used to brilliance on the South Club courts as they had been for decades, this was a very special occasion. Coming through a draw that boasted Sandy Meyer, Mike Cahill, Ramanathan Krishnan, Premjit Lall and Jaidip Mukherjea, meeting top-seed Manuel Orantes in the final on the Sunday was India's own Vijay Amritraj.

But before the final could be played, there were issues to be sorted out. Manuel Orantes and his doubles partner Juan Gisbert needed to get to Stockholm for the Commercial Union Masters that was due to start forty-eight hours later, and the only way they could do that was to be in Delhi by Sunday evening to catch the SAS flight, which did not fly daily. The singles and doubles finals (both of which featured the Spaniards) were thus slated for the Sunday morning, to start at 10 a.m. so that they could fly to Delhi on the afternoon's Indian Airlines flight.

News came the previous evening which would throw a major spanner into the works. The president of India, Fakhruddin Ali Ahmed, a big tennis fan, wanted to see the finals, and he had to come from Delhi, so play could only start in the afternoon.

Amritraj tells me the inside story of what happened that Saturday evening. 'Manuel didn't know what to do. So I called up the aide-de-camp of the president and told him that we would love to have the president watch us play, but could the president do us a huge favour? The ADC said he would check with the president, but what was the favour? So I asked if Manuel and Juan could fly back to Delhi after the match in the presidential plane. The president, being the tennis fan that he was, agreed immediately, and the match was played that afternoon.'[79]

The *Associated Press* carried a report that night which read: 'Vijay Amritraj of India delighted his countrymen Sunday by overpowering US Open champion Manuel Orantes of Spain 7-5, 6-3 for the men's singles title at the $50,000 Indian Grand Prix Lawn Tennis Championships in Calcutta. The second-seeded Amritraj took the closely-fought first set from the stocky left-hander, who tried to keep the Indian off balance with accurate placements and off speed shots, just as in the US Open final against Jimmy Connors. Leading 4-3 in the second, Amritraj broke Orantes' serve and easily ran out the match.' It had been a huge upset on clay, always the favoured surface of the Spaniards.

The flight to Delhi that evening carried two relieved, thrilled and happy Spaniards. Relieved and thrilled to be flying in the presidential aircraft, and happy to have won the doubles against the Amritraj brothers.

I asked Vijay Amritraj during our conversation whether Orantes ever managed to return the favour, and pat came the typically tongue-in-cheek Amritraj reply accompanied by that trademark smile—'Well, I won the match!'

The rest of the 1970s would unfortunately not go as well for Amritraj as the start to the decade had promised. A persistent elbow injury and subsequent treatments ranging from Filipino faith healers to the surgeon's knife meant that the Indian was only intermittently on the circuit. The change to a lighter Donnay racquet (thanks to a new management contract with IMG) took the pressure off the elbow and Amritraj's ranking which had dropped from 26 after the Calcutta victory to 46 at the end of 1977 started to slowly recover.

In the summer of 1979, leading Bjorn Borg by two sets to one and 5-4 in the tiebreaker of the fourth set at Wimbledon, it looked like Vijay Amritraj was once again at the cusp of fulfilling his promise. But as he would tell David McMohan in an interview a year later, 'There was no way Borg could have won, but he did. I've watched the match time and again on film and I just can't believe it. I've watched at normal speed, and in slow motion; I've stopped the film at certain key points and I cannot explain how I lost.'[80]

But he had, and the climb to the top 20 would take another couple of years. It was only by 1980 that Amritraj would once again start to get back into reckoning for Grand Slam glory. But the ABC of tennis was now history. In the intervening years, Bjorn Borg had taken the tennis world by the scruff of its neck and picked up ten Grand Slam titles, and Connors, while less prolific, had five trophies on his mantelpiece. To make matters worse, now in the mix was the mercurial but supremely talented John McEnroe.

THE LAST HURRAHS

If the exploits of Connors, Borg and McEnroe over the past few years had made the fans forget Vijay Amritraj, he would serve them a timely reminder of his talent as the new decade dawned. Wimbledon 1981 would see a rejuvenated and fit-again Amritraj.

Beginning his campaign by brushing aside an ageing former multiple Grand Slam winner Jan Kodes in straight sets, Amritraj then came out of the blocks serving magnificently, volleying and drop-shotting his way past a bewildered sixth seed Brian Teacher from the United States in the third round.

In the quarter-finals, waiting for him, was Jimmy Connors. While Connors may have piled up the silverware on his mantelpiece as Amritraj struggled on the outside courts and medical clinics, when it came to facing each other, the two men had always been evenly matched.

Amritraj would later say about Connors in an interview to *Sportstar*: 'Jimmy was extremely competitive. He hated playing against anyone he got along with and he hated the fact he got along with me. There are certain games that fit into the other person's games. Connors' game fit into the way I played. On a slightly quicker court, if a right-hander had a pretty decent wide serve on the deuce court, a lefty two-hander struggles on the return that opens up the volley side of the court. Also when the left-hander's backhand was stronger than his forehand which was how it was with Jimmy, I was able to attack his second serve and jump into the net.'[81]

The New York Times in its Wimbledon report the next morning would write: 'Amritraj, twenty-seven, is a graciously gifted player who grew up with grass courts in India. He had beaten Connors in their last two meetings, and he took advantage of his rival's service uncertainty by attacking early, often and effectively.'

For the first two sets, Amritraj was in his elements. He served wide on the deuce court, and followed up at the net to put it away. The more Connors tried to get a sense of the game, the less he could, stretched from corner to corner by the Indian's deeply angled serves. The more frustrated Connors got, the less first serves he put in. His second serves were easy meat for an Amritraj who seemed omnipresent across the net.

Not since 1974, when Ken Rosewall came back against Stan Smith in the semi-finals, had a player won a match from a two-set deficit in the last three rounds of Wimbledon. Surely, a Connors comeback from this stage was unlikely? But as had happened to the Indian often on the Grand Slam stage, the unthinkable could very quickly turn into unpalatable reality.

The New York Times describes what happened: 'With Amritraj serving at 1-2, 30-all in the third set, Connors hit a deep forehand placement that ended a long rally and told him he was still in the fight. Amritraj held from deuce, but Connors broke at 15 for 3-2 with a forehand crosscourt service return winner and a running forehand pass down the line. What followed was a classic example of how momentum often dictates the tempo of grass-court play. Connors served out the third set from deuce. Then, from 2-3 in the fourth set, he won sixteen of the next eighteen points, breaking to even the match with four winners that seemed to leave Amritraj almost motionless on the court. The bite was gone from his first serve. He volleyed and returned serve straight-legged and glided late to ground strokes. Connors broke serve for the last time at 15, sweeping forty-two of the last sixty points in the three-hour-thirty-two-minute match.' The scoreline read 2-6, 5-7, 6-4, 6-3, 6-2.

As we sit and talk about the match thirty-three years after the event, Amritraj is wistful for the first time in the conversation. He tells me, 'It remains the only regret I have ever had in tennis.'[82]

Then shaking himself out of it, with that broad smile back in place, he adds, 'And it wasn't just me. I had two friends who had flown over and bought the most expensive Centre Court seats available for the match. They told me later the money had been worth it only for the first two sets!'

Wimbledon 1981 was the last shot Amritraj was to have at Grand Slam glory, and although he stayed in the top tier and won several ATP tournaments, he would never again reach the last eight stage of a Major.

Ramanathan Krishnan, the only Indian till date to reach the semi-finals of Wimbledon, has this observation on why Amritraj did not fulfil his potential: 'Vijay was the most aggressive of all the Indian players I have seen. But he lacked a sound defence that he could fall back on, something that is very vital in a two-week tournament. This apart, he was not capable of the sort of one-pointed focus that you need to stay competitive through two weeks in a Slam.'[83]

But there remained one last hurrah to come in the Amritraj career.

By 1987, Vijay Amritraj had embarked on a Hollywood career, going off for shoots between tournaments. He had famously appeared in the James Bond film *Octopussy* alongside Roger Moore in 1983 and in *Star Trek IV: The Voyage Home* in 1986 as a starship captain. He was also appearing on NBC TV shows. Tennis had become a part of life that he was almost ready to let go.

Then Davis Cup time came around and India was in the semi-finals for the first time since 1974. As Amritraj evocatively describes it, India found itself there 'against all odds known to man, a team with a thirty-three-year-old part-time actor (Vijay) as captain, a semi-retired thirty-five-year-old (Anand) as his doubles partner, and one top-class singles player (Ramesh Krishnan) who was not, even then, ranked in the world's top thirty'.[84]

This disparate group of has-beens and under-achievers would, against all odds, take India to a victory over mighty Australia on their own turf, and into the finals of the Davis Cup.

A few months before, Amritraj had borne the responsibility

of taking India past Argentina in the first round. Down match point against world no. 15 Martin Jaite, he had fought back magnificently, wearing deep national pride on his sleeve, and taken India through.

When India met Australia at Sydney, the chips were stacked in favour of the hosts. Australia was led by reigning Wimbledon champion Pat Cash, backed up by world no. 23, Wally Masur. An injured Cash did not eventually play, and after Krishnan had beaten John Fitzgerald in the opener, Amritraj, now ranked outside the top 100, took care of Wally Masur in four sets, coming back from a set down. Even though Amritraj would lose the reverse singles to Fitzgerald, Krishnan prevailed over Masur to clinch the tie and catapult India into an unexpected final encounter with Sweden.

India would go on to lose 0-5 to Sweden on the freezing clay courts of Gothenburg, but there was no shame in a defeat to the world's top team with four players then ranked in the top ten of men's tennis.

Over a few glorious days in 1987, captain Vijay Amritraj had turned a rag-tag group of career underachievers into a team that dared to dream the impossible, and almost made it. There could have been no better high for what had been, despite the lack of a Grand Slam title, a remarkable career that would for all time link the Amritraj name with the most precious moments in Indian tennis.

It is easy to forget a few facts in our collective disappointment of the uber talented Amritraj not becoming the first Indian Grand Slam Singles champion.

First, in the Open Era, there have been few Asian players who have risen to the heights this man did—winning 15 ATP singles titles. Kei Nishikori, who reached No. 4 in the world, only won 12 in his career, and Paradorn Srichaphan, who broke into the Top 10, had only 5. Second, Amritraj spent a significant time in the Top 20 rankings, the last Indian and only one of three Asians to do so since 1968 when the Open Era began, rising to No. 18 in 1980. And for good measure, he led his country to two Davis Cup finals, one of which, in 1974, but for a political decision, legitimate and appropriate as it may have been, would rightfully have been India's to lose.

A Gentleman and Mr Nice Guy

If early indications of his health were anything to go by, Vijay Amritraj should have spent his life in and out of hospitals. Instead, the boy whose earliest memories are of lying on an ironing board at home in Madras, feet in the air, face down, head pointing to the floor to relieve the chronic chest congestion he was born with, became an icon of elite sport. As he inspirationally remarks in his book, 'I suppose I have achieved enough as an international athlete by now to prove that a robust beginning to life is not a prerequisite to success.'

His parents' determination to change the course of his life, the sacrifices they made in not taking vacations and investing all their time and money on the younger son's health and tennis lessons, would have an enormous impact on the man he would become. The focus on tennis was not to create world champions of their boys, but rather to ensure that the cerebral elder son Anand (he was a chess prodigy as a child) got some much-needed exercise, and Vijay's health improved with the outdoor activity.

When eighteen-year-old Vijay Amritraj got past India no. 2 Jaidip Mukherjea in five sets in the semi-finals of the National Championships in 1972, bagged the doubles title with Anand and then beat Ramanathan Krishnan in four sets in the singles final to lift the cup, life had made a hundred-eighty-degree turn and was poised to go well beyond the goals his parents had set.

As Amritraj would write at the end of his career, 'I suppose you could say we flew our kites pretty well, my brothers and I, but none of us needed to be reminded who got us off the ground.'[85]

Eventually, the sacrifices of his parents, Amritraj's natural ability to get on with people, and the inner strength he developed from battling adversity at a young age, would mould him into the person he became, off and on court—a gentleman, and Mr Nice Guy.

Years later, when Amritraj had already become a professional tennis player on the WCT—World Championship Tennis circuit (the predecessor of the ATP Tour), their guidebook would say about him, '(Vijay Amritraj is) probably the most popular player among his peers on the pro tour ... an articulate gentleman who is also a great ambassador for his sport and his country.'

Amritraj is undoubtedly one of the most polite, friendly and unassuming elite sportspersons I have met and there is no doubting the fact that he is a thorough gentleman off the court. But it is his calm smiling demeanour through terrible calls and opponents' tantrums on court that has always intrigued those who have seen him play. The insights that he provides in his book on this aspect of his personality are fascinating.

Talking about his opponents' behaviour and linesmen making doubtful calls, Amritraj charmingly says, 'I suppose it is a part of my Indian way of looking at things that makes me feel that anyone who behaves badly will get their comeuppance.' While he may have put down that acceptance of bad line calls to his belief in karma, as he matured as a player, Amritraj would discover that his calmness and smiling visage sometimes worked on its own to his advantage on court, and at other times, could be made to do so.

In his fascinating book, *Short Circuit: Borg, McEnroe and Connors, The Era of Bribes, Match-Fixing and Drugs*, on the unsavoury dealings on the tennis circuit in the 1980s, journalist Michael Mewshaw talks about a match between Ivan Lendl and Vijay Amritraj:

> In the second semi-final that evening Vijay Amritraj managed to stay on even terms with Ivan Lendl by forcing him to rush his groundstrokes. On almost every point the tall, graceful Indian swooped to the net and volleyed. Once, late in the second set, Vijay had hit a short shot, giving Lendl an easy put-away. As the Czech charged forward to murder it, Amritraj raised his arms in amiable submission, then was astonished when Lendl clobbered the ball wide. The crowd laughed. So did Vijay. But the Czech saw nothing funny about it. He complained to the umpire that Amritraj's submissive gesture had distracted him. Ivan Lendl seemed to have everything a tennis champion needed except a sense of perspective and a sense of humour.[86]

Amritraj himself talks in his book about the time he met Illie Nastase in the second round of a WCT tournament. By this time Amritraj and Nastase were good friends and playing

World Team Tennis together for the Los Angeles Strings. This friendship did make it a bit harder for Nastase to be his usual 'Nasty' self against the Indian, but did not materially alter his behaviour when he first came on court.

'I compounded his problem for him by killing every argument stone dead through the simple expedient of giving him the point. That took the wind out of his sails completely. Suddenly there was no one to argue with. As soon as I conceded a point, the umpire was calling the score in his favour and that was that. There was nothing left to do but play tennis. At courtside, Illie's lovely wife, Dominique, a long-limbed French brunette with a smile as wide as the Champs-Elysses, was laughing her head off. She knew exactly what was happening on court. "You naughty boy, you were so nice to him," Dominique giggled in her delicious French accent when we came off with the scoreboard showing a straight-set defeat for the defused Nastase.'

Another Nastase story is well worth telling. Amritraj and Nastase, both reaching the end of their careers at the time, came into the 1984 Stockholm Open as an unseeded pair, and ran into the top seeds John McEnroe and Peter Fleming in the round of sixteen. A hard-fought first set went to the Americans, 7-6. Amritraj tells me what happened next:

> At the changeover, one set down, Nastase leans over to me and says, 'Let's win this quickly.' I was a bit taken aback because I didn't think we had a great chance of winning at all. Here we were one set down against the top doubles pair in the world. Nastase tells me, 'You just play well and leave the rest to me.' I decide to go along. From the start of the second set he starts harassing McEnroe. Every time McEnroe is about to

serve, Nastase puts his hand up, stops him and laughs at him, completely putting him off. Then as we are changing sides, he dramatically pauses next to McEnroe and turning to me says, 'Look at him. With a face like that, I wouldn't go near a zoo.' The easy-to-rile McEnroe completely loses his cool and starts making mistakes. We win 6-7, 6-2, 6-4.[87]

As he writes, 'On court, in the heat of the battle, there was no way you could make Nasty nice. Nor, conversely, was there any way you could turn me into a tantrum-throwing lunatic. I claim no credit for it. It's just the way one happens to be.'[88]

THERE IS LIFE AFTER TENNIS

By the time he decided to lay down his racquet, six years had passed after the 1987 Davis Cup finals, and Vijay Amritraj was already a part-time actor in films and TV shows. For a time he tried to turn that into a second career, but that proved difficult. The link with tennis, the sport that had made him the man and celebrity he was, Amritraj decided was what would launch his second career. And that was the right call.

Television coverage of tennis was growing at a phenomenal pace and Amritraj was signed up on a five-year contract by Prime Sports in 1991 for all four Grand Slam events, starting with their first-ever live telecast of the US Open. He had no live television experience, but would go on to become one of the most respected tennis analysts and commentators over the next three decades. As he told *Sportstar* in a 2018 interview, 'It (the Prime Sports stint) taught me how to generate more interest to make people who don't watch tennis watch and give the seasoned viewers what they are expecting.'[89]

It also gave him the confidence to host a talk show called *Dimensions with Vijay Amritraj* on CNN-IBN that would feature personalities from all walks of life, from Donald Trump to boxer Sugar Ray Leonard and supermodel Cindy Crawford.

Continuing to give back to the sport that had given him everything, Amritraj became the president of the Association of Tennis Professionals in 1989. He would have a significant role to play in the improvements that guaranteed a better and fairer deal to players and a far more professional tour, now called the ATP Tour, than the sport had ever had.

When he started the Britannia Amritraj Tennis Scheme (BAT) in Madras in partnership with Rajan Pillai, the chairman of Britannia Industries, Amritraj could scarcely have guessed how important that step would turn out to be for Indian tennis. The emergence of Leander Paes from the practice courts of BAT into the show courts of the greatest Grand Slam venues could by itself count as Vijay Amritraj's greatest gift to Indian tennis.

At the age of sixty-nine, Vijay Amritraj continues to crisscross the world for his business and tennis commitments, making a difference to the world of tennis with every hat he dons. As this edition goes to print, Amritraj is shuttling between LA, Mumbai and Chennai, working to ensure the success of the return of the WTA circuit to his hometown Chennai, while fulfilling his television commitments for the US Open. As we wrap up the conversation about his career and the future of Indian tennis, and he gets ready to leave his Mumbai hotel for the airport, our final exchange is on how to make the WTA event a financial success so that it benefits Indian tennis. There is no doubt that he is one man who has given back as much to the sport as he got from it, if not more.

Vijay Amritraj, on and off court, is truly the ultimate 'A' of tennis.

Ramanathan Krishnan in action in 1959—at the peak of his
brilliant tennis career.

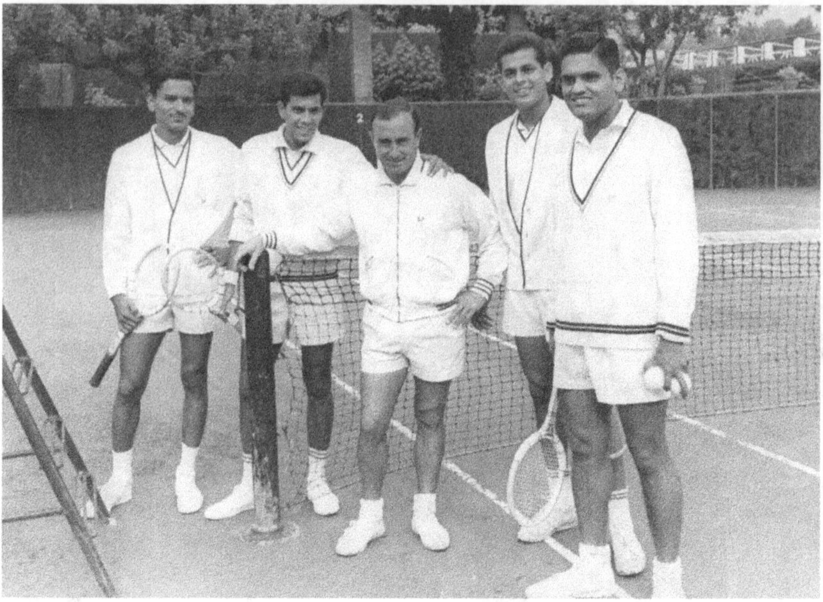

The team for the 1965 Davis Cup tie against Spain. (From left) S.P. Misra, Jaidip Mukerjea, Premjit Lall and Ramanathan Krishnan with an unidentified person (middle).

Courtesy: Family of Sumant Misra

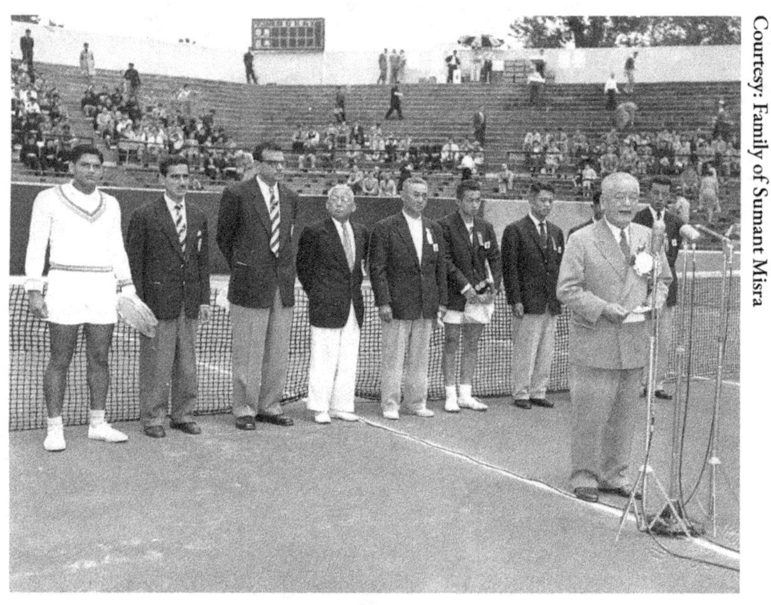

Krishnan, Naresh Kumar and Sumant Misra prior to the Davis Cup tie against Japan in 1959.

Vijay Amritraj at Wimbledon in 1982.

Rod Laver (extreme left) and Vijay Amritraj in Barcelona in 1988.

Somdev Devvarman in the Wimbledon Qualifying Rounds in 2015.

Ramesh Krishnan at Wimbledon in 1988.

Leander Paes at Wimbledon in 2013.

Mahesh Bhupathi at the
French Open in 2013.

Rohan Bopanna at the
French Open in 2013.

Sania Mirza at the Citi Open championships in Washington DC in 2011.

RAMESH KRISHNAN
THE MASTER OF TOUCH PLAY

The game of tennis has been the most influential teacher in my life.[90]

—Ramesh Krishnan

FREJUS, 19 JULY 1993

It is sometimes better not to start at the beginning, for the story of an elite sportsperson is often best told from its most extraordinary moment.

That moment in the career of Ramesh Krishnan came on the fourth morning of the 1993 Davis Cup quarter-final tie between France and India. The venue was Frejus on the magnificent Cote d'Azur (literally, if inadequately, translated as the 'Blue Coast'). At stake, the unthinkable—a victory over France on its most favoured surface, red clay, in an arena, the Colosseum, which, almost two thousand years before had been used for Roman gladiatorial contests. The red clay and the once blood-caked arena was no doubt symbolic of what the hosts expected to do to their hapless visitors.

India and France line up at Frejus before the tie

The story began three days earlier as twenty-year-old Leander Paes, ranked 208 in the world, took on one of France's legendary players, Henri Leconte. Ramesh, the senior partner, playing the opening match of the tie, had lost tamely in straight sets to the world no. 23, Arnaud Boetsch. Ramesh's tongue-in-cheek answer at the press conference before the tie—Jean Borotra—to a French reporter's question about who he would like to play on the first day now sounded almost serious.* As the first day of the tie drew to a close, the French crowd was ready to wind up early, certain of a 2-0 result, going into the next day.

But with a magnificent 6-3, 6-2, 3-6, 6-3 victory over a stunned Leconte, Paes would throw a major spanner into

---

*One of France's greatest tennis players and a part of the famous 'Three Musketeers' of the 1920s who dominated world tennis for over a decade.

the French works. When Boetsch and Leconte got together the next day and stitched together a straight sets doubles victory against Krishnan and Paes, parity appeared to have been restored.

The Indians, however, had other ideas.

Playing some magnificent tennis, Paes upset Boetsch in straight sets, and then India had a stroke of luck. Henri Leconte pulled out of the next match, and was replaced by debutante Rodolphe Gilbert. The official reason given for the withdrawal was Leconte's bad back, but very few on or off the court believed that to be the real reason. Enrico Piperno, India's Davis Cup coach at the time, believes Leconte was shocked by the loss to Paes and didn't want to take on the responsibility of a tie decider. Naresh Kumar, India's non-playing captain for the tie, agrees.

Be that as it may, when Ramesh Krishnan came out to play the decider, the court was a battleground of nerves. Krishnan would later write about the first part of the match. 'When he ran up a 2-1 (sets) and a 5-2 lead against me, things looked bleak.'[91] But the nerves of the debutante kicked in at that point, and the experienced Krishnan pulled things back to tie the match 2-2.

Krishnan goes on: 'I sensed an opportunity and went for broke. In semi-darkness, we battled it out to 4-4 in the decider. I had the momentum and did not want to stop. I wasn't sure about my physical condition on the morrow. Indeed, I had to be literally dragged off the court. And instead of spending the night on a yacht in the Mediterranean—as had been planned—I was lying on a table dazed and exhausted in my hotel room with the French masseur Jean George Cellier working on my tired muscle.'

While Krishnan was recuperating in his room, Naresh Kumar, the master strategist, was busy preparing for the morrow. He tells me, 'I went to the person who ran the gym at the practice arena and asked him for advice on how to get someone to his peak cardio level very quickly. I was advised to make the person run until he was ready to drop, then make him take a cold shower and put him on court immediately.'[92]

The next morning, Ramesh Krishnan woke up feeling better after the massage and the sleep, but as Piperno tells me, 'He was most reluctant to run or work out hard before the match, but Naresh would have none of it.'[93]

Piperno and Ramesh practising in Frejus

Naresh Kumar continues, 'I called young Leander and told him to get on court with him and make the bugger run!

Leander, with his youthful energy, followed my instructions, and in no time, Ramesh was drenched with sweat. I then made him take a cold shower, and put him on court.'[94]

Krishnan was all warmed up but down 15-40 on serve in the ninth game—things did not look good. He was giving the captain and the coach some anxious moments, and that is when the difference in experience and physical preparedness between the two players kicked in. Krishnan talks us through that. 'I came through that and then attacked Gilbert with relish. He fell to pieces. It was as quick a knockout punch as I might have expected to land.'

Piperno adds, 'Gilbert had no warm up, and had only had some light hits on court. When it came to the crunch, his tight muscles and frayed nerves made him freeze.'[95]

Leander and Piperno cheer Ramesh as he plays the final match of the tie for the victory

Krishnan had won 2-6, 6-4, 4-6, 7-5, 6-4, and clinched for India a tie that the ITF observer Thomas Hallberg would later call the 'greatest upset in the history of World Group Davis Cup'.

The semi-finals would be as high as India would go in the Davis Cup in 1993 after that magnificent victory against France. At home in Chandigarh on grass, two months later, the Ramesh–Paes duo would be blown away in no uncertain manner by Wally Masur and Jason Stoltenberg, ranked no. 15 and 44 in the world respectively. A 0-5 scoreline so soon after Frejus, while embarrassing, was perhaps in line with the rankings of the two teams and their players. Miracles done, status quo had been restored.

SYDNEY, 4 OCTOBER 1987

Six years before in Sydney, it had, however, been a different result, with Masur and Krishnan's roles reversed. The story starts earlier that year (1987) in the opening round against Argentina at New Delhi.

Krishnan had been up 6-1, 5-0 against Martin Jaite, ranked no. 15 in the world, and had then found a way to lose the match. Thanks to Vijay Amritraj's heroics against Jaite in the reverse singles, India had drawn level 2-2 and a nervous Ramesh, with captain Vijay giving instructions at the breaks, had taken India to a straight sets victory in the final match of the tie against Horacio de La Pena.

With a win over Israel in the next round, India squared up against the mighty Australians at Sydney in the southern spring of 1987. Leading the Australians was Pat Cash, the reigning Wimbledon champion, the captain—was the wily Neale Fraser and the surface for the tie—unsurprisingly—grass.

To everyone's surprise, at the draw ceremony, Pat Cash's name was missing from the first two singles. He had an injury that the Aussie captain Fraser had cleverly not let on earlier. Krishnan would face John Fitzgerald and Amritraj would do battle against Wally Masur.

Day one unexpectedly went to the Indians. An in-form Krishnan prevailed over the grass court specialist, Fitzgerald, in four sets, and Amritraj, on the last legs of a magnificent career and ranked outside the Top 100, came back from a set down to upset world no. 23, Masur.

Krishnan recalls, 'With a 2-0 lead, we were in the driver's seat. Vijay did not want to hurt his back by playing doubles and we decided to write off the second day's rubber.'

Amritraj writes his version of the story: 'My body does not bounce back well after a long struggle against a player of Masur's ability and even though I was prepared to throw our young reserve, Vasudevan, into the doubles with Anand, I knew deep down that my chances of beating as experienced a grass-court player as Fitzgerald first up on the Sunday would be slim. I think everyone on the team recognised this, so we were all mentally prepared for the likelihood that Ramesh would have to handle the fifth and deciding rubber for us. The fact that everyone was happy for Ramesh to be saddled with this responsibility, and quite confident in his ability to pull it off, showed just how far we had progressed as a team.'[96]

The Indians may have been confident, but the Aussies were not ready to be written off yet. Krishnan recounts what happened at the official dinner at the end of Day two: 'Fraser, whose team was still down 1-2 after winning the doubles, tried to wrest the psychological initiative from us. He said his players would do what was necessary on the morrow and he would tell us all about their (Australian team's) visit to Sweden for the final.'

When Fitzgerald unsurprisingly beat a tired Amritraj, all eyes were on Krishnan as he walked out to do battle with Wally Masur in the decider. Sitting in the captain's chair was Vijay Amritraj.

Amritraj talks us through the match. 'Masur, a nice guy with a droll line in humour, has never been able to exploit his natural talent to its utmost because he lacks a killer shot ... but in Davis Cup, logic can be blown to the winds, and as Ramesh trailed 1-4 in the first set and 1-4 again in the second, it was obvious that Masur was not going to give it away.'

From Krishnan's movements it was clear his legs felt like they were made of lead.

Amritraj continues, 'Ramesh was so nervous that his feet wouldn't leave the ground ... I knew I had to get him moving physically before he could start putting any pressure on Masur. "Exaggerate your movements," I told him. "Follow through all the way on each stroke." "Mmm," said Ramesh, absorbed in the task of getting his hand up to his mouth, so he could take a sip of water. "Move your feet," I went on, talking up a storm. "Jump up and down when you receive serve. Move, loosen up. Go for it." "Mmm," said Ramesh.'

Krishnan was an introvert. No one who has ever interacted with him will tell you otherwise. And his response to Amritraj's advice was typical. But like all clever men, he was internalising his captain's message, and Amritraj knew it.

Amritraj says again, 'The lack of verbal response is offset by the amount of eye-to-eye contact Krishnan likes to establish with me once he is back on court. In tight situations, he will look at me after every point and will want to draw encouragement from the fact that I am looking straight back at him. So you play the match with him, point by point, and by the end, of course, you are just as exhausted. But that's what Davis Cup captains are for.'

As Masur seized up, Krishnan grew from strength to strength. Eventually he would prevail 8-6, 8-6, 6-4 in a match he would call 'one of the finest matches of my career', to take India into the Davis Cup final for the second time.

Krishnan would later write, 'The euphoria in the locker room had to be seen to be believed. Neale and his boys came in to congratulate us and he said to me, "Your old man would be proud of you." The Aussies were never ones to carry any hard feelings and I appreciated this gesture very much. Champagne flowed and Vijay was in no position to drive us back to the hotel. I moved into the driver's seat for the journey back to the Regent. *It was a day when I was always in the driver's seat.*'

There was also another thought that went through Krishnan's mind as he lay on his hotel bed that night, too pumped up to sleep, that he would pen later:

As I grew up, getting to know more about the significance of the Davis Cup success, watching a few matches in which my father played, little did I realise that one day dream and reality would meet in the same place and time and earn the Krishnans a special place in David Cup folklore—as the only father and son to have won fifth rubbers to take the country into the Davis Cup Final![97]

In 1974, the last time India had reached the finals, the Indian Tennis Federation had prevented the Indian team from playing South Africa, given India's stance on apartheid. This time, there was no such danger. Sweden beckoned.

The Swedes had the promotional material for the final ready—'Swedes vs Cash'. That they had to change. But the slow indoor clay courts that had been prepared in freezing Gothenburg for the Aussies would do just as well for the Indians.

As Krishnan would say years later, 'We faced formidable odds. With one player in the top thirty-five (myself) and two part-time players, we were going up against the world's best team, a team that had four top ten players.'*

The great Roy Emerson, a friend of Ramesh's father Ramanathan Krishnan, had sent him a message: 'Get blood on your knees.' But against a Swedish side which had conceded just one set in five matches in 1984 against the Americans, boasting Jimmy Connors and John McEnroe, the Indians were on their knees on the blood-red court. As Krishnan put it with disarming honesty, 'We barely got clay on our socks.' The 0-5 result was hardly a surprise.

Krishnan would ruefully concede later: 'It was simply a case of a bunch of over-achievers being blown away by the favourite in a festive ambience.' Nonetheless, that bunch of over-achievers had beaten the Aussies on their home turf, and with a sole top fifty player in their ranks, had rubbed shoulders with the mighty Swedes in the finals of the Davis Cup. It was a feeling no Indian tennis player was to experience again for decades to come.

---

*Vijay and Anand were for all practical purposes done with their professional careers by this time.

THE BEGINNINGS

The Aussie great Ken Rosewall once told Ramanathan Krishnan after his son had broken into the top twenty-five, 'You know, Krish, your greatest achievement is passing your talent successfully to your son. It is very difficult. And so few of us have managed it.'[98]

These words are true not only in the case of tennis players but indeed anyone who plays elite sports. It is not obvious that all or any of Roger Federer's four children will emulate their father. Rohan Gavaskar, despite his talent, struggled to live up to the dizzyingly high standards set by father Sunil. Arjun Tendulkar's best bet at future sporting success is that he is not a batsman. So what made Ramesh Krishnan different?

Krishnan recalls asking himself the question as an adult, whether he could have been anything but a professional tennis player. And he provides us the answer:

> The truth is, I probably did not have a choice. How could it have been otherwise when you are the first-born son of India's top tennis player who, at the time I was born, was at the zenith of his career? What kind of a choice do you have when you are living in a house where half the land is set apart for a tennis court, where every wall reverberates to the sounds of forehands and backhands ... when you grow up under the wings of a benevolent dictator of a grandfather who was a cross between Harry Hopman and a British Army Sergeant Major stereotype?

But just as much as the family background and support, it was the love for tennis that was transmitted in the genes, and that would make the ultimate difference.

In a sober moment of his otherwise rip-roaring account of tennis on the circuit, *A Handful of Summers*, South African tennis player Gordon Forbes talks about evenings spent with his father that would shape how he felt about the sport. 'In the evenings, my father would tell us stories of the genius of the great players of that time. He had a way of making their deeds seem so marvellous that we'd be out at first light, giving them a try. Tennis stories became, for us, heady draughts quite early in our lives. Raptly we listened to them, savoured them, re-enacted them and stored them away in our memories.'

The Krishnan household was no different. In addition, Ramesh had a father who was still actively playing the sport as the son made his foray into competitive tennis. So tennis talk at home was soon to be complemented by tennis on the tournament courts.

At the Haryana State Championship semi-finals in Chandigarh in 1976, the newspapers had screamed— *Krishnan beats Lall.* This, in itself was not unusual, except that this was Ramesh, and not his father, beating Premjit Lall. Krishnan talks about that evening. 'I called my mother in Madras to tell her about the victory when Premjit dashed in and grabbed the phone. "All these years I've been losing to the father, now I am losing to the son," he said to my mother.'

In the finals, Krishnan would go on to beat his father to win his first senior championship. He was fifteen, Ramanathan Krishnan thirty-nine. The following year Krishnan won the National Championships for the first time. He was sixteen years and six months old, and he bested his father's long-standing record by two months.

In 1978, after his Class X exams, Ramesh travelled to Europe as part of a group of Indian Juniors under the care of coach Akhtar Ali for the summer circuit. Ali, who was well networked among the former players, got the greats of the game, like Stan Smith and Pancho Gonzales, to take a look at young Krishnan and knock around with him. It would be invaluable for the growth of the young man.

Krishnan self-deprecatingly recounts his encounter with Gonzalez, one of the greatest servers in the history of tennis, 'The great man gave me a serving lesson, although those who have watched me through my career—and judged my service prowess—would not believe that I learnt anything from Pancho at all!'

The serve would continue to be Krishnan's Achilles heel through his career and indeed make him a part of tennis folklore that is recounted whenever raconteurs sit down over a few beers. But to put the remark on Gonzalez's service lesson in context, one needs to go forward a few years to 1981. That year Krishnan ran into John McEnroe in the quarter-finals of the US Open.

It had been a remarkable start for the young man. He had beaten an ageing Stan Smith and then stunned no. 7 seed Gene Mayer in the fourth round. McEnroe was the top-ranked player in the world and in supreme form, but Krishnan and the American had run into each other a few times in the junior and senior circuits over the years, so there was no question of being overawed.

Krishnan won the first set on tiebreak. Midway through the second set when Krishnan was a break up was to come a famous McEnroe rant on his opponent's service: 'The guy serves at ten miles an hour and I still can't return it.'

The American would, however, find a way to manage his angst. Krishnan served for the second set at 5-4 but McEnroe pulled it back from 30-30, showing grit and determination, going on to win the set in a tiebreak and eventually the match, 6-7, 7-6, 6-4, 6-2. That was the closest Ramesh Krishnan would get to a Grand Slam singles title in his career.

McEnroe would march into the finals of the US Open that year and beat Bjorn Borg in four sets to lift the title, one of the seven singles titles at Grand Slam events he eventually picked up in the course of his career.

Vijay Amritraj tells me another Krishnan–McEnroe story. In that instance, Krishnan frustrated McEnroe into making multiple mistakes, and after the match, McEnroe told Amritraj, 'I got so tired of waiting for his serve to arrive, that when it finally did, I didn't know what to do with it!'[99]

In the course of writing this book I asked Krishnan how he coped at the highest level with a serve that even he felt compelled to joke about. He modestly answered, 'The rest of my game was quite okay. I had good ground strokes and volleys. I think the best parts of my game were my return of serve and taking the ball early.'[100]

Making an Impact

In 1979 when Krishnan flew into Paris for the French Open, he knew that at almost eighteen, this was his last chance at making an impact at the juniors, even though he was slated to play in both events.

In the seniors event he had beaten Peter Fleming (John McEnroe's long-time doubles partner) in the first round before losing to Jimmy Connors. But this experience was to serve him well when he played the juniors a week later, running through the field before defeating Ben Testerman of the United States in the final.

The French Open juniors was his, but this was not a time for celebration, as he left for London to play the juniors' event at Wimbledon. That was the main course. The junior title on clay, as far as Ramesh was concerned, was merely what the French would call hors d'oeuvre.*

At Wimbledon, Krishnan came from 2-6, 0-3 behind to beat Schalk Van Der Merwe of South Africa in the quarter-finals, showing the fighting spirit that would see him bring about some remarkable come-from-behind Davis Cup victories in the years to follow. The straight sets victory in the final over David Siegler of the US was almost a formality after that.

Ramesh Krishnan had become the second Indian after his father to hold aloft the Junior Wimbledon title. Having won the French and Wimbledon in a span of a few weeks, Ramesh also reached the semi-finals of the junior event at the US Open, and finished the year as the top-ranked junior in the world.

He was now eighteen, and it was time to deliver as a senior what he promised as a junior. That, as Krishnan would soon discover, was easier said than done. He would later say about this transition, 'For a vast majority of players, the move from junior tennis to the men's game is seldom easily accomplished. The men's game is an ocean compared to the small lake in which we were splashing about merrily as juniors.'[101]

---

*An appetiser

Continuing on this theme, and talking about the lack of success for Indian players in recent times at the senior level, he would tell me, 'Transitioning from juniors to the senior ranks is tricky business. And it continues to be so. In fact, it is more so now with players well into their thirties performing well and staying on top of the rankings. At the moment, tennis is being dominated by Europe and a youngster from India is at a big disadvantage. The cost of producing a world class player has increased manifold.'

It would be two years of toil for Krishnan as he struggled to establish himself among the seniors, fading away from the limelight and going back to the satellite events to wet his feet before stepping back among the big boys. In the meantime he appeared for his BA exams and obtained his degree.

In a reflection of the Indian family circumstances he came from, four years later when a survey was done on the ATP tour after Becker sensationally won Wimbledon at the age of seventeen, there was found to be only one college graduate among the top 100. That man was Ramesh Krishnan.

The 1981 US Open, and the Canadian Open that preceded it, would give Krishnan the confidence that he was good enough to be in the big league. He won his first ATP tour title in Manila that year and was signed up by IMG as a client. The finances were now taken care of and he could concentrate on the tennis.

It was, however, not until 1983, when Ramesh lost a close five-setter against Vitas Gerulaitis at Wimbledon and his old coach Harry Holman suggested he start running to improve his fitness, that there was a change in Ramesh's fortunes that would play out over the next four years.

In 1984 Krishnan became the second Indian after Vijay Amritraj and only the third since his father to break into the official top twenty-five rankings, appearing at no. 23.

In 1986, he entered the quarter-finals of Wimbledon for the first time. Krishnan beat sixth-seeded Joakim Nystrom of Sweden in the third round on the way to his encounter with the big-serving Serbian, the 6'6" tall Slobodan Zivojinovic. In an unequal match up of power and big serving versus touch play and subtlety, Krishnan bowed out in four sets.

The following year at Flushing Meadows would turn out to be the last chance Krishnan would get to emulate his father at a Grand Slam event, and perhaps surpass his semi-final record. In the first four rounds, Krishnan was in the form of his life, beating Paul Annacone, Joakim Nystrom (then a top twenty player), Johan Kriek and Andrei Chesnakov, without losing a set.

The previous year, he had narrowly lost to Stefan Edberg, and given his own current form, Krishnan fancied his chances in the return match against the world no. 4. But as he ruefully writes, 'Edberg had improved remarkably in a year's time and he simply demolished me this time.' Thankfully, the Davis Cup victory over the Aussies and the sheer exhilaration of taking his country into the finals, just as his father had done, would make 1987 a year to cherish.

In October 1988 Krishnan suffered a back injury that would eventually convince him a few years later to retire from the game. But there were a few things still left to achieve.

At the 1989 Australian Open, Krishnan met the world no. 1 Mats Wilander in the second round and pulled off a stunning straight sets victory over the Swede. Despite a few more ATP tour titles in the next couple of years, he realised his career was coming to an end. An ankle injury at Wimbledon in 1991, for all practical purposes, ended Krishnan's run at the Grand Slams.

But two years later when the French team walked across with the huge bottle of champagne that had been put on ice for them at Frejus, and handed it over to the Indians, it was a poignant and exhilarating moment at the same time. Ramesh Krishnan, brought out of semi-retirement, had led his country to one of its most remarkable victories in the history of the Davis Cup. It would prove to be the icing on the cake of a magnificent career.

While Paes and Krishnan may have been expected to perform another miracle in the semi-finals of the Davis Cup that year, it was sadly not to be. The Australians blew away India 5-0 at Chandigarh. The experienced Wally Masur, ranked no. 15 in the world, was at the helm, determined to avenge the upset six years before.

The toll on the body from the years on the tour, the lack of family time and his constant battles with the Indian tennis administration on behalf of the players was all coming to a head for Ramesh by this time. When the administrators unfairly pointed fingers at him after the loss to Australia, Krishnan had had enough. He announced his retirement from the game.

Krishnan made a return to the Davis Cup arena as the non-playing captain in 2007. It was time to give back to the game that had given him so much. As he told me recently, 'As a Davis Cup team captain, you would like to motivate the younger players and pass on some of your experience. I enjoyed my stint as a Davis Cup captain very much.'[102]

Beyond the Davis Cup captaincy which he relinquished a few years ago, Krishnan continues to give back to the sport with his endeavour of producing future champions at the Krishnan Tennis Centre in Chennai which he has run since his retirement from the sport.

THE ALMOST MEN

I have been one of the coaches who has been working with three generations. Leander Paes is my trainee. I have worked with Ramesh Krishnan, Zeeshan Ali, and I was a private coach of Vijay Amritraj. I have produced more national champions and Davis Cup players in the country than any other coach. My success as a coach is because I try to keep learning and still I am learning.[103]

—Akhtar Ali

It is indubitably true that the names of Ramanathan Krishnan, Vijay Amritraj and Ramesh Krishnan are the ones that bring instant recognition among aficionados when one talks about Indian tennis in the five decades between independence and the turn of the century.

But it is also a fact that these three and the equally talented but oft-forgotten Naresh Kumar, Sumant Misra, Jaidip Mukherjea and Premjit Lall could not have risen just on their own if they did not have a high level of robust domestic competitors to fight their way through as they went up the ranks. Some of these unheralded players would also go on to make significant contributions in India's Davis Cup campaigns.

The fact that many of them did not make a mark on the international scene often had more to do with the unique financial challenges of the international sport that living and earning in India presented, rather than the talent that they possessed.

This is a tribute to that group of players with indomitable spirit who, largely unheralded now, kept the tricolour flying through some very difficult decades for Indian tennis.

AKHTAR ALI

It is only fitting that the first name that this chapter throws up is that of Akhtar Ali, for in terms of his contribution to the development of the sport in the country, Ali can rightfully be described as the 'First Man of Indian Tennis'.

Akhtar Ali's tennis skills first came to the notice of the tennis fraternity when he won the Junior Nationals at the age of sixteen in 1955 and reached the Junior Wimbledon semifinals the same year. The following summer he would make his first appearance on the senior stage at the same venue, reaching the second round.

Between 1958 and 1964, Ali was a regular in the Indian Davis Cup squad alongside Ramanathan Krishnan, Jaidip Mukherjea and Premjit Lall. His 9-2 overall and 4-0 unbeaten doubles record speaks volumes of his contribution. The fact that he didn't reach greater heights as a player can probably be put down to a physical shortcoming rather than talent. As Ramanathan Krishnan tells me, 'Lack of height affected his tennis.'[104]

But Akhtar's greatest contribution would come after he lay down his racquet as a player. His decision to turn to coaching is one Indian tennis will alway be grateful for. Treading on the footsteps of the legendary Dilip Bose, Akhtar Ali would excel as a talent spotter and coach in much the same vein as Bose. The boys he trained would go on to become some of India's greatest tennis players over the next few decades.

Gaurav Misra, the 1972 national champion, tells me, 'I can't now pinpoint exactly what it was, but Akhtar's suggestions and tweaks took my game to the next level. He was a very good coach.'[105] Vijay and Anand Amritraj, new entrants to the Davis Cup team while Ali was leading it, would also benefit from his wisdom.

The next star of Indian tennis who came under his wings was Ramesh Krishnan. Krishnan explains in his book *A Touch of Tennis* that Akhtar Ali's contributions went well beyond being just a coach. It also lay in his unique quality that, 'he never hesitated to approach anyone for a favour, whether it was for himself or a friend'.[106] This would be very beneficial for his trainees.

In 1977, at the age of sixteen, the junior Krishnan set out with Akhtar Ali and the rest of the junior team to play in Europe starting with the French Junior Championships at Roland Garros, which was won that year by John McEnroe.

Going on to the Queen's Club in London after that, Ali would bring all his social skills to bear in order to benefit his ward. 'It was at Queen's that I often stood amazed, watching Akhtar waltz across to say hello to all sorts of top players—present or past—in sight. One day he found out that Stan Smith was looking for a practice partner and introduced me to the 1972 Wimbledon champion so that I got a chance to play him. Another day it was the great Pancho Gonzales who Akhtar dragged onto court to take a look at me. The great man gave me a serving lesson,' Krishnan writes in his book.

But perhaps the most precious gift of Akhtar Ali to Indian tennis was a man who would dominate the sport and take Indian doubles to dizzying heights it had never before experienced—Leander Paes.

Paes had wielded his little racquet for the first time as an eight-year-old on the South Club courts under the watchful eyes of Akhtar Ali's brother, Anwar. But soon he was hitting with the seniors, Jaidip Mukherjea, Premjit Lall and Ali himself. While Ali worked on him, it was obvious that Paes was slated for bigger things. So when the Amritraj brothers came looking for talent in 1986 for their Britannia Amritraj Tennis Academy in Chennai, Akhtar Ali asked Anand Amritraj to hit a few balls with Paes. The young boy's physique and sharp reflexes caught the eyes of the elder Amritraj, and the rest, as they say, is history.

Akhtar Ali is now retired but continues to be involved with the sport and South Club. He lives in Kolkata.

S.P. Misra

Growing up in Hyderabad where the tennis exploits of Ghaus Mohammad were still a part of the lore, Shiv Prakash (S.P.) Misra and his brother took to tennis at the Secunderabad Club. Brother S.S. Misra, now a successful entrepreneur, would tell *Business Standard* years later, 'We used to be ball boys when my father and his cousins used to play at the club.

Slowly, we started to emulate them and learnt the game. During those days, though it was very expensive, my father always encouraged us to play.'[107]

Between 1964 and 1969, Misra was a vital cog in the wheel of the formidable Indian Davis Cup squad of the time. In fact, it is a travesty that his name is rarely mentioned alongside Ramanathan Krishnan, Premjit Lall, Jaidip Mukherjea and Akhtar Ali. Of all Indian Davis Cup players to play more than ten matches, no one in the history of the sport in India has a better win-loss record than S.P. Misra. Appearing in nineteen matches across eleven ties, Misra racked up an incredible record of eighteen victories and one loss.

It was often up to him to take India through the early rounds, partnering Premjit Lall in the doubles and shouldering the burden of one and often two singles matches on his broad shoulders. When India progressed to the higher rounds in certain years like 1966 for example, the big guns—Krishnan, Lall and Mukherjea—took over.

For the past five decades, Misra has been an administrator, a national selector and the non-playing captain of the Indian team. This includes the ill-fated outing to the 2012 London Olympics when he was asked to manage a team of disgruntled and warring superstars after their ugly public fights had already caused irreversible damage to the country's chances.

While taking on the job, fully cognisant of what he was getting into, Misra had said, 'I have the highest respect for them and will try my best to keep them in right spirit ahead of the huge challenge.'[108] But when the following year, Somdev Devvarman, a man with a far less stellar Davis Cup record (fourteen wins and eleven losses over fourteen ties) called him 'not up to the mark', Misra resigned as captain with the words: 'I am deeply saddened by the developments of the past few days.'

In late 2018 when he was replaced as chairman of the national selection committee without any prior notice, Misra bowed out with the words, 'Everything has to end one day. Nothing can go on forever.'[109]

Through everything that has happened, as he did through his playing career, Misra, in the best traditions of sport, has remained quietly dignified and done the job assigned to him, putting Indian tennis before everything else.

GAURAV MISRA

It was early March of 1972, there was still a nip in the Calcutta air, and the court side at the South Club was filling up quickly. After many years the much-loved Ramanathan Krishnan was in the final of the National Championships, and facing him was a young man who had grown up around the club. Misra had first played here with his grandfather (one of the founders of the club) at the age of six, and often heard accounts of his father Sumant Misra's on-court brilliance, told and re-told to him by the likes of Premjit Lall, Jaidip Mukherjea and Krishnan.

In the semi-finals, Misra had beaten Lall, the no. 2 seed, a victory that gave him enormous confidence, and one that he savours to this day. In the final, for Gaurav Misra, whose talent had been originally identified by Stan Edwards, the Australian coach who had taken over from Dilip Bose, and then been groomed by Akhtar Ali, it was time to stand up and be counted. Misra was under no illusion that this would be anything but a bruising battle against the man who may have been past his prime, but was already a living legend.

Two years before, Misra had won the National Hard Courts at Trivandrum, announcing his arrival on the Indian tennis scene beating the very talented Vijay Amritraj and then his brother Anand in five sets. But this was different. It was the National Championships, on his home turf, and facing him was India's Davis Cup captain and indubitably the greatest player in the annals of Indian tennis.

It would, in fact, be a marathon tussle between the twenty-one-year-old Misra and the veteran Krishnan. Three bruising hours later, history had been made. With his 4-6, 6-4, 8-10, 7-5, 6-2 win over Krishnan, Gaurav Misra had earned a permanent place in Indian tennis lore alongside his father by becoming the first father–son duo to win the National Championships.

Sports India reported: 'It was a victory for aggressive youth over rich experience crowned by artistry and superlative skill. Misra, seeded seventh, was in brilliant form and justified the high hopes his captain had entertained about his ward, one of the six in the Davis Cup squad nominated for India. It is the first case in India of father and son winning the national (championship) and wearing national colours too.'[110]

For Misra it was undoubtedly the high point of his career, but as he tells me during our conversation earlier this year, his semi-final win against Premjit Lall at his peak had given him greater fulfilment. 'If anything, it was for me an even more satisfying win than the final, given Krishnan was past his prime.'[111]

Sadly, soon after this Misra was diagnosed with an overactive thyroid gland condition and was physically unable to get back to a level of fitness this elite sport demanded. After gamely trying for six months he realised that his body was not going to be able to cope up with the rigours of the sport and gave up playing competitively. It was a sad and sudden end to what promised to be an exciting career.

After working for a few years at Balmer Lawrie in Calcutta, Misra moved to Mumbai where he briefly coached the likes of Gaurav Natekar at the MSLTA courts. Soon after, he moved to the United States as a coach at an academy. A few years later, his old friend from Calcutta, Bidyut Goswami, who was coaching at Columbia University, got in touch with Misra. Goswami had won the U-14 event in 1967 at the Junior National Championships when Misra had picked up the U-18 title. They had stayed in touch and remain fast friends.

In 1999, Misra joined as director of tennis of Columbia's Dick Savitt Tennis Centre on Goswami's insistence, and built up that programme alongside Goswami. The duo would guide the school to several national titles. Misra is now retired and continues to live in the United States.

Jasjit Singh

While athletics, hockey, cricket and football have seen their fair share of turbaned men, notwithstanding the fact that tennis in India was first introduced in Punjab, the sport would have to await its turn to welcome the first Sikh to play for the tricolour. When Jasjit Singh stepped onto the South Club grass to do battle against Australia's Bob Giltinan in 1974, the long wait would be rewarded in dramatic fashion.

By reposing his faith on Singh as India's no. 2 singles player ahead of the shocked Anand Amritraj, Ramanathan Krishnan had put his ward permanently in the record books. Singh, in turn, justified his captain's trust by playing inspired tennis and went on to beat world no. 16, Giltinan, 11-9, 9-11, 12-10, 8-6 in the opening match of the tie.

That would, however, be the only Davis Cup match he would win of the three that he played that year. It was also the only year he would make the team. In an international career that was active for four years between 1973 and 1977 (with a sole US Open appearance in 1969 where he lost in the second round to John Newcombe), Singh rose to no. 89 in the ATP rankings in 1974.

In 1973, Singh and his mixed doubles partner, South African Ilana Kloss, stormed into the quarter-finals of the US Open. Kloss was to become the World's no. 1 women's doubles player a couple of years later. In the quarters, the Indo-South African pair lost to the ultimate winners of the Slam event—Australia's Owen Davidson, winner of thirteen Grand Slam doubles and mixed doubles titles, and his partner, Billie Jean King, with twenty-seven such titles under her belt.

Singh lives in New York.

SASHI MENON

Twice national champion in 1980 and 1981, Shashi Menon's would perhaps have been a more familiar name to Indian tennis fans if he had been born a decade later. As it would happen, however, his talent was often hidden behind the flamboyant and dominant Amritraj brothers who had taken over the mantle of leading Indian tennis from Krishnan, Lall and Mukherjea.

In 1974, as India progressed on an unlikely journey to the Davis Cup final against South Africa, only to concede the tie, taking a strong stand against apartheid, Menon would find himself on the sidelines.

In the quarter-finals, while it was Jasjit Singh who got the nod from captain Ramanathan Krishnan to play the second singles against Australia, in the semi-finals against the Soviet Union, as far as Menon was concerned, it would be unfortunate sibling politicking that edged him out. Menon would wistfully say years later, 'Vijay pushed for his brother. Unfortunately, it got to the point where if Anand didn't play (singles), then he (Vijay) didn't want to play.'[112] For the record, Anand did justify the captain and his brother's faith in him by coming back from the edge and beating Alex Metreveli, taking India into the final.

Notwithstanding that disappointment, Menon was to be India's Davis Cup warhorse between 1970 and 1985, playing thirteen Davis Cup matches and winning eight of them.

In ATP tournaments over a thirteen-year-long career between 1970 and 1983, he played 217 matches, winning 100. In 1975 and 1976 he briefly broke into the top 100 in the world in singles, but success would be more forthcoming in the doubles format, picking up three titles in 1978.

Menon currently lives in the United States.

CHIRADIP MUKHERJEA

Chiradip Mukherjea's name is often lost in the shadow of his more accomplished tennis-playing brother, Jaidip. But in the 1970s, the junior Mukherjea was one of the bright sparks on the Indian tennis scene. While his four Davis Cup appearances may have been against 'lesser' teams—Pakistan, Thailand and Philippines, his unbeaten record, that few men before or after him have managed, even against similar opposition, is well worth mentioning.

In a short career, he reached the second round of Wimbledon on both occasions he played there. On the second occasion in 1975, he beat Poland's Wojtek Fibak in the first round. Fibak would rise to world no. 10 soon after. Mukherjea also won the Asian Games bronze in 1978 at Bangkok, partnering Shyam Minotra. He retired from tennis soon after to concentrate on a corporate career. He lives in the United States.

Srinivasan Vasudevan

Born in Madras and following in the illustrious footsteps of Ramanathan Krishnan and the Amritraj brothers came a man who would not quite rise to the heights of his illustrious predecessors. But Srinivasan Vasudevan did do his best to keep the Indian flag flying through the 1980s as the Amritraj brothers came to the end of their careers.

In 1987, when India stormed into the Davis Cup final with a magnificent and largely unexpected semi-finals triumph against much-fancied Australia in their own backyard, Vasudevan was a part of the campaign that year and partnered Anand Amritraj in the doubles, giving Vijay a break after India had taken a 2-0 lead after day one. A straight sets loss to the strong Aussie pairing of Pat Cash and Peter Doohan for the scratch Indian pair was hardly a surprise.

Vasudevan appeared in ten Davis Cup matches between 1983 and 1991, winning six of them. He was also part of the Asian Games silver medal winning team of 1982 alongside Nandan Bal, Enrico Piperno and Jayant Rikhye and the bronze winning team eight years later.

Vasudevan retired from professional tennis in 1994 and lives in the United States.

NANDAN BAL

Watching Nandan Bal's booming serves on the grass courts of South Club was a sight for sore eyes as I was growing up in Kolkata. What gave me secret hope was that he looked like a (much) bigger version of my then chubby self and yet managed to sweep aside all comers with his brilliant tennis.

In 1979, drafted into the Indian Davis Cup squad at the last minute as the Amritraj brothers and Ramesh Krishnan pulled out of the tie against South Korea, it was baptism by fire. In the freezing cold of Seoul in December, debutant Nandan Bal, a grass court specialist, stepped onto the unfamiliar slow clay for the second match of the tie.

India was one match down, Shankar Krishnan (Ramesh Krishnan's cousin) having lost the opening encounter. Facing Bal was Kim Choon-Ho, who, two years later, would win two golds and a silver at the Asian Games in New Delhi.

'We are in this boat and we need to sail. Put up the best performance you are capable of producing. Don't worry about the crowds and don't worry about the results. Remember two things that will always help you—think big, and have a large heart. Now just go out and enjoy your game,' was the advice from Ramanathan Krishnan, the non-playing captain.[113]

As Bal tells me, 'In the 1980s, when the fear of loss and how the nation would react was what coaches and captains burdened you with, Krish's calm and unfazed approach and sage advice was a breath of fresh air.'[114] The advice would work wonders and Bal won his opening match in four sets, and then combined with Shashi Menon the next day to take the doubles in straight sets. India went into day three with an unexpected 2-1 lead.

'Hearing "Advantage India", instead of "Advantage Mr Bal", that I had been used to before, is what I remember most, those words bringing home to me what it meant to play for your country,' Bal recounts, his voice still heavy with emotion after all these years.

Unfortunately, the greater experience of the Koreans and the vociferous crowd support would tilt the tie in their favour in the reverse singles with Young-Jai Deong, the clay court specialist, defeating Bal in the final reverse singles in four hard-fought sets.

Notwithstanding the outstanding performance, given the presence of the senior players, the only other Davis Cup match Bal would get to play in his career was in the Zonal semi-final against Thailand in 1983, which he won.

In 1982, the Asian Games came to India. The hopes were high from the young Indian squad—Nandan Bal, Enrico Piperno, S. Vasudevan and Jayant Rikhye. A week before the Games, the whole team came down with food poisoning, Bal the worst affected. With Rajiv Gandhi taking a personal interest and coming in multiple times to check on the players—'he was a man who genuinely cared'—Bal recalls, the doctors at AIIMS in Delhi managed to put the team back on its feet. Although Bal, still weak from the illness, lost in the men's singles, the foursome picked up the silver in the team competition, losing to the strong Indonesian outfit in the final after beating China in the semis. 'That was a real team effort and unlike some Indian teams over the last decade or two, we genuinely enjoyed our time together and bonded well, and it showed in our performance at the Games.'

Between 1983 and 1986, Nandan Bal ruled Indian tennis, winning four successive national championships. But like many before and after him, international exposure would be limited by a lack of financial backing. The middle-class Bal family, with his father an employee of the Life Insurance Corporation of India, did as much as they could, but could not afford to send him abroad to improve his game against better players for thirty to forty weeks a year. By the time he was at his peak, the Indian circuit was a thing of the past, so world class players were not coming to India any more.

With a break into the top 200 in the world but unable to go further, Bal decided that he needed to move on and secure his future. He left tennis and took up coaching, a profession that would give him a new lease of life in the sport. 'I believe I am a far better coach than I ever was as a player,' Bal tells me with candour.

Having coached the Indian Davis Cup team for thirteen years and the Fed Cup team as well, Bal now runs his own academy at Pune, preparing the new generation of players for a shot at glory.

ENRICO PIPERNO

Emerging from the South Club lawns and the Bengal Lawn Tennis Association Coaching Programme run by Akhtar Ali in the 1980s came another contender for the next big hope of Indian tennis. At first glance, the mildly chubby Enrico Piperno may not have looked a contender for the title of national champion, but he would soon show that looks can be deceptive.

Why Rohit Brijnath referred to Piperno as 'one of the smartest players on the tennis court'[115] was soon apparent to all his opponents on the national stage. Backed by a very supportive father, one of the most respected bookmakers in the Indian horse racing fraternity, Piperno's game evolved because of who he watched and played against at the South Club.

Piperno talks me through what it was like during the period. 'I was junior national champion and I could only get to play at Court 6 at the South Club. There was Premjit Lall and Jaidip Mukherjea on Court 1, Bidyut Goswami and Chiradip Mukherjea on Court 2, and so on. That was the sheer depth of tennis at the club. The locker room environment was amazing.'[116]

In a long career that followed, despite his initial years on grass, Piperno would play seven National Grass Court finals without ever winning one. But any disappointment on this count was put to rest by his record in the National Hard Court Championships where he emerged champion a staggering six times. Brijnath tells me, 'Until Leander arrived, year after year I kept asking myself the question as to who could beat Rico here. There were faster and more talented players who appeared, but none with the court smarts of Rico.'

When I mention this to Piperno during our long and delightful chat one winter afternoon at the Royal Calcutta

Turf Club where he has now replaced his father as a steward, he laughs and says self-deprecatingly, 'Rohit is right. I didn't have the speed of the others, so the only weapon I could use was my brains. Outsmarting my opponents was the best way for me to succeed on the tennis court.'

Between 1979 and 1990 Piperno played in the national circuit and the Challengers and smaller tournaments in Europe and as he says, 'made a decent living, but didn't make it big'. During this entire period, the Davis Cup team was the domain of the Amritraj brothers and Ramesh Krishnan, and like Bal, Piperno largely did not get a look in.

But unknown to Piperno then, a second unexpected career awaited him.

When Leander Paes fell out with the Amritraj brothers and the Britannia Amritraj Tennis Academy in 1990, it was to Piperno that Dr Vece Paes turned to, become young Leander Paes' first professional coach. At Digboi in Assam a few weeks later, Piperno, still ranked no. 8 in the country, but now Paes' coach, in a startling turn of events, would meet his ward in the final of his seventh National Hard Court Championship, and lose.

The match signalled a new dawn for Indian tennis, as Leander Paes began his march into the ranks of senior tennis following up with a victory over Australia's Wally Masur at the ATP tournament in Singapore. A few months later, Paes, not yet eighteen years old, won the US Open Junior title.

Naresh Kumar took over as the Davis Cup captain after that and handed Paes his debut in the doubles at Chandigarh against Korea alongside Zeeshan Ali. Paes and Ali lost the match, but the talent was evident for all to see. Twenty-four months after he started, as Paes grew in stature, Dr Paes and Naresh Kumar found Bob Carmichael and Tony Roche, coaches who could take Paes to the next level, into the top 100, which was the first target. The association with Piperno came to an end.

By this time, Piperno had been appointed the coach of the Davis Cup team, a position he would hold for the next several years. In 1993, Piperno and Kumar would guide the team that caused one of the most famous Davis Cup upsets of all time, beating favourites France on clay at Frejus. Ramesh Krishnan and Leander Paes, under the guidance of the captain-coach duo from Calcutta, would stun Henri Leconte's France, and the world of tennis.

In 1996, Mahesh Bhupathi had made his debut, and early the following year, C.G.K Bhupathi, Mahesh Bhupathi's father, and former player himself, asked Piperno to take over as his son's coach. Later that year Bhupathi became India's first-ever Grand Slam winner, lifting the mixed doubles title with Rika Hiraki at Roland Garros.

A few months before this, Paes, the winner of the bronze in singles at the Atlanta Olympics the previous year, and now coached by Bob Carmichael, had invited Bhupathi to become his doubles partner on the circuit. It was a decision that would change the course of Indian tennis history, in more ways than one.

Over the next three years, as the Paes–Bhupathi relationship went through its ups and downs, Piperno continued to coach Bhupathi as well as the Davis Cup team. But in late 2000 he quit as the Davis Cup coach to take over as captain of the struggling Fed Cup team. The baby of that team, making her debut for India, was the youngest player on court, fourteen-year-old Sania Mirza. The association with Bhupathi continued for the next few years, and during the time the two men worked together, Bhupathi would win six Grand Slam doubles and mixed doubles titles. When they parted after eight years of association, it had been a richly rewarding relationship.

Piperno continued with the Fed Cup team for thirteen years, as Sania Mirza grew into the greatest women's player in the history of Indian tennis. But sadly, a Fed Cup breakthrough into the World Group would be difficult to come by with no one of similar stature in the team to support her. Under Piperno, India's best-ever Fed Cup performance came in 2006 when India was the runners-up in Asia/Oceania Zone Group I. Only in March 2020 would an Indian team surpass that by moving into the World Group playoffs.

Piperno took to television commentary after leaving the Fed Cup team in 2013, and now devotes his time to his stewardship at the RCTC, the occasional television stint, and the Enrico Piperno Tennis Trust run out of the Ordnance Club at Kolkata, helping kids who could not otherwise afford it, play tennis. And most of all, he indulges his great passion and love for the stray dogs of Central Kolkata, many of whom know him by his voice, and he in turn their names, making sure to spend a few hours with them every day.

ZEESHAN ALI

Yet another talent to come out of the South Club lawns in the latter half of the 1980s was a man indubitably born to play tennis. With a father like the legendary Akhtar Ali, one of the finest coaches India has ever produced, Zeeshan Ali's emergence on the tennis circuit was perhaps as predictable as day following night.

Between 1986 and 1991, Ali won five national championships, including four in a row between 1986 and 1989. In 1986, he was the highest ranked junior in Asia and the Asian Junior Champion. He was also ranked World Junior no. 2, reaching the semi-finals of the junior singles event at Wimbledon, and finals of the doubles at the US Open.

But like thousands of players before him, Ali found it difficult to translate the success in the junior ranks into sustained international performances. Achieving a highest ATP singles ranking of 126 in 1988 at the age of eighteen, his performances dropped off the following year.

Between 1987 and 1994, Ali was a member of the Davis Cup team, usually appearing in the Asia zonal matches alongside Paes in the doubles and in some of the singles rubbers, including the dead fifth rubber against Jason Stoltenberg in India's 0-5 loss to Australia in the 1993 World Group semi-final. The following year, as India made a first-round exit from the World Group, Ali lost both his singles matches in straight sets to Jim Courier and Todd Martin in one-sided encounters against the United States.

He retired in 1995 after an injury and was, for many years, the non-playing captain of India's Davis Cup team.

GAURAV NATEKAR

Gaurav Natekar was a part of the 'Almost Generation' of the 1990s who raised hopes that Indian tennis had a bright international future beyond Leander Paes, only to dash those very expectations after a scintillating start.

Natekar was born with a famous last name, his father Nandu Natekar being one of the legends of Indian badminton. An eight-time national champion, Nandu Natekar, in a career spanning fifteen years, won over 100 national and international titles. He was the recipient of India's first Arjuna Award in 1961, the first Indian badminton player to get an international medal at the Selangor International in Malaysia in 1956 and a quarter-finalist at the All England Championship.

The senior Natekar, in fact, had first burst into prominence as a tennis player. He faced up to Ramanathan Krishnan in the final of India's Junior National Championships where the young Krishnan won 6-1, 6-2 to launch his own career as one of the greatest players of his age. Natekar, equally adept at badminton, took the decision to switch to the latter.

His son Gaurav would choose tennis as his sport and excel at it. Winning his first national championship at the age of twenty, Natekar went on to win it a further six times. He was part of India's Davis Cup team from 1992 to 1997. In 1993, at Frejus, he watched Ramesh Krishnan and Leander Paes take India into the semi-finals against Australia, but was not required to play an active part in that campaign. In the 0-5 loss to Australia that year, he partnered Paes in a four-setter loss to Patrick McEnroe and Richie Reneberg. The following year he won the gold medal at the Hiroshima Asian Games singles event and then the doubles in tandem with Leander Paes. In 1996, his Arjuna Award joined his father's on the family mantelpiece.

Natekar retired from professional tennis in 1998 and moved into coaching and sports management. He is currently CEO of Mahesh Bhupathi Tennis Academies and married to Arati Ponnappa, herself a seven-time national champion and India no. 1 between 1997 and 1998.

HARSH MANKAD

In July 2000, twenty-one-year-old Harsh Mankad stepped onto the clay courts at Bastad in Sweden to play India's opening World Group qualifying match in the Davis Cup against Sweden. He may not have been aware of the fact, but he was making sporting history. His legendary grandfather Vinoo Mankad had become one of India's cricketing greats after debuting against England in 1946, father Ashok Mankad had also played cricket for India with distinction and mother Nirupama Mankad (see *Women's Tennis Comes of Age* chapter later in this book) had been India's greatest tennis player of her time. By following in their footsteps and representing his country, it would be the first time in the history of Indian sports that four members from three successive generations of a single family had represented the country.

While Mankad's Davis Cup record is not stellar, with six wins and ten losses in singles, he was India's leading male player for a number of years in the early part of the new millennium, emerging from the NCAA Collegiate tennis system in the United States as its no. 1 ranked player in 2001-02. By 2005, when he was winning a few important singles matches for India, Mankad was India's highest ranked ATP player and became only the second player after Leander Paes to win a Challenger event when he prevailed in Manchester in 2006.

After retiring from the ATP tour, Mankad lives in the United States and works as a tennis coach and is an entrepreneur running a tennis technology web and mobile-based player development platform called Tenicity.

Vishal Uppal

In March 2020, Vishal Uppal from New Delhi found himself back in the limelight almost two decades after his last hurrah on the world tennis stage. Unlike in 2000 when the young debutant was drafted into the doubles combination at the last minute to play his first Davis Cup match partnering Leander Paes, and helped India beat the much-fancied Koreans, or 2002 when he won the Asian Games doubles bronze alongside Mustafa Ghouse, this time it wasn't for his skills on the court.

The Indian Fed Cup team, against all expectations, with Uppal as the non-playing captain and Sania Mirza playing the doubles after her comeback, had fought their way through to the World Group playoffs for the first time in the history of women's tennis. While at the time of writing this chapter, there is no clarity on if and when the tie against Latvia will be played given the COVID-19 pandemic, the move up to this level is as significant a breakthrough as anything women's tennis has witnessed thus far in the country. And Vishal Uppal has been an important cog in that wheel of success.

In a story reflective of many young Indian boys, Uppal's first love was cricket, and his heroes were Kapil Dev and Roger Binny. 'I fancied myself as an all-rounder and they were my idols. I took to tennis at eleven only because playing cricket during breaks at school was becoming tough. Being a fast runner, I would be the first on the tennis court. Gradually, tennis became my first love even though I follow cricket closely even today,'[117] says Uppal.

In 2000, when India took on unfancied Lebanon in the Davis Cup, Uppal was a part of the squad, but didn't play. A less than stellar display from Paes' partner Fazaluddin Syed resulted in an unexpected doubles loss in the tie. With the crucial semi-final tie against Korea scheduled to be played on grass at New Delhi, a change was made.

Uppal talks me through his debut. 'I had been practising from the deuce court for ten days, when just before the tie, captain Ramesh Krishnan walked up to me and told me I would be partnering Leander in the doubles. He had seen me practising and asked if I was sure I could play the ad court since Leander would play the deuce. I answered that I was normally an ad court player anyway, so would be very happy to play from there.'[118]

Uppal would go on to play the match of his life, as the pair won 6-7, 6-4, 6-4, 7-6 to take India into the World Group playoffs. The only other doubles match the pair played together was two years later as they lost to the formidable combination of Lleyton Hewitt and Todd Woodbridge in the first round of the World Group playoffs.

In 2002, when Uppal and Ghose won the doubles bronze at the Busan Asian Games while the Paes–Bhupathi combine picked up the gold, it would be the icing on the cake in what was finally a short career. 'It was a memorable moment which I live every day,' says Uppal.

Four years later, as the Delhi air grew thick with dust from the construction activities for the Commonwealth Games, Uppal found it increasingly difficult to play and was diagnosed with severe chronic dust allergy. Forced to quit the sport he loved so much, Uppal moved on to coaching and has become one of India's much-sought-after coaches over the past decade. If the Fed Cup success is anything to go by, he has much to contribute to the future of the sport in the country.

DOUBLES: INDIAN TENNIS FINDS ITS PLACE

WHAT IS IT ABOUT INDIANS AND DOUBLES?

Doubles came naturally to me, as it does to most Indian tennis players.[119]

—Sania Mirza

I had never given much thought to why we Indians have traditionally excelled in doubles, until I was asked the question a few years ago by an Australian colleague who was partnering me at a corporate tournament. 'What is it about Indians and doubles?'

He had reluctantly asked me to come in as a partner at the last minute (his regular partner had dropped out with an injury) but had been surprised at the quickness of my reflexes at the net, something my less-than-toned physique had given no hint of. Those reflexes and my ability to put away winners at the net, aided by his booming serves, had taken us to the semi-finals, where, playing our third successive match on a hot Singapore afternoon, we finally, literally, ran out of steam.

I had no obvious answer, but decided to ask the question to the wide spectrum of players and coaches that I spoke to while writing this book. Their answers ranged from the obvious to the unexpected. They also made me realise that answering the innocent question asked by my Aussie partner all those years ago was also the best way of leading into a discussion about the unprecedented and indeed unexpected success of Indians at the highest levels of this format of the sport.

Notwithstanding the rare successes of a Ramanathan Krishnan, a Vijay Amritraj or a Ramesh Krishnan in singles, the undeniable fact is that from the Fyzee brothers in the early years of Indian tennis to the Krishnan–Lall and Krishnan–Mukherjea duo, the Amritraj and the Paes–Bhupathi combine, the most memorable Indian victories on the tennis circuit have often come from the doubles combines. So my first port of call was Ramanathan Krishnan who, in the company of Jaidip Mukherjea and Premjit Lall, brought India some of her greatest Davis Cup victories.

Krishnan's response was as crisp as his ground strokes and as well-directed as his drop shots. 'Subtle movements, good reactions and supple wrists. Add to that quick thinking on the court. And there you have your answer.'

He spoke with fondness and admiration about his doubles partners, particularly Naresh Kumar, Premjit Lall and Jaidip Mukherjea, in answer to my question about whom he enjoyed playing the most with and why. I hoped this would give me further clues on what made good pairs tick. 'Each of them were good in their own way. Premjit hit the ball harder, whereas Naresh and Jaideep were quick around the court. I enjoyed playing with Jaideep most because in times of crisis, he was bold and fearless.'

'Bold and fearless' were words that would be used time and again to describe India's best doubles players by scribes and fellow players alike. It certainly explains why in later years, Leander Paes and Sania Mirza were much sought after by some of the greatest tennis players of all time as partners for Grand Slam events. For a Martina Navratilova or Martina Hingis to seek out Leander Paes as partner and almost instantly win a Grand Slam, surely says something about this, as does the sustained success Martina Hingis had, partnering Mirza in the women's doubles.

The gift of 'quick thinking' is valuable indeed in the doubles format. When a person is standing right in front of you across the net, it is often quick thinking that comes to the rescue. Having wearied of the reach of my opponents in my social matches, I asked Leander Paes how he deals with two tall opponents on the other side. 'Straight down the middle,' he said. 'There is no way they can get down fast enough.'

Paes then got up from the chair on his Bandra terrace where we were spending a lovely afternoon together with his father, chatting about life and tennis. He picked up the racquet lying nearby, and told me as he demonstrated the shot, 'On the next rally, when the ball comes to you, follow up by rolling the wrists and make the ball spin and drop just out of reach of the opponent staring at you across the net.'[120] It was a precious and surreal moment in my chats with the legends.

I have often heard disparaging comments from amateur players and fans, scribes and professionals—'a doubles Grand Slam is not a real Grand Slam', or 'only they play doubles who cannot make it in singles'. This reasoning is flawed and certainly exposes a narrow-minded approach to the sport.

Playing doubles is absolutely vital in developing into a high-performance tennis player. It gives you lessons on serves, returns and point construction. Learning specific serving patterns, and the percentages of where those returns will be hit, is something great tennis players implement into their singles match play.

In doubles, you focus harder on your shot-making because you are trying to avoid the net player on the other side, so the target you are aiming for becomes much smaller. Naturally, the precision with which you must return is much greater. When you play doubles, you are also forced to learn how to volley. The alternative is getting hit on the body. As a consequence, you learn how to anticipate where balls are likely to go, get used to uncomfortable situations, and this immediately improves your anticipation.

Finally, in doubles, you inevitably work on shots that you wouldn't ordinarily hit very often. The chip, the topspin lob, the drop volley, the low-dipping passing shot, the serve and volley game, the chip and charge are tactics that are par for the course in doubles but whose implementation in crucial singles matches is what separates the men from the boys. One just needs to watch Roger Federer and Rafael Nadal at work to realise this.

But great doubles players are as rare and special as exponents of the singles format, and rarely do they excel at both. Sadly, the financial disparity between the two formats is so large now that it is just not economically viable for a Rafael Nadal or Roger Federer to play doubles and earn a tenth of what they could as singles champions in the same tournament. However, when they do play, as Nadal and Federer do at the

Olympics, the Davis Cup, the ATP Cup and the Laver Cup, the enjoyment and the skills on display are enough to make fans wish they appeared in the format more often. The two greats are almost equally adept at both formats, but choose to play only one.

Some singles players are so good they even carry their less gifted partners on the glory trail, as was arguably the case with John McEnroe and Peter Fleming. Fleming had once famously remarked: 'The best doubles team in the world is John McEnroe and anyone.'[121]

Most gifted singles players do not, however, make good doubles partners, often because their game is tailored to individualism rather than teamwork. There are examples galore.

Gilles Simon, ranked no. 6 in the world in singles partnered with Jeremy Chardy ranked no. 25. Together they played twenty-four matches and only won nine of them, with no titles to show for their efforts. Novak Djokovic, one of the greatest tennis players of all time, with a 83 per cent singles win–loss record, has a 43 per cent doubles record, having played 126 matches as of January 2020.[122] Stan Wawrinka, once world no. 3 in singles, has a 64 per cent win–loss record but only 44 per cent in doubles from 160 attempts at the format.

Leander Paes, the most prolific and successful Davis Cup doubles player in the history of the sport, had this to say about teamwork in the context of his successful partnership with Martina Hingis after they won the US Open in 2015, 'Sometimes the chips are against you, sometimes they fool you. What I love about this teamwork is that in any partnership there's got to be one person who brings the energy to the team. There's got to be one person who takes all the pressure on their shoulder and drives the team forward. I know if I can keep Martina happy, if I can keep her relaxed, the tennis I don't even have to worry about. This young girl is phenomenal on the tennis court and off it.'[123]

Sania Mirza talks about herself as a fifteen-year-old playing the 2002 Asian Games doubles at Busan in South Korea alongside Paes. 'I remember thinking to myself, no matter what happens, no matter how I play, if we lose, it will be because of me. But Leander has the knack of making you feel extremely comfortable on the court. As his partner, he ensured that I did not feel inferior in any way and that helped me play as best as I could.'[124]

And this is where the great exponents of the doubles format step up. For those few hours on court they cease to be individuals and become part of a greater whole, playing the role the circumstances on court demand, egos left behind in the changing room locker.

The circumstances that lead to them becoming doubles players might, however, often be beyond the control of the individuals themselves. Vijay Amritraj narrates this story of him and elder brother Anand growing up under the watchful eyes of their parents who were convinced that the older sibling was the one fated to reach the dizzying heights of tennis glory.

When the younger Amritraj made his way through the 1975 Asian Championships field consisting of Ramanathan Krishnan, Premjit Lall and Jaidip Mukherjea into the finals and blew away elder brother Anand in the final, a crisis arose in the Amritraj family. Vijay was severely admonished by his father when he came home. Robert Amritraj would later candidly confess to journalist and Amritraj's co-author Richard Evans, 'Neither my wife nor I said a word to Anand about it because we felt it was Vijay's mistake, but really it was ours. I know he felt that we did not seem to understand his point of view ... (and) we may well have hindered his progress by the stance we took over Anand. What we still considered the right order of things (the elder child having an inalienable right to win) got in the way of our judgement.'

What may have been a loss for the family was a gain for the nation. Not only did India get the better singles player to lead the nation's efforts in the sport for the next couple of decades, but it also gained a world-class doubles pair as Anand switched his allegiance largely to that format.

Sania Mirza switched to doubles because of an injury to her wrist. What she would achieve once that decision was made was unimaginable. That Mirza would bring back six Grand Slam doubles titles to a country which not long ago had marked Nirupama Vaidyanathan's second round Australian Open entry as a landmark was testimony to what Indian proficiency in the doubles format was capable of.

Leander Paes realised fairly early that he did not have either the physique or the technical ability to get to the top of the singles format. What he did have, however, was a game that was eminently suited for excellence in doubles—physical fitness, lightning quick reflexes, the ability to think quickly on his feet and play smartly. All he needed to succeed was a partner who complemented him and brought skills he did not have.

In the initial years, Mahesh Bhupathi was that man.

For Bhupathi, Paes, in turn, provided the superior reflexes and net play that he lacked. It was a combination made in tennis heaven. The genius of the pair on the ATP circuit, despite some incredible results, was destined not to outlast the detrimental effect of their combined egos. But in the Davis Cup, the Paes–Bhupathi combine established an incredible string of twenty-four consecutive doubles victories together, stitched over a fourteen-year period between 1997 and 2010, a record unlikely to be broken anytime in the foreseeable future.

With no immediate successors emerging after Rohan Bopanna, the assembly line of Indian doubles players seems to have temporarily ground to a halt. But given the interest and investment in the sport in recent years, it will only be a matter of time before a pair of worthy successors to the Fyzees, the Amritrajs and the Paes–Bhupathi combines emerges.

Taking the liberty of paraphrasing cricket writer Sujit Mukherjee's words about Indian spin bowling, we can draw hope from the fact that there is some aspect of our national character that finds fullest expression in hitting the tennis ball in a hundred slow and devious ways.[125] Perhaps it is that which will ensure the quasi-dry riverbed of doubles champions soon turns the trickle into a flood of talent, bringing succour to the thirst of Indian fans seeking the next Paes and Bhupathi.

THE GENIUS OF LEANDER PAES

Eventually our relationships with athletes over time are not only to do with winning but also how they win, the way they move on court and how they wear defeat, the manner in which they speak of opponents and toss their hair, the art they offer and the resolve they exude, the little peculiarities they own and the adversity they encounter, the people we are when they come into our lives and the spaces they fill. For they are fulfilling something fundamental we crave, slaking some complicated, private demand we have of champions and sport. In the end, it's not about the score, you see, but how they make us feel.

—Rohit Brijnath

It is difficult to fit him into a pre-conceived box.

If you try it on the tennis court, he will find a way to break out of the confines and deliver counterpunches that will not only knock you out, but do it in a manner that you would never envisage. American baseball legend Babe Ruth could well have been talking about him when he said, 'It's hard to beat a person who never gives up.'

Off the court, you could hate his guts (and some unfortunately do), but as you spew invective at his latest antic, you would, in all likelihood, be shaking your head at the tears pouring down his cheeks as he talks about his love for the Indian flag and how it drives him more than anything else in this world.

Within these walls of seeming contradictions thrives one of the greatest doubles players in the history of tennis. Thirty years as a professional tennis player. 148 different doubles partners.[126] Eighteen Grand Slam doubles titles. Five Asian Games gold medals. One Olympics medal. Forty-five Davis Cup doubles victories. And a heart that beats in tune with the strains of the Indian national anthem.

A man about whom one of the greatest sports writers of our times, Rohit Brijnath, says, 'He makes tennis personal, he affects you, he demands your involvement, till you're on your feet before you can stop.'[127]

His name: Leander Adrian Paes.

Atlanta 1996

The 1990s was not a decade that had given Indian sports much to cheer about. As Brijnath quips, 'Covering the sporting 1990s was often like a tired investigation into mediocrity.' [128]

The summer of '96 would change that forever.

It started (as sporting fairy tales often do) on the hallowed turf of Lord's Cricket Ground in London with the Test debut of two men—Sourav Ganguly and Rahul Dravid, who, along with Sachin Tendulkar, and soon to be joined by V.V.S. Laxman and Virender Sehwag, would form the core of the greatest batting line-up in the history of Indian cricket. It would culminate 6,500 kilometres away on the hard courts of the Stone Mountain Tennis Centre in Atlanta, two months later.

Back to Brijnath, 'So there we are, the Atlanta Olympics. He's twenty-three. Never won a round in a Grand Slam singles event. Ranked no. 126 or thereabouts. I'm not even watching him. But, at different venues, the hockey, the athletics, news leaks in from the tennis centre. The kid won again. He beats Richey Reneberg, world no. 20, beats Nicolas Pereira, world no. 74, beats Thomas Enqvist, world no. 10. We know he thinks rankings are only to be disrespected, but this is ridiculous. I start making the trek to the tennis centre because it's beginning. The pressure. Forty-four years is how long India hasn't won an individual Olympic medal, forty-four years which everyone wants him to erase. Even Mahesh Bhupathi can feel it and stays on to help his friend. The friend beats Renzo Furlan, world no. 26, he forces world no. 6 Andre Agassi to a first-set tiebreaker in the semis.'

Agassi himself describes what happened next in his book *Open: An Autobiography*. 'In the semis I meet Leander Paes, from India. He's a flying jumping bean, a bundle of hyperkinetic energy, with the tour's quickest hands. Still, he's never learned to hit a tennis ball. He hits off-speed, hacks, chips, lobs—he's the Brad of Bombay. Then, behind all his junk, he flies to the net, covers so well that it seems to work. After an hour, you feel as if he hasn't hit one ball cleanly— and yet he's beating you soundly. Because I'm prepared, I stay patient, stay calm, and beat Paes 7-6, 6-3.'[129]

The gold and silver were out of reach, but there was one more metal still up for grabs, and one last chance of seeing the tricolour fluttering on American soil. Waiting for Paes in the play-off for the bronze medal was Fernando Meligeni, world no. 93. In his state of nervous excitement, the flying jumping bean would lose the first set to Meligeni. A decade later, talking to journalist Mark Malinowski of *Tennis Magazine*, Paes would reveal what few realised at the time: 'In my bronze medal match I played Meligeni with a torn wrist tendon—it was 60 per cent torn. I was like bandaged up completely.'

But this was the flag he was playing for, and as he would do time and again in the years to come, Paes stormed back to take the second set. One set all, an Olympic medal at stake, and the silent roar of a billion people in his ears, Paes stepped back onto the court, the wrist all but forgotten.

Rohit Brijnath talks us through to the climax. 'By the third I keep slipping out, walking the perimeter of the stadium outside, drawing deeply on a Gold Flake, listening to the scores on the loudspeaker. I am too nervous to watch. It's as if I still don't believe this child from the neighbourhood, who used to sleep with his football boots—he played everything— is now on the verge of an Olympic medal. But he believes, he swallows his anxiety, he runs, he chases, he volleys, he exults, he wins, and what the hell else do you do at such a moment but quietly cry for this boy who refuses to go deaf to the voice within?'

The image of Leander Paes standing on the podium, an Olympic medal around his neck, the tricolour fluttering behind, would do as much to inspire individual sporting achievements in India as the iconic photo of Kapil Dev holding aloft the Prudential Cup on the Lord's balcony had done for Indian cricket in 1983. The invisible but constricting ceiling had been pierced by a raised fist. An individual Olympic medal, not just qualification, would become an achievable goal. Twelve years later, a single shot from the unwavering rifle of Abhinav Bindra would finally shatter the ceiling first breached by Leander Paes.

THE BEGINNINGS—CALCUTTA

A year before Leander was born into the Paes family, something would happen that was destined to shape his life. Dr Vece Paes, born in Goa, trained as a medical doctor in Calcutta, and one of the finest hockey centre-halves of his time, brought back an Olympic medal that would inspire the young Paes as he grew up in Calcutta.

Through his schooling at Calcutta's La Martiniere School and his early lessons in tennis at the South Club, the fascination with the medal would never go away. As seven-year-old Paes hit tennis balls powerfully across the net at whoever father Doc Paes put in front of him and demonstrated reflexes and anticipation far beyond his years, he began to be noticed. Paes tells me about how 'Premjit (Lall) uncle' would play with him and give him pointers, and Jaidip Mukherjea would do the same. He realised only when he grew up how lucky he had been to learn from these legends, blissfully unaware of their achievements.

As if the genes on one side of the family was not enough, on the other there was mother Jennifer. Great-grand-daughter of Michael Madhusudan Dutt, the legendary and colourful poet from Bengal, Jennifer's achievements ran much more to the sporting than the cerebral. Three years before Leander's birth, she had led the Indian basketball team to the 1970 Asian Championships at Kuala Lumpur and she would do the same a decade later, this time at Calcutta.

From the two parents came the genes, the passion and respect for the flag that would become synonymous with the name of Leander Paes for generations of Indian tennis fans. As he says in a *Sportstar* interview, 'When I started playing I had great role models. In my house, I had my mom and dad who were both phenomenal athletes, very passionate about their sports and playing for the flag. They played at a time when commerce was not a relevant reason to play sports. They played because they wanted to make sure that the Indian flag was flying high on international shores.'[130]

By the age of twelve, the multiple sports Paes played had been tried and discarded by his parents, and the final battle came down to football and tennis. Football almost won out.

As a junior, he was good enough to be selected for a stint at the Barcelona Junior Programme. The problem arose in the second month of the three-month programme when he was asked, assuming they decided he was good enough, was he ready to give up his Indian passport and use his father's Portuguese roots to get a passport that would then be converted to a Catalan one? If he was agreeable to that, and eventually turned out to be good enough, then he might be allowed to continue in the junior programme for the long term. Barcelona's investment in him as a Catalan club would only make sense if he eventually represented Catalonia and Spain.

Paes would say years later, 'I ironed my father's no. 10 India jersey and my mother's no. 7 India jersey, as a kid. My biggest dream was to wear India colours and be an Olympian like them. So the conversation at Barcelona convinced me that I had to give up my football dreams. When I came back my father asked me what I wanted to do now, and I said—play tennis.'[131]

The final decision his parents would eventually take to make Leander Paes a tennis player had as much to do with the young boy's talent for tennis and the fateful football conversation at Barcelona as it did with their own experience of Indian sports administrators. Speaking to journalist Gautam Bhattacharyya, Jennifer would explain, 'As his father and I both played team games, we knew the amount of politics involved in the team games in our country.'[132]

It was a decision that would change the trajectory of Indian tennis.

In early 1986, months after the fateful decision, Vijay and Anand Amritraj went to Calcutta to play the Davis Cup tie at South Club against Czechoslovakia. At the Club, coach Akhtar Ali, former India Davis Cupper, asked Anand Amritraj to hit a few balls with the promising youngster. Paes' physique and quick reflexes made an immediate impression. Months earlier, the Britannia Amritraj Tennis Academy had been established, and the Amritraj brothers were on the lookout for promising youngsters between thirteen and seventeen. Paes' talent was too much to pass by, and a few months before his thirteenth birthday he moved to Madras, joining the likes of Gaurav Natekar, Rohit Rajpal and Asif Ismail as a part of the first batch of eight. All four would go on to play the Davis Cup for India.

THE JOURNEY BEGINS

In 1990, as Rohit Brijnath and his fellow scribes despaired about the future of Indian sports, Leander Paes reached the finals of the Australian Open juniors, and a few months later, stormed into the final of Junior Wimbledon. There he beat South African Marcus Ondruska, becoming the first Indian since Ramesh Krishnan to claim the Junior Wimbledon title.

Merely entering the Junior US Open draw that year would have made Paes world junior no. 1, but that was not to be. BAT management felt he should move on to the senior circuit. India's Davis Cup captain Naresh Kumar (a family friend who had seen Paes grow up) and Doc Paes disagreed with BAT, as no preparations had been made to enter the ATP tour. They together made the decision to take Paes away from BAT.

The following year Paes turned professional. His long, hard journey as a lonely tennis player, forever on the move, was about to begin.

While the decision had been taken, the finances were to be arranged. This, in itself, was no easy matter for a family based in Calcutta with limited resources, but in a period of great economic stress and low foreign exchange reserves in India, getting permission to remit money out was equally challenging.

Paes had been deeply influenced by Dave O'Meara, his coach at BAT. But having a foreign coach at this juncture was financially out of the question. So, in a moment of inspiration, Doc Paes turned to fellow South Club member and multiple national hard court champion, Enrico Piperno.

Flying back together from an invitation tournament at Delhi where Piperno had beaten his son, Doc Paes told Piperno, 'Rico, look, you are thirty years old, you've been on the circuit for a while and you have a great tennis brain, why don't you now start coaching?'[133]

Piperno tells me he thought about it for a long time. 'I had no formal training as a coach, and taking on someone like Leander who had won Junior Wimbledon by then was a big responsibility. But I decided to go for it.' The association that started in 1990 would last for about two years in the formative phase of Leander Paes.

Piperno tells me the story about Paes' first national championship at Digboi that year. Accompanying Paes to Digboi, he was told that the hospitality did not extend to him, but only to the player. With his national ranking still at no. 8, Piperno decided to participate in the tournament and found himself in the finals. On the other side of the net was Leander Paes. Paes won in four sets.

In April 1991 at his first ATP tournament as a professional, Leander beat Wally Masur, then ranked no. 50 in the world, in Singapore.

The journey had begun. It would last for three magical decades.

PLAYING FOR INDIA

'You ask me why I do this? Because my love for the India flag, the country and the people is unconditional. Unconditional, no matter what.'[134]

These are not idle words. They were uttered by a man who had won a tournament on Monday in Mexico, received word that he may (just may) be needed to play for his country in the Davis Cup in under a week, travelled for twenty-four hours to get to India, and stepped onto the practice courts on Wednesday morning. It was 2017, the player—forty-four-year-old Leander Paes.

Rohit Brijnath had signed off the article in *Mint* about the Atlanta Olympics with the words: 'I hope I never forget that day in 1996. The day he dissolved an Indian cynicism, the day he produced such charismatic courage that he had the capacity to move, the day when that strangest of things happened. Athletes win for themselves first. But that day, he let us think he was winning for us.'

It wasn't just that day. For three decades, Leander Paes has elevated his game beyond the artificial shackles of his physical ability every time he has heard the strains of the national anthem and seen the fluttering tricolour. 'Leander in the Davis Cup plays well above himself and the performances in his early years is one of the top five things I have seen in Indian sports,' says Brijnath, a man who has been following Indian sports for well over three decades.[135]

One of the performances Brijnath refers to came in 1993 in India's famous victory against France in 1993.

Naresh Kumar and Enrico Piperno, the captain and coach of that team, talk me through it. 'When Leander stepped onto the practice courts in Frejus about ten days before the tie, his game seemed to have come apart. He was playing pathetic tennis. It was unrecognisable from a few months before,' says Piperno. Naresh Kumar adds, 'His eyes were strangely bloodshot. He looked very tense and he seemed to have worked himself up to a pitch where he couldn't possibly perform on a tennis court.'

For the next few days captain and coach concentrated on Paes, giving him back his confidence, and helping him raise his game back to where it needed to be. On the first day of the tie, with India down 0-1, when Paes stepped onto the court against the much-fancied Henri Leconte, in Piperno's words, 'He was absolutely on fire.'

Leconte won the toss and elected to serve. The left-hander's first serve came into Paes' backhand, and in a stunning return to start the match, the Indian softly dropped it over the net. The more Leconte tried to turn it into a clay court game of baseline rallies, the more Paes served, chipped and volleyed, and occasionally sent stunning forehands past the French player.

'Leconte was a passionate and experienced player who thrived in Davis Cup conditions. I attacked from the beginning, and by the time I took the first two sets, the crowd was appreciating my tennis. It was much easier from that stage,' recalls Paes. He would pull off a stunning 6-1, 6-2, 3-6, 6-3 win.

After India lost the doubles, at 1-2 down it was again up to the twenty-year-old Paes to pull something out of his hat. He would not disappoint. Playing against Arnaud Boetsch, world no. 23 and a past master of the baseline clay court game with his heavy, top spin drives, Paes went in all guns blazing, chipping and charging with well-directed shots from unexpected angles, interspersed with delicately tossed grenades drifting over the net. After his stunning victory in straight sets, Paes would simply say, 'We were down 1-2. I had to beat Arnaud to give Ramesh a shot at winning the decisive fifth rubber.'

Leander Paes, twice in three days, had done what all of France had considered impossible at the outset—beaten the two top French singles players on red clay. In doing so, ironically he had merely invoked the words of the greatest French general of all time, Napoleon Bonaparte, 'Impossible is a word to be found only in the dictionary of fools.'

But how had he achieved the nigh impossible, not once but twice?

Paes' interview to journalist Marc Malinowski about his preparations for a typical match, given years later, provides a clue and a lesson to any aspiring elite sportsperson. 'I leave everything that I walked into the locker room with, out of my mind. And then I just leave my thoughts blank, with just a few tactical thoughts. And then I let my mind react. I let my mind be instinctive. I let my mind control my body. And just let all that muscle memory come in. And breathe the air slowly, take in the flavors of the court. Just feel those sweat beads coming down me and let my muscles roll. And I know that once I find my rhythm, which is basically what I was looking for, if I find my rhythm on a certain day, it'll be hard for anyone to beat me.'[136]

Two years later when India went up against mighty Croatia, Paes would turn what might have seemed a one-off performance against France into the new normal. Indian fans would now forever believe that with Leander Paes in the Davis Cup team, anything was possible.

Croatia, led by world no. 7 (he had been world no. 2 the previous year) Goran Ivanisevic, arrived in sweltering New Delhi to play the team that in their view was one of the minnows—India. The surface was grass. Ivanisevic was a two-time Wimbledon finalist at that stage (he would finally lift the trophy at SW19 six years later), and by the tenth month of 1995 had hit 777 aces in tournament play. Facing him was world no. 123, Leander Paes.

Rarely had an opening match of a Davis Cup presented such a lopsided prospect. And at 6-7, 4-6, 0-3, 30-40, the writing appeared to be etched on the wall.

Sanjit Misra, now a banker, then a teenager watching his first Davis Cup match, recalls with awe watching Goran Ivanisevic at his destructive best. 'Leander had displayed sheer brilliance the previous day in the doubles against Ivanisevic and Sasa Hirszon. But on this day, Goran was unplayable. His serves, after landing on the court, were taking off and hitting the back wall of the spectator stands, then dropping back into Leander's court at the bat of an eyelid. Never seen anything like that in my life. The crowd was actually clapping for Goran rather than Leander.'[137]

And then it happened.

Leander Paes—two sets down—convulsed with diarrhoea that had sent him running to the bathroom after the third set, and wilting in the heat (he had never ever played a five-set singles match), refused to quit. He talks about what went through his mind. 'One part of me was telling me it's over, but another was telling me, give effort, and I was thumping my heart and saying, "Fight, fight!"'

On the first day of the tie, Ivanisevic had labelled Paes 'a limited player'. He was not incorrect, but the limit was merely physical. Mentally, no such mortal boundaries existed for Leander Paes, by then already known in tennis circles as the 'Davis Cup Miracle Man'.

As the heat mounted (literally and figuratively), Ivanisevic wilted. Complaining frequently about the heat, the line calls, and anything else that he could think of, out in the court, mentally he melted, and at one point, upset with his father who was berating him for lack of effort, zipped his racket in the bag and told the chair umpire it was over. He eventually played on, reluctantly.

Five hours and thirty-eight minutes after they had stepped onto the court, Paes leaned back to serve for the match. He was crying as he tossed the ball up. He had to stop himself in mid-swing. 'I couldn't believe I had got so far and it just got too much.' He would finally get that serve in and pull off one of the most unlikely victories in the history of the Davis Cup.

Reflecting on the incredible face-off, in his match report in *India Today*, Rohit Brijnath evocatively wrote about the young Indian, 'He is a fragile genius. And sometimes an ordinary man with extraordinary courage is the better face of sport.'[138]

DOUBLING UP FOR SUCCESS

By 1996, Leander had figured out that at five feet ten and a half inches and without the tremendous technical ability of a Michael Chang, he was not going to win any singles Grand Slam events.

Years later he would explain in an interview to *The Telegraph*, 'I don't believe that I am a talented tennis player, I don't have good technique with my backhand. And I am only five feet ten and a half when most modern tennis players are over six feet tall. My strengths are my passion, my dedication and hard work and my hunger and desire to be the best that I can be. I am also an out-and-out perfectionist.'[139]

Given his athletic ability and tremendous reflexes, he knew could excel in the doubles format, which put less constraints on the height and build of a tennis player. So he decided to ease off on his engagements on the singles circuit and devote more time to doubles instead.

It was a decision that would change his life, and transport Leander Paes from an occasional miracle man in the Davis Cup to an all-time great of the doubles format.

THE 'INDIAN EXPRESS'

1996 was a watershed year not just for Paes' decision to concentrate on doubles. It was also about who he chose to partner with. Mahesh Bhupathi had emerged from the NCAA system in the US, and joined the Indian Davis Cup team on Paes' recommendation. Paes and Bhupathi were now beginning to finally fill the void left by retirement of the Amritraj brothers. While Paes had reached the semis of the US Open doubles in 1993 partnering Sebastien Lareau, in the intervening three years he had got no further. The two young Indians, inseparable friends by now, fancied their chances on the ATP circuit.

The first year was a difficult one and success was hard to come by. It was Bhupathi who breached the final barrier and became India's first champion at a Grand Slam tournament. But this was in mixed doubles, partnering Rika Hiraki of Japan at the French Open in 1997.

Two years after they paired up, Paes and Bhupathi would finally start providing a glimpse of what might come. In 1998, they reached the semi-finals of three Grand Slam events, the Australian, French and US Opens. The 'Indian Express' was knocking at the doors of history. The following year, they kicked it wide open.

In January 1999, the Indian pair reached the final of the Australian Open, seeded no. 1, despite never having won a Grand Slam together. But after a seesaw five-set battle, it was the Swede-Aussie combine of Jonas Bjorkman and Patrick Rafter that walked away with the trophy 6-3, 4-6, 6-4, 6-7, 6-4.

Four months later, with a 6-2, 7-5 win over Goran Ivanisevic and Jeff Tarango at Roland Garros, Leander Paes and Mahesh Bhupathi became the first Indian pair to win a Grand Slam title. Less than two months later, the pair added the Wimbledon doubles trophy to their respective mantelpieces. Wimbledon, the holy grail of every Indian tennis player since Sardar Nihal Singh in 1908, finally had not one, but two Indian winners.

Naresh Kumar, writing in *Frontline* that year, would say: 'Normally, doubles partners have different, complementary roles to play. One partner is solid and keeps the partnership on an even keel with consistent play (Bhupathi), while the other is the opportunist who puts pressure on the opposition with frequent interceptions and takes chances—a swashbuckling role tailor-made for Paes. The fact that Paes is considered to be one of the quickest men on the circuit, if not the quickest in the world, more than makes up for any of his other shortcomings. Together the Indians are a formidable team.'[140]

They indeed were. Over the next two years, the pair who had by then been formally dubbed the 'Indian Express' by the media, would win twenty-two doubles titles together on the circuit, including another French Open that they added in 2001. By doing so they had snatched away the mantle of the most formidable doubles pair in the world from the greatest of them all, the 'Woodies'—Mark Woodforde and Todd Woodbridge, the famous Australian pair who had dominated the format for over a decade.

Paul Oberjuerge would write in *The National*: 'Even at Grand Slams, doubles tennis is enthusiastically ignored. For any doubles team to appear on the international radar requires special circumstances.'[141]

The on-court chest-thump became a signature mark of the Paes–Bhupathi combine. As Paes told me recently with a laugh, it started as a tactic to distract the Woodies who were otherwise quiet and unflappable. It worked, and eventually became a part of their routine.

For four years, Paes and Bhupathi represented the best in Indian sport. The hunger, the passion, Paes' volleys at the net, Bhupathi's booming double-handed backhand from the baseline, the chest-thumps, the hundreds of tricolour-waving supporters thronging tennis stadiums, from Melbourne to Rio, represented the ambitions of the new India.

But after 2001, it all fell apart. The bosom friends who understood each other so well suddenly found the cacophony of clashing egos too much to bear. Paes blamed his former coach, now in Bhupathi's corner—Enrico Piperno—for the break up.[142] Piperno tells me that Paes still does. Bhupathi cited irreconcilable differences. There was talk of 'woman trouble' between the two.

I had numerous conversations on this topic in the course of writing the book, with coaches, former players and scribes who have covered the sport in India for decades. Paes and Bhupathi themselves sought to pinpoint the exact reason for their break up in the recent web series *Break Point*, but in the end, as I had concluded from my conversations, overwhelmingly the blame has to be attributed to their egos. They speak about the misunderstandings, and the fact that they didn't directly talk to each other. Bhupathi expresses his anguish over the fact that 'all the emotion and frustration turned to pure anger, and I had mentally and physically checked out of that relationship after that.' Paes talks about how Mahesh would not return his texts and it came to a situation that even before a Grand Slam he didn't know if Mahesh would show up because he hadn't responded to his texts. But the reality is that once the egos came into play, people close to the two took sides, and accusations and counter-accusations flew freely, sullying the atmosphere beyond redemption.

In 2011, a decade after the break up, having tried and had various degrees of success with multiple partners, the pair would come together for one last dance. 'Time is the best healer. We both take responsibility for whatever happened in the past, and now we're a lot more mature about it,' Paes would tell *The Wall Street Journal.* [143] It was, however, too late to recreate the magic, and despite winning three more ATP titles, further Grand Slam glory would not be forthcoming.

The pair would, however, continue to serve the country, putting aside their differences when they stepped on court for India. In 2002 and 2006 they won the Asian Games doubles gold medals. In the Davis Cup the Paes–Bhupathi combine established an incredible record of twenty-four consecutive doubles victories together, stitched over a fourteen-year period between 1997 and 2010. It is a record that is unlikely to be challenged anytime in the near future.

Making *Break Point* may have been cathartic for the two, but it doesn't take away from the fact that as it often happens in sport, ego combined with breakdown in communications between two human beings deprives the players and their nation of years of glory at the highest level. As Greek philosopher Heraclitus adroitly pointed out three thousand years ago: 'No man ever steps in the same river twice, for it's not the same river and he's not the same man.'

REACHING FOR GREATNESS

While he may not be referred to as India's first Grand Slam title winner, over the course of the two decades since winning the first Major, Leander Paes has unequivocally established himself as the nation's greatest-ever doubles player.

In 2003, the Australian Open saw the unusual pairing of Leander Paes and the legendary Martina Navratilova, in the mixed doubles event. 'She chose me as her mixed doubles partner at the Australian Open in 2003 and wouldn't take no for an answer,'[144] Paes would later say. That year, against all odds, the thirty-year-old Paes and forty-seven-year-old legend who had last won a Grand Slam title eight years earlier, blew away everyone in their path, picking up the titles at Melbourne and Wimbledon. They would also reach the finals of the Australian Open the following year and the French Open in 2005.

Navratilova would remark years later, 'Of all the mixed doubles partners I played with, Leander is my favourite.'[145] That's a huge statement. Consider the list of Navratilova's partners over the years—Heinz Gunthardt, Paul McNamee, Emilio Sanchez, Jonathan Stark, Bob Bryan. Not a list to scoff at.

Paes and Navratilova have remained firm friends and Paes credits her with teaching him the valuable life lesson—'age is just a number'—and helping him achieve longevity in the sport. 'Navratilova taught me the importance of physical fitness and that is the reason I had such a long career,' says Paes.[146] The fact that she won her last Grand Slam title at the age of forty-nine and Leander is only now considering laying down his racquet at forty-seven is testament to how useful that lesson has been.

In 2006, five years after his break up with Bhupathi, Paes won his fourth men's doubles Grand Slam title at the US Open, partnering Martin Damm of the Czech Republic. They beat Max Mirnyi and Jonas Bjorkman in the final. Two years later when Paes held aloft his next US Open crown, it was with partner Cara Black in the mixed doubles event.

In 2009, four years after his last tango in Paris, Paes climbed the platform at Roland Garros to receive his fifth career Grand Slam men's doubles title. His partner this time was Lukas Dlouhy of the Czech Republic. From the clay of Paris to the hard court of Flushing Meadows, 2009 was the year of Dlouhy and Paes as they beat the Bryan brothers in the semis. In the final, the pair came from behind to beat Bhupathi and Knowles 3-6, 6-3, 6-2, a result that understandably would give Paes more than the usual satisfaction associated with a Grand Slam title.

Knowles, who was also to partner him to a Grand Slam final, has this to say about Paes as a doubles player, 'He reads the game of doubles as well as anyone. What I think he does the best of anyone is getting the most out of his partners.'[147]

It was again with Cara Black that Paes would turn 2010 into a personal triumph, picking up the Australian Open and Wimbledon titles.

In 2012, thirteen years after his first men's doubles title at Roland Garros, Paes completed a career Grand Slam in the format, winning the Australian Open title. Coming into the tournament unseeded, the Paes and Radek Stepanek combination upset the three-time defending champions Bob and Mike Bryan 7-6, 6-2 in the final.

Stepanek tells this story about that final to explain why partners enjoy playing with Paes, 'Before the finals of the 2012 Australian Open, Leander and I were waiting in our locker room. I switched on my laptop to read Czech newspapers online. Leander, who was standing next to me, began to read them, despite having no clue as to what he was reading. On top of that Leander's accent he had put on made the whole situation pretty hilarious and took away the stress from both of us before a major Grand Slam finals. It's always fun playing with Leander ... be it in practice or in a Grand Slam final.'[148]

Melbourne 2012 would be Paes' last triumph in the men's doubles format. But there was glory yet to come.

Three years later, in 2015, two decades after turning professional, forty-two-year-old Leander Paes would have his pinnacle year on the Grand Slam circuit. Partnering him was one of the greatest players on the women's circuit, thirty-five-year-old Martina Hingis.

Hingis had been the youngest-ever Grand Slam champion and youngest-ever world no. 1. By the age of twenty-two, she had won forty singles titles and thirty-six doubles titles. Then in early 2003, she suffered a cruel blow. Diagnosed with ligament injuries in both ankles, she had to withdraw from professional tennis. In 2006 she made a comeback, rose to world no. 6, then had to retire with a hip injury besides being handed a two-year suspension for testing positive for cocaine.

In 2013, at the age of thirty-two, Hingis made her comeback, this time purely as a doubles player. But it was only in 2015 that she would find the right partners who would accompany her to the pinnacle of the doubles format. In the mixed doubles format, she did not have to look further than Leander Paes.

As it had been with the other Martina, Paes' success started in Melbourne. Ranked no. 7, the Hingis–Paes combine laid low all in their path before imperiously brushing aside the challenge of defending champions Kristina Mladenovic and Daniel Nestor in the finals 6-4, 6-3. Coming into Wimbledon, still ranked no. 7, Hingis and Paes did not drop a single set on their path to glory at SW19, sealing the final with a dominating 6-1, 6-1 demolition of third seeds Alexander Peya and Time Babos. They wrapped up the year at Flushing Meadows. Now seeded fourth, they beat Sam Querrey and Bethanie Matek–Sands 6-4, 3-6, 10-7 to lift the US Open. But they were not done yet. There was one hurrah yet to come from this incredible pair.

The following year, the Hingis–Paes pair came into the French Open, unseeded. They took out the no. 4 seeds in the second round and no. 5 seeded Elena Vesnina and Bruno

Soares in the quarter-finals. In the semis they got past no. 6 seeds Andrea Hlavackova and Roger–Vasselin after a hard-fought encounter, 6-3, 3-6, 10-7. Awaiting them in the finals were the no. 2 seeds Sania Mirza and Ivan Dodig. In an intense and emotionally draining encounter that lasted well over two hours, the unseeded Indo–Swiss pair prevailed, coming from a set down to take the title 4-6, 6-4, 10-8.

A year later when Hingis announced her final retirement from the sport, Paes would say, 'Martina has been a true champion of our sport and, personally, it has been an absolute delight to have won all four Grand Slams with her and, indeed, to have completed the career Slam as a mixed doubles team. We won the four Grand Slams in a space of sixteen months, which would be considered quite remarkable. As an achievement on the biggest stage, it's huge.'[149]

The 2016 French Open would also turn out to be Leander Paes' swan song on the Grand Slam stage.

One Last Roar

The last four years of Paes' career were an exhibition in grit, determination and the mental ambitions that often exceeded physical reality. Success on the circuit had been incredibly hard to come by. Playing obscure tournaments to garner points, travelling, staying fit and practising ceaselessly, Paes continued to show up at major tournaments with a bewildering array of partners to add to the already incredibly long list.

But every time Indian tennis needed him he left everything behind and showed up to be counted.

In November 2019 when the captain and top players of India's Davis Cup team refused to travel to Pakistan citing security concerns, there was a real danger that India would face the penalty of default. Once more, Leander Paes stepped up. He volunteered to be a part of the side that would travel to Pakistan, used his powers of persuasion and undeniable charm to get a reluctant Indian government to agree to the tie and even provide special security and an Air Force plane that would be at the disposal of the team the entire time. Diplomatic efforts ensured that there was full cooperation and agreement from the Pakistan government to this plan. In the end, the plan would not need to be executed as the world body moved the tie to neutral Uzbekistan, where Paes helped India make a clean sweep of the encounter.

On Christmas Day 2019, a few weeks after I spent a delightful evening with Paes and his father on the terrace of their Bandra apartment in Mumbai, reminiscing about his unbelievable career, Paes announced on Twitter that 2020 would be his last year on the circuit. In a reflection of his never-say-die spirit, he even created a hashtag that fans could use to chat with him and follow him as he bid farewell to the sport that has meant everything to him. He called it #OneLastRoar.

With the postponed Tokyo Olympics coming up in 2021, and knowing how he wears national pride on his sleeve, the #OneLastRoar was clearly directed at a second Olympics medal. The retirement plan looked to have been moved out a year thanks to the pandemic that derailed sports activities, and indeed brought life itself to a standstill in 2020.

In his dreams every single night over the next few months,

there was a gold medal dangling from his neck, the tricolour going up to the tune of the Indian national anthem, hand on heart, and tears of joy cascading down his cheeks.

The dream could have turned to reality, and with Leander Paes on the court, one would have had to be a brave punter to entirely dismiss the possibility, the #OneLastRoar would have reverberated across the country and propelled Paes to sporting immortality.

But as it turned out, Paes did not make it to Tokyo and a disappointed nation found it had indeed been just a dream. Notwithstanding that final disappointment of a muted roar, this journey of three decades that started on the green lawns of South Club in Calcutta, gathered eighteen Grand Slam titles and added an Olympic medal for good measure on the way has given far more to both Paes and his country than 1.4 billion Indians could ever have hoped for.

MAHESH BHUPATHI AND ROHAN BOPANNA

THE UNLIKELY TWIN AND
THE WORTHY SUCCESSOR

We kind of conquered a white man's game, which was never done before. It led to a lot of success. Sania (Mirza), Rohan (Bopanna), all you guys now, we go in there believing that you can win. I think we were instrumental in putting the flag down for Indian tennis.[150]

—Mahesh Bhupathi (to Purav Raja on the importance
of his achievements with Leander Paes)

MAHESH BHUPATHI

Roland Garros, 7 June 1997

Wimbledon victories may be our national obsession, but it is France that has long been the real happy hunting ground for Indian tennis.

A hundred years ago, an Indian team making its first-ever Davis Cup appearance in 1921 had shocked a strong French side on clay in Paris and stormed into the semi-finals of the competition. Seven decades later, in 1993, Ramesh Krishnan, a man on the verge of hanging up his racquet, would combine with Leander Paes, a talented but wild and unpredictable teenage genius, to stun the hosts, once again on red clay at Frejus.

It was but natural that four years after Frejus, when a young Indian doubles specialist—Mahesh Shrinivas Bhupathi, brought into the Indian Davis Cup squad two years before on the insistence of Leander Paes—reached the finals of the mixed doubles event at Roland Garros, the nation would sit up and take note.

Before the French Open started, few had paid attention to the sixteenth seeded Indo-Japanese pair of Mahesh Bhupathi and Rika Hiraki. Neither player had thus far shown signs that they were going to fulfil the potential of the talent each undoubtedly possessed. But all that would change over the two weeks of the competition.

The unheralded pair brushed aside the competition, taking care of the sixth seeds, the ninth seeds and the fourth seeds on their remarkable journey to the final, losing only two sets the entire way. In the final, Hiraki–Bhupathi stunned the top-seeded pair of Lisa Raymond and Patrick Galbraith of the United States in straight sets, 6-4, 6-1.

This was a game changer for both nations. Rika Hiraki became the first Japanese woman to win a Grand Slam event. Mahesh Bhupathi became the first Indian, male or female, to achieve the same feat. Japan would have to wait for two decades before another woman, Naomi Osaka, went past Hiraki's achievement to win multiple Grand Slam singles titles. For India, the wait would be much shorter.

Over the next decade and a half, the nation would hail a Grand Slam winner, all in doubles, thirty-seven times. But the man who had shown the way was Mahesh Bhupathi, eventually laying claim to twelve of them.

A Career Launched by the Davis Cup

In 1994, when nineteen-year-old Mahesh Bhupathi, then a student in the United States, won his first national championship and defended it the following year, his strong serve and much improved powerful baseline play was noted by Leander Paes, at twenty-one, already a veteran of the Davis Cup side. Rafael Nadal, a man who knows a thing or two about tennis nuances, had also commented about how Bhupathi's strong backhand makes him best for an ad court player.

Paes had first seen fourteen-year-old Bhupathi play five years earlier in Sri Lanka, and even then the supremely effective backhand had stood out. The intervening years, and the height and muscle that came with them, had added a booming serve to the package. With his own deuce court skills clearly in sight, and in search of a partner who would complement his quickness and expertise at the net, Paes lost no time in teaming up with Bhupathi. His very personal, selfish dream that was the driver in approaching the strapping young Bhupathi, as Paes would freely admit in the future, was to win Wimbledon.

Paes, in a recent interview alongside his old partner, recalled his conversation with Bhupathi at the time, that went like this:

Paes: 'Do you want to win Wimbledon?'

Bhupathi: 'No'

Paes: 'Do you want to be No.1 in the world?'

Bhupathi: *Laughs*

Paes: 'Give us ten-years of hard work and we will win Wimbledon and we will be No. 1 in the world.'

Bhupathi eventually signed up to the dream. The pair's decision would be a game changer for Indian tennis. An unsuspecting world did not know it yet, but the Indian Express was ready to levitate.

In the World Group tie against Croatia in 1995, as Paes once again demonstrated that in singles matches he is a different player when the tricolour is aflutter, Bhupathi quietly played his part, combining with Paes in a crucial four-setter doubles win against Ivanisevic and Hirszon to give India a 3-2 victory. It was to be the beginning of an incredible association.

In the 1997 World Group clash with the Czech Republic, Paes and Bhupathi pulled off a straight sets win against Martin Damm and Petr Korda. Damm was a semi-finalist at Wimbledon that year and would climb to world no. 5, while Korda was to win the Australian Open doubles title a few months later.

Over the next fourteen years, the Paes–Bhupathi pair would remain undefeated in Davis Cup ties, winning twenty-four successive matches against the best teams in the world. This remains the longest winning streak in doubles in the hundred-and-twenty-year history of the Davis Cup. Playing for the flag, Bhupathi and Paes added the gold medals in doubles at the 2002 and 2006 Asian Games to complement their Davis Cup triumphs.

Outside the Davis Cup and Asian Games arena, the pair would go on to achieve even more, as the positive experience of the Davis Cup pairing convinced the two young men to cement their association on the ATP circuit.

The 'Indian Express' Years

From 1996, in the tradition of Australia's Woodies, the Bryan brothers and McEnroe–Fleming from the United States, the Bhupathi–Paes combine would put their nation on the world doubles map, wearing proudly on their sleeves the moniker— 'Indian Express'.

The breakthrough as a pair did not, however, come easily. After much heartbreak over the next two years, in 1998 they reached the semi-finals of three Grand Slam events—the Australian, French and US Opens. The following year, the Indian Express made the move from rails to Maglev.

Until Bhupathi won his first title with Hiraki, no Indian had ever reached the final of a Grand Slam event. Just two years later, in 1999, two Indians would be in the final of every single Grand Slam doubles event. In the best summer of all time for Indian tennis, the pair won both the French Open and Wimbledon titles.

Perhaps most importantly for Indian fans, they found

not one, but two Wimbledon champions, nine decades after Sardar Nihal Singh became the first Indian to play at Wimbledon.

'1999 was the peak. We were the titans of the doubles world, it was a lot of fun,' recalls Bhupathi. Indeed they were. As a pair, in another first for Indian tennis, Bhupathi and Paes entered the first Grand Slam of the year as the no. 1 seeds. Losing to Pat Rafter and Jonas Bjorkman in five hard-fought sets in the final may have been heartbreaking, but the Indians had seen the finish line and knew it was a matter of time before they breached it. At Roland Garros, they crossed the finish line first, and a month later, they picked up the Holy Grail of tennis, at least as far as the adoring Indian fans were concerned—the Wimbledon trophy.

Rocketing to no. 1 in the world that year, the pair had also incredibly become the first doubles team in the Open Era and indeed the first in four decades to reach the final of all four Grand Slams in a single calendar year. To cap off the year, Bhupathi won the mixed doubles title at the US Open, partnering Ai Sugiyama of Japan.

Paes and Bhupathi would win twenty-two doubles titles together on the circuit over the next two years, including another French Open that they added in 2001. That very year, in one of the most infamous flare-ups in tennis history, the Indian Express broke the magnetic field that kept them on the Maglev.

Although they attempted to get back together in the coming years, the damage proved to be irreparable. In 2011, a last attempt at recreating the magic only resulted in three ATP titles, but not a Grand Slam as both had hoped. The closest they would come to a title was the final of the Australian Open that year.

Notwithstanding the problems, the sheer magnitude of what the pair achieved would only be realised in 2015 when a mathematics professor at the International School for Social and Business Studies, Kristijan Breznik, released his extensive study—'Revealing the best doubles teams and player in tennis history'.[151]

The aim of the study was to identify the best male doubles teams and the best male doubles individual players in the Open Era of tennis. It took official ATP data and studied 58,365 male doubles teams (10,717 individual male doubles players) that played 128,195 matches, in the period from 1968 to the end of 2014.

As previously stated, Peter Fleming, John McEnroe's long-term doubles partner had once said: 'The best doubles team in the world is John McEnroe and anyone.'[152] Breznik, with a more mathematical approach, found that it was the Bryan brothers who had won that accolade.

From an Indian perspective, for a pair that had, for all practical purposes, been at the top of the world only for a period of two years, Mahesh Bhupathi and Leander Paes were ranked the tenth best doubles pair in the history of the sport. In terms of the best individual lifetime performances in a field of over ten thousand players, the study puts Paes at no. 10 and Bhupathi at no. 13.

For a nation starved of sporting heroes, the findings of this study come as a shot of much-needed optimism and only elevate the iconic status of these two remarkable players.

Doubles Beyond Paes—A Mixed Success

In an international career that was a few years shorter than Paes', Mahesh Bhupathi's doubles partners of both sexes numbered an incredible 102. While that may have been shy of Paes' record 148, it is a number that reflects the attractiveness that Bhupathi held as a partner.

It would not, however, be until he had found his forty-fifth male partner, Max Mirnyi of Belarus, that in 2002, a year after the Indian Express parted ways, Bhupathi would win his first men's doubles Grand Slam title with a partner other than Paes. Sadly, it would also be the last.

At the US Open that year, Mirnyi and Bhupathi, seeded third, got past the Bryan brothers in the semi-finals and took out the Czech pair of Jiri Novak and Radek Stepanek in the final to land Bhupathi his fourth, and what turned out to be his final men's doubles title at a Grand Slam event.

At Wimbledon in 2003, the Mirnyi–Bhupathi combine would have its last chance at glory, but lose in four sets. At the Australian Open and US Open in 2009, combining with Mark Knowles, who had been a partner off and on since 1998, Bhupathi reached the finals only to fall short.

The men's doubles titles may have dried up, but Mahesh Bhupathi's Grand Slam-winning habits would be kept alive and well (appropriately enough, given his first success with Hiraki), by his pairings with some of the greats of women's tennis. In the end, the tally of eight mixed doubles titles from the twelve finals he made an appearance in is a record few can boast of.

The Japanese connection that started with Rita Hiraki

would prove to be fruitful once again in 1999 when Bhupathi combined with Ai Sugiyama to win his first US Open title, even as he and Paes disappointingly lost the men's doubles final.

In 2002, Bhupathi picked up his second Wimbledon title and first in mixed doubles, partnering Russian doubles specialist Elena Likhotseva. Three years later, he wrested back the title, this time partnering French multiple Grand Slam winner, Mary Pierce.

For Pierce, it was an important moment in her career, having tried and failed thus far to add a Wimbledon crown to her cabinet of Grand Slam trophies. She would say a few years later, 'I am a big fan of Mahesh Bhupathi. I was honoured and privileged to play mixed doubles with him. I had so much fun while playing with him. I learnt a lot and was sometimes in awe while sharing the court with him. Winning the mixed doubles in Wimbledon was like a dream come true for me.'[153] Having achieved her goal, Pierce laid down her racquet the following year. She was inducted into the International Hall of Fame in 2019.

Bhupathi was, however, far from being done. That year he paired with Daniela Hantuchova to win the US Open. A few months later, at the 2006 Australian Open, he paired with Martina Hingis, who was making her second comeback to professional tennis.

The Hingis–Bhupathi pair came into the draw as wild card entrants. Hingis had few expectations, but Bhupathi knew he was partnering a legend of the sport. He would say about her, '(Hingis is) the greatest doubles player in our sport. (I) have never seen the creativity and ability she has on court with any of my other partners. She always hit the right shot in the open space.'[154] In the second round came the first upset of the tournament when the Hingis–Bhupathi pair beat the no. 2 seeds Lisa Raymond and Jonas Bjorkman. Then they got past the no. 5 seeded Aussie pair of Samantha Stosur and Paul Hanley to storm into the finals. Waiting there was the sixth-seeded pair of Elena Likhotseva and Daniel Nestor. A straight sets demolition of the pair, and Hingis had a Grand Slam mixed doubles title on her comeback, and Bhupathi, his sixth.

If the Paes–Bhupathi combo had been the Indian Express, then the period between 2008 and 2012 saw the emergence of the 'Palace on Wheels'. The elegant and effective combination of Sania Mirza and Mahesh Bhupathi once again put an Indian pair at the top of the world doubles charts. Starting with a loss in the Australian Open final in 2008, the pair would soon taste success. The following year they had reversed the results at the same tournament, and in 2012 they won the French Open title.

Mirza tells me about the pairing. 'In mixed doubles, Mahesh Bhupathi may be the best partner I had. I won my first Grand Slam with him and we went on to win another Grand Slam together.'[155]

Sadly, right after they had won that second title, the fiasco of the London 2012 Olympics ensued. The partnership broke under the strain as Mirza sent out a press release after she had been made a sacrificial lamb in the dispute between the AITA, Bhupathi and Paes. 'Mahesh Bhupathi has firmly stood by his commitment to play together with his men's doubles partner, Rohan Bopanna, as he genuinely believed it was good for India. However, in the process, he sacrificed the commitment he made to me to try and win an Olympic medal together for India.'[156]

The AITA reacted forcefully after the Olympics was over with an announcement, 'It is further decided not to consider Mahesh Bhupathi and Rohan Bopanna for selection to play for India till 30 June 2014.'[157]

Bhupathi tweeted in response. 'The cranky old grandfathers on the executive committee, who have never played tennis, waiting for a reaction? There is one coming. Stay tuned!'[158]

Away from these controversies, with his last ATP doubles final having come in 2013, partnering Rohan Bopanna, and his career at a standstill, in 2016 Bhupathi announced his retirement from the sport.

In 2017 Mahesh Bhupathi became the captain of India's Davis Cup team. His tenure that ended in 2019 saw a weakened team struggling to make their presence felt on the world stage. His continued ego clashes with Leander Paes with accusations of deliberately slighting his former partner being bandied around, it was a difficult period for Bhupathi. While the young members of his team, Ramkumar Ramanathan, Prajnesh Gunneswaran and Divij Sharan all have good things to say about him, disagreements with the senior players and the AITA crept up from time to time.

Entrepreneur Beyond Tennis

Beyond the tennis arena, Bhupathi is a serial entrepreneur. He runs a management and brand solutions company, Globosports. Married to actress and former Miss Universe Lara Dutta, Bhupathi now also runs a beauty company, Scentials Beauty Care and Wellness Pvt Ltd.

He has also been an investor in tennis academies and tournaments, ventures that appear to have had mixed success.

While his tennis academy run by former national champion and Davis Cupper Gaurav Natekar is doing stellar work, ambitious ventures like the IPTL appear to have had less financial success.

Still in his forties, Bhupathi undoubtedly has much to give to Indian tennis, and one hopes that in the years to come, the contributions that he makes alongside Sania Mirza and Leander Paes will help carry on the legacy of Indian tennis and take the sport to greater heights.

ROHAN BOPANNA

The Last of the Mohicans

If there is a reason that Indian tennis fans did not despair after the retirement of Mahesh Bhupathi and the naturally infrequent triumphs of an ageing Leander Paes, it was the success of Rohan Bopanna, the natural successor to the duo.

Rapidly rising to no. 3 in the world in the doubles rankings, Bopanna raised hopes that he would take up where Paes and Bhupathi had left Indian tennis. While that would prove to be a heavy cross for him to bear as far as the Davis Cup is concerned, he was destined to have a sterling career on the ATP circuit.

Playing for India

Bopanna made his Davis Cup debut in 2002 to join, what seemed on paper, the strongest Indian squad to appear in the competition in a few years. With a big serve and strong ground strokes, the team management could have been forgiven for thinking that he would be a perfect complement to the Bhupathi–Paes duo as the second singles player after Paes.

But his record of only ten wins in twenty-seven singles matches over the course of a eighteen-year career speaks volumes about how that experiment went. A five-set win over a nineteen-year-old Kei Nishikori in 2008, years before the young Japanese would make his way to no. 4 in the world, was one of Bopanna's rare triumphs. In doubles, he met with more success, racking up a 11-8 win–loss record, five of those wins coming in partnership with Leander Paes.

While Davis Cup wins were difficult to come by, the Hopman Cup in 2007 made Bopanna a popular man among Indian fans. In this mixed gender competition, Bopanna, replacing an injured Paes, was partnering Sania Mirza. Bopanna's efforts in the singles would once again be disappointing, but the combination with Mirza would prove effective.

Ranked no. 27 in the world in singles and at the peak of her prowess in the format, Mirza won her singles match against Lucie Safarova of the Czech Republic and then combined with Bopanna to run away with the decisive mixed doubles. In the next round, the pattern was repeated. Suddenly, unexpectedly, India was battling Spain for supremacy in their group and a place in the final against Australia. In the end, with Mirza unable to win her singles match this time against an opponent ranked ten places above her, and Bopanna losing his third successive one, this time to Tony Robredo, the mixed doubles victory was not good enough to take them past the powerful Spaniards. Nonetheless, it was a remarkable performance from the unseeded Indians and the best India would ever do in the competition.

Grand Slam Title and a Stellar ATP Career

In 2007, Bopanna took the most unusual step of getting into what turned out to be a long and fruitful doubles partnership with Aisam-ul-Haq Qureshi of Pakistan. Over the next few years, the duo would come to be nicknamed the 'Indo-Pak Express' by the media in the two perpetually warring nations, as they won a few Challengers, the Johannesburg Open ATP event, finished runners-up at the US Open and five ATP Tour events, and reached the quarter-finals at Wimbledon. Most of these successes came in 2010. A Grand Slam title, however, would prove elusive.

With the London Olympics in mind, Bopanna got together with Bhupathi and won the Paris Open in 2012, finishing runners-up at Cincinnati and Shanghai. At the Olympics, it was a fiasco, when after all the drama had played out in full gaze of the world's media and a shocked nation, the pair was knocked out embarrassingly early. Nonetheless, they continued to play together, their best result coming at the Rome Masters the following year when they lost in two tiebreaks to the Bryan brothers in the final.

Bopanna would have to wait for his time in the sun—that elusive Grand Slam title, until 2017. That year, at thirty-seven, fourteen years after turning professional, Rohan Bopanna finally held aloft his first Grand Slam title. The venue, as has for a century been the case, was Indian tennis' happy hunting ground—France.

At Roland Garros, partnering Gabriela Dabrowski of Canada, the seventh seeded pair met and vanquished the second seeds Sania Mirza and Ivan Dodig in the quarter-finals. They then got past the third seeds Andrea Hlavackova of Czech Republic and Roger–Vasselin of France. In the final they triumphed over the unseeded German–Columbian pair of Anna–Lena Gronefeld and Robert Farah to stand on the podium holding aloft the trophy.

At the age of forty-two, Rohan Bopanna continues to play at the highest level with his ATP doubles ranking now up to 19.

In January 2023, Mirza and Bopanna once again rekindled India's hopes of a Grand Slam title. The pair, who had first played together when Mirza was fourteen, and Bopanna twenty, came together one last time at the Australian Open. But, alas, their dream run to the final was not destined to turn into a Championship win.

Even so, Bopanna continues to make young Indians believe that winning at the highest level in tennis is an achievable dream.

THE RISE OF THE INDIAN WOMAN

THE EARLY PIONEERS OF WOMEN'S TENNIS

Tennis has been around for so long—women have been playing the majors since the 1800s. Other sports have not had professional leagues for women for as long.

—Venus Williams

The broken pony roller at Wimbledon may have brought the British men to the soon-to-be hallowed turf of Wimbledon, but it would be another seven years before women made their appearance on the courts at the club. In 1884, when Miss Maud Watson won the inaugural women's singles title, tennis had truly transcended the gender barrier.

Three years later, the women's sport would take off in two far-flung corners of British influence—the US National Championships at Philadelphia and the Punjab Lawn Tennis Championships at Lahore, both inaugurating their respective ladies singles events in 1887.

While women made their way into competitive tennis at the other major tournaments in India through the mixed doubles, it would take another twenty-three years after

Lahore showed the way, for the All-India Lawn Tennis Championships at Allahabad to introduce the ladies singles event in 1910. The Bengal Lawn Tennis Championships at Calcutta only opened up to women in 1916. By 1922 and 1924 respectively, the Sind Lawn Tennis Championships at Karachi and the Western India Championships at Bombay had also added the ladies singles event.

It was hardly surprising that just as in the case of the men, the early women competitors were drawn from the European populace who had the access to the club courts and the competitive events where they could hone their game. Foremost among them was Nora Polley, the first woman to ever represent India at the Olympics Games. Born in Bengal in 1894, Nora Margaret Fischer was educated largely in England and married (later to be) Major Sydney Trepess Polley in 1915.

At Paris, in 1924, Polley reached the pre-quarter-finals of the ladies singles event before losing to Lily Alvarez of Spain, and partnering Sydney Jacob, bowed out at the same stage of the mixed doubles competition after a hard-fought 7-9, 6-4, 7-9 loss to Ireland's D'Ancy and Hilda Wallis. After the Olympics she played two tournaments in England at Tunbridge Wells and Bexhill-on-Sea (where the 6 September 1924 edition of *Bexhill-on-Sea Observer* described her as one of 'the most dangerous competitors').[159] That would sadly remain the last record of her playing competitive tennis.

The Indian origin pioneers of the women's sport in India would largely arrive in the 1920s, when the sport spread across the country. It would require that the social prejudices that worked against playing tennis freely in public view, while adorned in western outfits, be met head on by some women.

E.M. Newson (nee Sandison)

Born into an Anglo–Indian family in the Railway Settlement at Kharagpur, E.M. Sandison became the first woman of Indian origin to win a major singles title.

In 1925, she created a sensation by lifting the Bengal Lawn Tennis Championships title, becoming the first non-European to do so, a decade after the event had been introduced. Three years later she once again appeared in the finals of the championship, but was to finish runner-up on this occasion. In the meantime, she had won the ladies doubles, partnering her younger sister Jenny in both 1926 and 1928, the pair finishing runners-up in 1927.

While Jenny would go on to become the more famous sportsperson in the family, the name of the elder sister will always remain in the annals of Indian tennis as the true pioneer of the sport among Indian women.

Kshama Row

Pandita Kshama Rao is remembered today more for her role in the 'modernism' movement of Sanskrit literature. In *Modern Indian Literature: An Anthology*, author K.M. George says about Row, 'She had an inborn love and flair for Sanskrit ... She became virtually the voice of India to herald the Gandhian struggle for freedom and the attainment of independence in memorable poems like "Satyagrahagita", "Uttarasatyagrahagita" and "Svarajyavijaya".'

Hailing from Indore, where both she and her doctor husband Raghavendra Row's families were landlords bearing allegiance to the Holkars, Kshama Row's other, less-remembered identity was as one of India's finest tennis players of the time.

In 1921, Kshama won her first mixed doubles title partnering R.A. Wagle at the Western Indian Championship in Bombay. Three years later, she won her second mixed doubles title with the same partner at the Bombay Presidency Hard Court Championship.

In 1927, at the very tournament, Kshama would create tennis history by becoming the first ladies singles champion hailing from an orthodox Indian family. The shackles of tradition had finally been broken.

Less than a decade later, Kshama Row scripted a stunning conclusion to her tennis career when she partnered her teenage daughter, Leela, to win four doubles titles—the Bombay Presidency Hard Court Championships in 1933, 1937 and 1940 and the Bombay Parsi Gymkhana Tournament in 1935.

Nearly a century later, this feat of a mother–daughter doubles combination winning multiple prestigious tournaments remains unparalleled in the annals of not merely Indian tennis, but in all accounts of the sport.

RAJKUMARI AMRIT KAUR

1954 to 1958 was a remarkable period in the annals of Indian sport. When Rajkumari Amrit Kaur was appointed the president of the All-India Lawn Tennis Association in 1954, an Indian sports body had at the helm a person who had actually played that sport at the highest level. (Sadly, this novel experiment would rarely be repeated, unable to survive the test of bureaucratic and political intrigue that has plagued Indian sports since.)

Soon afterwards, Kaur would write to India's first Chief of Army Staff, General K.M. Cariappa, the two divided by political affiliation and connected by a common love of sports. The letter, addressed to the general when he was India's ambassador to Australia, and found by historian Ramachandra Guha in the National Archives at New Delhi, read, 'Like all other sports organizations I found it (AILTA) completely bankrupt and full of intrigue.'[160] Notwithstanding how she found it, once she was at the helm of affairs, Kaur would transform the sport in India in the 1950s.

In 1953, she founded the 'Rajkumari Amrit Kaur Coaching Scheme' that engaged the services of four Indian and one foreign coach to cover athletics, hockey, tennis, cricket and table tennis. The scheme, supported by a government grant, would, in the next few years, bring a host of international coaches to India. Benefiting from this system, Indian tennis would see the rise of a generation of brilliant players, led by Premjit Lall and Jaidip Mukherjea.

Kaur's commitment to the sport would also encourage the South Club administration in Calcutta to invite the best players in the world to India during the European off season and give the opportunity to a generation of Indian players to hone their skills against the very best in the world, without the financial drain of constant tours abroad.

But to understand the deep association of Kaur, the first health minister of independent India, with the sport whose administration was entrusted to her in 1954, we need to go back four decades.

Born on 2 February 1889 to Raja Harnam Singh, the younger brother of the prince of the Kapurthala state, Amrit Kaur was one of two sisters and eight brothers. Singh had lost out on his chance to succeed as heir to the throne when he converted to Christianity as a teenager. He raised his young family in Lucknow where he took up the job of managing the Oudh estates.

Young Amrit was to have the benefits of not only a royal upbringing in an enlightened environment, but also an education at the best institutions in England—Sherborne School for Girls in Dorset where she captained the cricket, hockey and lacrosse teams, and at Oxford University.

At Oxford, Kaur had honed her skills on the tennis courts. On her return to India at the age of twenty, unable to pursue the other sports given the social restrictions, she plunged into the more genteel and brand new world of women's tennis.

Shimla, the summer capital of British India, was unsurprisingly a favoured destination for tennis aficionados. It was here, on the beautiful lawns in crisp autumn weather, that the Simla Open Handicap Tennis Tournament was played every year.* It was in this very British setting that Rajkumari Amrit Kaur was to taste her first successes in the sport.

For three successive years between 1911 and 1913, young Kaur would partner her brother Kunwar Maharaj Singh to win the mixed doubles tournament, becoming the first Indian woman to win a tennis title in any format (singles or doubles). It would be a decade before any other Indian woman would achieve the same feat.

---

*Simla was the old spelling and has been retained for purposes of historical accuracy in the name of the tournament.

In 1912 and 1913, besides partnering his sister, Maharaj would, in fact, also win the men's singles title in the tournament. He also reached the finals of the 1912 Bengal Lawn Tennis Championships, losing narrowly in a four-set encounter to Charles Scroope, an Irish player who appeared with some success in the main draw at Wimbledon for many years.

After 1913, Kaur would not be seen on the tennis courts for more than a decade as she found a new calling—the fight against social evils—the purdah system, child marriage and the devadasi system. The Jallianwalla Bagh massacre of 1919 and her growing admiration for Mahatma Gandhi whom she met in the aftermath of the tragedy drove her to join the freedom struggle. Her parents' objection to her joining the freedom struggle would, however, keep her from being formally associated with the movement until 1930, when her father passed on.[161] In 1926 Amrit Kaur decided to return to competitive tennis.

Over the next two years, Kaur would notch up the two biggest victories of her career, winning the women's doubles title at the prestigious Punjab Lawn Tennis Championships at Lahore. Her partner in both cases was Ms E. Row. Between the two victories, in 1927, she helped found the All-India Women's Conference (AIWC), an organisation that has since dedicated itself to women's empowerment. In 1929, Amrit Kaur would end her tennis career at the very venue where she first emerged as the face of women's tennis in India—Shimla, winning the mixed doubles in the company of Jagat Mohan Lal, one of India's top male players of the time.

In 1930, Rajkumari Amrit Kaur moved to Mahatma

Gandhi's Sevagram in Wardha and accepted the post of his secretary, a responsibility she would hold for the next seventeen years, until India became independent. Aruna Asfa Ali would later write, 'Rajkumari Amrit Kaur belonged to a generation of pioneers. They belonged to well-to-do homes but gave up on their affluent and sheltered lives and flocked to Gandhiji's banner when he called women to join the national liberation struggle.'[162]

In 1947, Amrit Kaur joined the nation's first cabinet on the invitation of Pandit Jawaharlal Nehru. She was appointed independent India's first health minister, and was also one of the few women who were part of the Constituent Assembly. Kaur would hold the health portfolio for a decade, and helped found the All-India Institute of Medical Sciences (AIIMS) in Delhi. At the time of its founding, she spoke from the heart: 'It has been one of my cherished dreams that for post graduate study and for the maintenance of high standards of medical education in our country, we should have an institute of this nature which would enable our young men and women to have their post graduate education in their own country.' She donated her ancestral property in Shimla, called 'Manorville', to AIIMS. It serves as a holiday retreat and a rest home for its nurses.

Born a princess, becoming India's first successful women's tennis player, pioneering women's empowerment in the country, giving up her royal privileges to join the struggle to free her nation from the British, taking up the huge challenge of the nation's health after the devastation of the partition and the chaos of building a nation from its varied dysfunctional parts, to finally giving back to the sport she had pioneered by putting its future on strong administrative footing, Amrit Kaur's was truly a life worth living.

Rajkumari Amrit Kaur passed away in 1964 at the age of seventy-five, leaving Indian tennis immeasurably richer for her involvement with it.

JENNY SANDISON

When E.M. Sandison became the first Indian woman to win a major Indian singles championship, she was laying the groundwork for the Sandison name to be a recognisable one in the sport. The mantle would rest on the shoulders of younger sister Jenny, to forever etch the Sandison name in the annals of Indian tennis.

Notwithstanding Jenny Sandison's elder sister's solitary triumph, ladies singles titles at the major tournaments for the first three decades of the sport in India had largely adorned the cabinets of European women. The arrival of teenaged Jenny would change that forever. Her all-court serve and volley game accompanied by a powerful and immensely effective smash revolutionised women's sport in the country, thus far dominated by baseline players.

When seventeen-year-old Sandison defeated Lena McKenna, multiple championship winner and the most dominant singles player of the time at the All-India Lawn Tennis Championships held at Allahabad in 1927, the *London Lawn Tennis Almanac* reported, 'Miss J. Sandison, runner-up in the Bengal Championship a week earlier, gained well-deserved success in the ladies' singles, and thus achieved the distinction of being the youngest player to place her name on the championship roll. Possessing great mobility and variety of strokes, the Bengal girl has made considerable progress since last year and has now overcome her habit of reckless hitting.'[163]

For much of her career, given the times, and the difficulty of a single woman travelling widely across the country, Sandison confined herself to playing tournaments in eastern India, two of which happened to be the most prestigious in the country—the All-India Lawn Tennis Championships in Allahabad and the Bengal Lawn Tennis Championships in Calcutta.

Between 1927 and 1935, she won the singles event at the Allahabad tournament all seven times she made an appearance there (the 1928 tournament was abandoned due to rains and she did not play in 1931). For good measure, she picked up five doubles titles as well.

At the Bengal Lawn Tennis Championships, Jenny was a six-time singles champion between 1928 and 1937. She also won five doubles and four mixed doubles titles during the period. At the East India Championships at Calcutta (later to be merged with the All-India Lawn Tennis Championships), her record of winning the singles title twelve times between 1925 and 1938, of which seven were successive wins between 1925 and 1931, remains unmatched.

Jenny Sandison's dominance on the courts and her all-round game in the 1930s when she was ranked no. 1 in the country for six straight years would cause Ghaus Mohammed, perhaps India's greatest tennis player of the 1930s and 40s, to say that she 'possessed the spark of genius'.[164]

In 1929 and 1930, Jenny travelled to England to play at

Wimbledon and on the English summer circuit. The first year she had to dip into the family finances for the voyage, and in England she supported herself by working as a typist. But when she went back for the second time in 1930, the All-India Lawn Tennis Association would pick up the tab.

In 1929, Jenny had become the first woman of Indian origin to play at Wimbledon. However, on both occasions, largely due to her inexperience of the big stage, playing in alien conditions against the best players in the world, she could not progress beyond the first round.

She did, however, gain a significant victory in England at the prestigious Surrey Championships at Surbiton, where, in the Ladies finals in late May 1929, Jenny came up against Britain's Betty Nuthall, then ranked no. 4 in the world. In one of the most thrilling matches of her career, Jenny defeated Nuthall 3-6, 7-5, 6-4.

The *Aberdeen Press and Journal*, reporting on the match, would say, 'Miss Betty Nuthall was beaten by the champion of India, Miss Jenny Sandison, 3-6, 7-5, 6-4 in a remarkable match in which Miss Nuthall led 6-3 and 5-1.'[165]

Earlier in the tournament, Jenny had injured herself. The *Yorkshire Post and Leeds Intelligencer* reported, 'Sandison's hand was badly blistered during practice over the weekend, (and) bled profusely during the match.'[166] It was unlikely she was fully fit while playing the finals just two days later, which made her victory over Nuthall even more remarkable.

Betty Nuthall would go on to win the US National Championships ladies' singles title the following year and put her name on eight Grand Slam doubles and mixed doubles titles over the next four years. In 1930, she would also beat

Sandison in a close-fought title clash at the Middlesex Lawn Tennis Championships, which the British Press widely labelled her 'revenge'.

While Jenny Sandison may not have made headway at Wimbledon, her victory over Nuthall had earned her the attention of the British press, both on and off the court.

In September 1930 the *Lancashire Evening Post* reported, 'The Press Association understands that there is a likelihood of Miss Jennie Sandison, the lawn tennis champion of India, not visiting England next year. She is going to be married upon her return to India, and her plans for the future are uncertain. The identity of Miss Sandison's future husband is being kept a close secret. She is in business in India, and has been engaged for about two years. To a Press Association reporter today Miss Sandison said, "Of course, I hope to be married, but when I am unable to say. I cannot tell you his name." Mrs E.V. Simon, Miss Sandison's chaperone in this country, admitted that she knew all about Jenny's romance, but would not divulge any information.'[167]

Notwithstanding the speculation, it would be another five years before Jenny Sandison finally tied the knot. *The Hull Daily Mail* announced in September 1935, 'Miss Jenny Sandison, India no. 1 lawn tennis player, has been married to Mr T.P. Boland, a railway official, states a Reuters message from Calcutta.'[168]

Two years later, having won her last singles title at the Bengal Lawn Tennis Championships, twenty-seven-year-old Mrs Jenny Boland set sail for England with her husband. Given the lack of mention about her in the British press thereafter, it seems safe to assume that India's greatest pre-independence women's tennis player had played her last competitive match before she left her country's shores for the final time.

LEELA ROW DAYAL

When Jenny Sandison laid down her racquet after her marriage in 1935, she left the future of the sport in good hands. Stepping into Sandison's large shoes with consummate ease, and going several steps further than her own illustrious mother Kshama, was Leela Row. Row was to win six successive All-India Lawn Tennis Championships between 1936 and 1943.

At the age of eighteen, Row had already shown great promise and indeed had early success when she picked up her first ladies' singles title at the All-India Lawn Tennis Championships in 1931, defeating the dominant player of the 1920s, Lena McKenna, in straight sets. Jenny Sandison would have a stranglehold on this tournament for the next few years, while Row waited for her time in the sun.

In 1934, five years after Sandison became the first Indian woman to appear at Wimbledon, Row would do one better. She prevailed over Gladys Southwell of Britain 4-6, 10-8, 6-2 in a gruelling three-setter to move into the second round at the original Mecca of lawn tennis, but here she lost to Ida Adamoff of France in an equally hard-fought three-set encounter, 3-6, 7-5, 4-6.

It would take sixty-eight years for Row's feat to be matched. When Nirupama Vaidyanathan won her opening round encounter at the Australian Open in 1998, she became the first Indian woman in the Open Era to reach the second round at a Grand Slam event, and only the second woman to do so in the history of the sport in the country.

The following year, in 1935, Leela Row again made it to Wimbledon, but this time she lost rather tamely, 2-6, 1-6, to the British veteran Evelyn Dearman, appearing in her seventh Wimbledon Championships. The summer was not a complete washout as Row picked up the singles title at the East of London Championships held at the Felixstowe Lawn Tennis Club in Suffolk.

Over the next decade and a half, Leela Row would continue to play domestically, maintaining her national ranking between one and two over the period. Her last competitive match was recorded in 1952 when she lost to a young bespectacled Urmila Thapar at the finals of the Delhi Hard Court Championships.

In 1943, Row had been married to Harishwar Dayal, an ICS (Indian Civil Service) official, the two drawn together by their common love of mountaineering. Two decades later, it would be atop a mountain that the marriage would come to an abrupt end when Dayal died during an expedition to the Khumbu region near Mount Everest. His wife was by his side when the accident happened. Harishwar Dayal was at that time India's ambassador to Nepal.

Leela Row, like her mother, was not only a gifted tennis player, but also a scholar and a linguist. Apart from English and her mother tongue Marathi, she read and wrote French, Italian and Sanskrit. She also wrote two books on Indian classical dance—*Nritya Manjari* on Bharatnatyam and *Manipur Dances* on Manipuri dance.[169]

A 2018 article by Sidin Vadukut in *Mint* summed up Row's life aptly: 'Leela Row Dayal climbed mountains, wrote plays, was a dab hand at the violin, knew the Dalai Lama, and, of course, won a match at Wimbledon. It is what you might call a full life.'[170]

THE PARSI LADIES

The Olympics records show an M. Tata, aged forty-five, representing India at the Paris Games in 1924 alongside Nora Polley. This mysterious lady whose identity has never been delved into adequately was one of the seven tennis players that made up half the 1924 Olympics Indian squad. It can now safely be concluded from my research of the archives and media reports of the time that she was Bangalore-born Mehri, the wife of Dorab Tata, a member of the International Olympic Committee who later launched the Indian Olympic Association. Dorab was the son of the Tata Group founder Jamsetji Tata, the financier of the Indian team to the 1924 Olympics.

Mehri Tata, later to be known as Lady Meherbai, was however not in the team because of her Tata connection. Far from it. She was a gifted tennis player who had earned her place by winning a triple crown at the Western India Tennis Championships, and for good measure picked up titles at Kissingen and Baden-Baden in Germany. Incredibly, like a few of her contemporaries, she played tennis in a 'gara', the traditional Parsi sari.

At Paris, Tata paired with Mohammed Sleem in the mixed doubles and received a bye into the second round. *The Hindu*, in its 17 July 1924 edition, reported, 'In the third round of mixed doubles, Flaquer and Lili Alvarez walked over Sleem and Lady Tata (India) scratched.'

There is no explanation in the records as to why they conceded a walkover to their opponents. Journalist Stan Rayan of *The Hindu* speculated in 2012, 'Did Tata pull out to allow Mohd Sleem to concentrate on his singles? Or was she unwell? Did the organisers stop her because she wanted to play in a saree? Was she around for the first round? It sure will be interesting to know.' Indeed it would, but sadly it's unlikely we will.

Five years after the Olympics, Lady Meherbai Tata was to play a significant role in campaigning for the Child Marriage Restraint Act (popularly known as Sharda Act) in both India and abroad, and getting it passed. She remained at the forefront of social change for women and children in India throughout her life.

At about the time when Jenny Sandison was the luminary on India's eastern tennis horizon and the mother–daughter Row duo ruled the western waves, Karachi in the north-west was producing its own set of female tennis talent.

The Dinshaw sisters—Parin Gustadji Dinshaw and M.H. Dinshaw—were a force to reckon with. Parin Dinshaw became the first Indian woman to win the Sind Championship in 1931, and won the title again in 1934. Her sister M.H. Dinshaw won the Bombay Parsi Gymkhana tournament, dethroning Leela Row in 1937, the two sisters also combining to win the doubles that year.

The Dinshaw sisters came from one of the most prominent families in Karachi. The patriarch of the family, Edulji

Dinshaw, a very successful businessman, was responsible for building twelve hospitals in the city during his lifetime, besides donating huge amounts to Bombay University to support needy students. His son Nadirshaw Edulji Dinshaw, a prominent philanthropist of his time, had the honour of lending his name to Pakistan's premier engineering college, NED University of Engineering and Technology (although few in Pakistan realise this today). There are still statues to this remarkable Parsi family scattered discreetly around Karachi, long removed from the prominent street corners they once adorned.

Meher Dubash, another Parsi lady from Karachi, with a strong forehand and a steady baseline game, won several North West India tournaments and Sind Championships between 1933 and 1937. She also combined with Leela Row to win the All-India Lawn Tennis Championships doubles in 1937 and the doubles and mixed doubles titles at the Punjab Championships in 1939.

Thanks to pioneers like the Sandison, Dinshaw and the Row families, women's tennis in India had got off to a flying start in the years immediately preceding independence. It would be left to the new breed of women emerging from the darkness of the struggle for independence to make their mark on a sport that owed its origins in India largely to the pleasure fields of colonialists.

WOMEN'S TENNIS COMES OF AGE

Hyderabad has an enviable record of producing sportspersons of international calibre. Khanum Haji, I remember vividly as an athletic young lass bouncing about the court, and, to the delight of Indians, thrashing memsahibs on her way to winning tournaments.[171]

—Khushwant Singh

KHANUM HAJI

Independent India's First Singles Champion

As the clock struck midnight on 15 August 1947 and India awoke to freedom from British rule, it was only fitting that the mantle of national champion would also pass on to an Indian woman. And so it came to pass at the first-ever grass court national championships held in India.

If there ever was a woman who could break off the dual shackles of colonialism and the social constraints of religious conservatism at once and make her way the 'new normal', it was young Khanum Haji.

Armed with a powerful serve, a graceful all-round game and a punishing forehand, Khanum Haji from Hyderabad powered her way to her first-ever national championship on the fast grass courts of South Club in Calcutta. In the finals, England's Laura Woodbridge, twice champion and two-time runner up over the past six years at the All-India Lawn Tennis Championships (which became the national championships), would give her a walk over, presumably due to ill health. Given the form that Haji had displayed through the tournament, it is safe to assume that the match, even if played out on the court, would, in all likelihood, have been hers.

Haji successfully defended her title the next two years, defeating the less talented but hardworking young left-hander Promilla Khanna in the final on both occasion. Haji then decided to take intermittent breaks from the sport over the next few years.

She would come storming back nine years later, now Mrs Khanum Singh, to claim the title back in 1957 at the age of thirty-five. As luck would have it, facing her across the net that year was, once again, Promilla Khanna, now a mature twenty-eight and on top of her game. But yet again Khanna would fall short to the determined lady from Hyderabad, 5-7, 5-7. The following year, the southpaw* would finally win her maiden singles title defeating Leela Panjabi in the finals.

1957 was a very productive year indeed for Haji, proving she had lost none of her skill and power in the intervening years. That year, besides the national championships on grass, she would also win the National Hard Court Championship, the South India Championship, the Bombay State Championship and Western India Championship. As if she

---

*A term that comes from boxing, but is often used to refer generally to a left-handed sportsperson

had anything left to prove, for good measure, she also picked up the doubles titles at the Asian Championship, the Western India and Bombay State Championships.

Providing one of the rare first-hand accounts of Haji's life on and off court, Khushwant Singh, in his inimitable style in *The Telegraph* in 2008, recalled his college contemporary thus, 'Khanum Haji, I remember vividly as an athletic young lass bouncing about the court, and, to the delight of Indians, thrashing memsahibs on her way to winning tournaments. She went through a succession of husbands, all non-Muslims.'

Confirming Singh's insight on her on-court prowess, Ramanathan Krishnan who saw her in action on the circuit in 1957 tells me, 'Mrs Khanum Singh became no. 1 because of her aggressive play.'[172]

Having proved that at thirty-five she was still the best in the country, Haji announced her retirement from the sport. Khanum Haji later settled in Maryland in the United States after her second marriage, her name now Mrs P.O. Cheryan.[173]

Urmila Thapar

The winter of 1951 would see the emergence of a precocious teenage talent on the tennis courts. Seventeen-year-old Urmila Thapar came down from the cool climes of Shimla to pick up both junior and senior titles at the Northern India Lawn Tennis Championship in Delhi, and followed it up with a stunning upset of Laura Woodbridge in the finals of the national championship at Calcutta. With these victories, Thapar became the no. 1 women's player in the country. She had just turned eighteen.

A powerful serve and a steady consistent game made

Thapar a force to reckon with in the 1950s in both singles and doubles. While she lost the national title to Davar two years in a row, she also partnered with her opponent to make a sweep of the doubles titles across the country in the first half of the 1950s.

Giving up on competitive tennis not long after her marriage in the mid-1950s, Urmila Sahay (nee Thapar) switched to golf. When in 1974 the fans stood up to applaud the new ladies' champion at the Western India Golf Championship, it would mark the second coming of a rare sporting talent born in the hills that surrounded colonial India's erstwhile summer capital.

RITA DAVAR

India's First Wimbledon Finalist

Khanum Haji may have been the first Indian woman to have made a mark on the domestic scene after independence, but it would take the emergence of seventeen-year-old Rita Davar from Calcutta in 1952 to put the nation firmly on the international tennis map.

That year at Wimbledon, the ladies juniors singles category had twelve entrants, India's Rita Davar among them. With a first-round bye, Davar, who didn't have a major domestic competition against her name yet, stormed through to the semi-finals, dropping only three games. In the final four she beat Annie Soisbault of France in straight sets, and suddenly, she was the first Indian, female or male, in the final of a Wimbledon event. There, Davar met Fanny ten Bosch from the Netherlands.

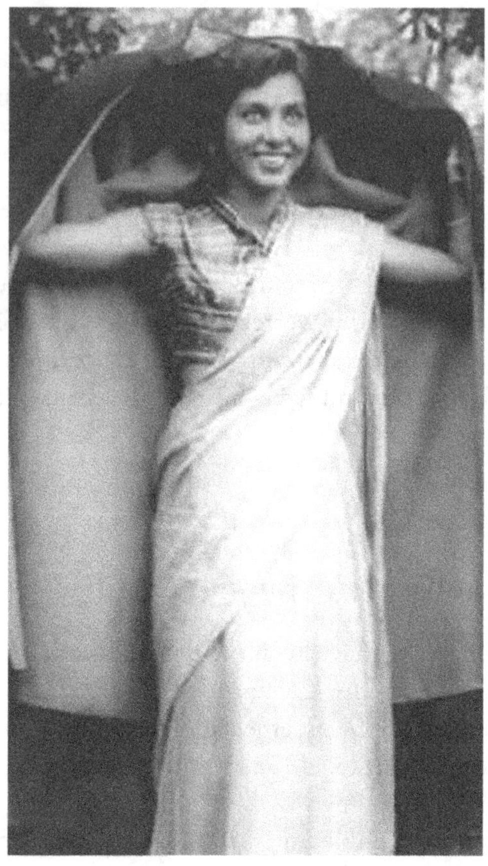

Rita Davar

After Davar had taken the first set 7-5, the nerves kicked in and the Dutch girl ran away 6-1 with the second. Ramanathan Krishnan, who appeared in the Wimbledon Boys' singles for the first time the same year, talks me through what happened. 'Rita Davar from Calcutta and I played in Junior Wimbledon singles for the first time in 1952. She reached the final and held match point. She could have been the only Indian girl to win that title. She choked at match point and lost the match.'[174]

The final scoreline read 7-5, 1-6, 5-7. It would be the first, and indeed thus far last time that an Indian woman would appear in the finals of a Wimbledon singles event.[175]

In 1953, India's two teenage tennis sensations, Rita Davar and Ramanathan Krishnan, would bring their growing form and confidence into the senior ranks and pick up the women's and men's national championships. That year at Wimbledon, Krishnan would go on to win the boys' title and become the first Indian to win a trophy at the iconic Grand Slam event, while Rita bowed out in the third round.

Between 1954 and 1956, Davar competed in the women's singles event at Wimbledon but without success. She did, however, win the national championships in 1954 for the second successive time. She also won the All-India Hard Court Championship twice.

In 1955, Davar partnered Krishnan to win the All-India Hard Court Championship. A few months later, the pair beat Jose Maria Draper of Spain and Margaret Grace of Great Britain to move into the third round of the mixed doubles event at Wimbledon. Here they met the eventual runner-up pairing of Morea of Argentina and Brough of the United States and lost 3-6, 4-6. It would be Davar's highest place finish in the main draw of the Championships. She didn't know it then, but at the age of twenty-one, Rita Davar had played her last major tournament.

A few months later, the prestigious tennis club at Baden-Baden in Germany had inaugurated a new clubhouse in their premises and introduced a tournament called the 'Internationals'. Davar became an affiliate of this reputed club, and there she would meet her future husband, a German national. Competitive tennis would cease to be a part of her life.

Rita Davar faded from the combined memories of tennis fans thereafter and it would be years later, that Naresh Kumar would bump into her. He remains the last person from the Indian tennis fraternity to have had contact with her. 'A long time ago I met her and her husband in Baden-Baden. She was a promising youngster,' Kumar tells me when I ask him about India's first Wimbledon finalist.[176]

LAKSHMI MAHADEVAN

The First Asian Champion from India

While Rita Davar garnered all the headlines as a junior prodigy and made an unexpectedly early exit from tennis when she was at the top of her game, there was a young girl in Chennai, quietly preparing to make her own mark on the sport. Her name was Lakshmi Mahadevan.

Through the latter part of the 1950s on the floodlit tennis court next to his house in Mandaveli in Chennai, T.K. Ramanathan had been putting Lakshmi through much the same regime that had already put his son Krishnan firmly on the world tennis map. 'I practiced in a skirt and a half saree tucked around my shoulders,' Lakshmi recalls in a recent conversation with me.

'TKR would kick off the session with a 15-minute rapid volleying with him. He would invariably call up and instruct me to sleep by 8.30 p.m. if I had a match the next day,' Lakshmi would recount in an interveiw to The Times of India in 2015. But it was not all work, and TKR took personal interest in all his trainees. 'Every Sunday we would be treated to a meal from Rayar's Mess or Ratna Cafe,' she recalled with a smile.

While Lakshmi had played her first tournament after she joined Presidency College in Chennai in 1956, it wasn't until she came under the TKR regime after graduating from college that she truly blossomed as a player. He took her strong forehand and used that as the anchor, streamlining and refining the rest, while allowing her natural style to drive her game.

By 1960, when she won the Madras State Championships at the Madras Gymkhana Club, there were no challenges that remained on the strong Chennai circuit. Lakshmi was ready to move on to competition at a higher level. Her on court dress had also evolved at the time, and wherever she went, her salwar-kameez clad figure hitting powerful forehands down the line was an immediate draw.

TKR's belief and Lakshmi Mahadevan's hard work would all pay off as the 1960's, arguably the most exciting decade in Indian tennis, kicked in. In 1963, Lakshmi played her first tournament abroad, the Ceylon Nationals, making the finals before losing to Ceylon's No. 1 player Ranjini Jeyasurya.

In January 1964, Calcutta's South Club was hosting the Asian Tennis Championships. Heading the men's line up was top-seeded Ramanathan Krishnan, and to TKR's immense satisfaction, in the list of unseeded players was a certain Lakshmi Mahadevan.

Less than two weeks later, the sounds of celebration rang

through the TKR household. While Krishnan's victory was not unexpected, the image of a beaming Lakshmi Mahadevan holding up the Ladies' trophy was on the front pages of all the Chennai papers. Lakshmi had caused one of the biggest upsets in Indian Women's tennis by beating top seed England's Mrs. Mills in straight sets.

Against all odds, Lakshmi Mahadevan had become the first Indian woman to win the Asian Tennis Championship.

That year both she and Krishnan were ranked No. 1 in the country. 'It must be the only instance in the history of Indian tennis,' Lakshmi tells me, (and one suspects she is right) 'that the same man [TKR] has coached both men's and women's reigning Asian Champions, who also happen to be the No.1 ranked players in the country that year.'

Over the next year, Lakshmi won the Ceylon National Championships, the All-India Hard Court at Hyderabad, the Western India Championships, and several other domestic tournaments. However, a medical issue was already cropping up that, unknown to Lakshmi, would cut short her career that was just ascending its peak.

A year later Lakshmi sought to defend the Asian Championships but lost in the finals to a seventeen-year old prodigy emerging from the south. A few months later Lakshmi, now struggling with the medical discomfort, once against lost to the young strapping girl in the semi-finals of the nationals, and announced that she was taking a break from the sport. That break would last eight long years, but it was a career not destined to be revived.

The baton had been passed on to the seventeen-year old. Her name was Nirupama Vasant.

Nirupama Mankad (nèe Vasant)

Seven Times National Champion

As Khanum Haji lifted the first national championship at Calcutta on a chilly January day in 1947, all the way across the country (and soon to be a universe apart) in Karachi was born a woman destined to be India's most dominant tennis player of the 1960s and '70s.

With father 'George' Vasant being one of India's leading players of his time, at one point ranked no. 2 behind Ramanathan Krishnan, Nirupama had the right DNA to excel in the sport. Vasant would coach hundreds of players after his own playing days were over, but few matched Nirupama's talent, hard work and ambition.

Vasant was a strong influence on her career, and like many 'tennis dads' before and after him, coaching became a part of the father-daughter relationship. Nirupama would laughingly tell Rajdeep Sardesai in an interview for the *Afternoon Despatch and Courier* in 1986, 'Even today my father coaches me. I have to remind him that I am almost forty now and retired.'

Even before she bagged her first national title at the age of seventeen in 1965, Nirupama Vasant won the Asian Championships. It had been a decade since an Indian woman had won an international title, and followers of Indian tennis had good reason to be excited.

She would not disappoint. That year she went on to win the Northern India Championship at Delhi, the Western India title at Bombay, and eventually ended the year with the national title. It was just the beginning. That national title would turn out to be the first of seven that had her name inscribed on it. She also bagged the no. 1 ranking in India that year and would hold on to it for the entire length of an incredible thirteen-year career.

In 1968 Vasant won her second Asian Championship title, defeating world no. 13 Alice Tym in three hard-fought sets. The following year she was given the Arjuna Award. In 1971 she partnered Anand Amritraj in the mixed doubles event at Wimbledon, losing to the Chilean pair of Jaime and Ana Maria Pinto Bravo in the second round.

Nirupama married into the illustrious Mankad family from Bombay. Cricket ran in their blood. Father-in-law Vinoo Mankad was India's first great all-rounder; husband Ashok Mankad would captain Bombay and be an important member of the Indian Test team for several years and brother-in-law Rahul Mankad played for Bombay for over a decade.

Two decades after Nirupama Mankad had hit the last ball over the net, in 2000, her son Harsh Mankad made his debut for India in the Davis Cup and would remain India's highest ATP-ranked player for over two years in the first decade of the new millennium.[177] The sporting genes in the Vasant–Mankad family were alive and well.

Kiran Bedi

Asian Champion to India's Top Cop and Beyond

One of India's pioneer generation of tennis players, Sydney Montague Jacob, had resigned from his post in Amritsar as director of agriculture after the Jallianwala Bagh massacre in

1919. Thirty years later, in one of the houses barely a stone's throw away from the infamous garden, was born a baby girl destined to defend the law, and prevent tragedies like the one inflicted by Brigadier General Dyer.

Growing up as one of four siblings who played at the nearby playground, Kiran Peshwaria was blissfully unaware that the grass beneath her racing feet had been nurtured on the blood of innocent martyrs. The sign, Jallianwala Bagh, held no significance for the siblings spending blissful afternoons in the garden.

What was in no doubt however, was her talent at tennis, a sport that she was introduced to at the Service Club in Amritsar where her father and grandfather were members. Winning the National Junior Championships in 1966, Kiran went on to become the Asian Champion in 1971 and picked up the National Hard Court Championship in 1973, defeating Nirupama Mankad in the semi-finals.

That would, however, also be her last national title, for 1973-74 turned out to be a watershed year not only for Kiran but thousands of women who came after her.

Passing the All-India Civil Services Examination with flying colours, Kiran Peshwaria became India's first female IPS (Indian Police Service) officer. The fight against injustice she had started waging even as a teenaged tennis player standing up to the Punjab Lawn Tennis Association for discriminating against female players with much lower compensation than the men would now be taken to the next level, as Kiran Bedi took up the broader fight for law and justice in India.

In a media interview as India's first female IPS officer trainee, she would say, 'Policing, for me, is about the power to reform, power to provide instant justice. This is my mission.' Twenty years later Kiran Bedi was promoted as Inspector General of Delhi Prisons. During this stint, she made wholesale reforms at Delhi's Tihar Jail and was the recipient of the Ramon Magsaysay Award in 1994 for her stellar work.

In 2003, Bedi became the first Indian woman to be appointed as a police advisor to the secretary-general of the United Nations, in the Department of Peace Keeping Operations. She resigned in 2007, to focus on social activism and writing. She has written several books, and runs the India Vision Foundation. In 2015 she joined politics as a member of the ruling BJP. At the time of writing this book, she is the governor of the Union Territory of Pondicherry.

She continues to play tennis socially.

Nirupama Vaidyanathan

The First Professional

The most prominent players of the 1980s wcrc Amreeta Ahluwalia and Kiran Bedi's younger sister, Anu Peshwaria. Ahluwalia won both national championships—on grass and hard courts—in 1978, and Peshwaria followed suit with successive national championships in 1981 and 1982. But for the rest of the decade, the titles were widely dispersed among multiple contenders.

It was not until the arrival of young Nirupama Vaidyanathan from the unlikely (but numerous) tennis courts of Coimbatore that Indian tennis fans again sat up to take notice of the sport then dominated by the Amritraj Brothers and the younger Krishnan.

Like many successful tennis players before and after her, Vaidyanathan was coached by her father. By the time she was ten, she was beating her father's friends at Coimbatore's Cosmopolitan Club. She recounts in her book *The Moonballer*, 'Playing against adults made me think like an adult on the tennis court.'[178] Off the court, the lessons came from her father who made her hit against the wall continually. 'The wall never misses, so try to outdo the wall.' The training regime was tough. As Vaidyanathan remembers, 'Mornings were meant for our coaching and afternoons for us to play against other players.'

At fourteen, Vaidyanathan burst into the tennis scene in an era when no woman dominated the Indian courts, won the senior national championship singles and doubles titles in 1991 and became the no. 1 player in the country. She dominated the national circuit until 1996, winning the grass court national championship four years in a row from 1992 to 1996 and the hard court version from 1991 to 1995.

In 1996, aged eighteen, she took a momentous decision, becoming India's first professional women's tennis player. Living alone in Belgium, braving the unfamiliar cold and playing in hundreds of local tournaments across Europe to gain experience and points was going to pay off. In January 1998, she was given a wild card entry into the Australian Open.

At Melbourne, her first round opponent was Gloria Pizzichini from Italy, ranked over a hundred places above Vaidyanathan. Her 5-7, 6-4, 6-2 victory was a stunning upset. *The Hindu* reported, 'Nirupama's tennis was something of a revelation. (She) stormed back in style, hitting lovely passes, going for her shots and bringing them off on the big points.'

With the victory, Vaidyanathan became only the second Indian to move into the second round of the women's singles draw at a Grand Slam event, sixty-four years after Leela Row had first recorded the feat at Wimbledon in 1934. She also became the first one in the Open Era to do so.

In the second round at Melbourne Park, she lost to Gryzbowska from Poland. Sadly, that would be as far as Nirupama Vaidyanathan would go at a Grand Slam event for the rest of her career. But what she had achieved was an important step forward for women's tennis in the country.

With immense faith in her own abilities, Vaidyanathan had gone outside the comfort zone of the small town environment of Coimbatore where she hailed from, braved an unfamiliar world and all the challenges of surviving there as a young girl, and showed that with intent and self-belief, it was possible to look beyond the horizon and be counted on the world stage.

The mantle would fall on a young girl from Hyderabad to pick up where Vaidyanathan left off, and take women's tennis in India to the next level.

Vaidyanathan (now Nirupama Sanjeev) is an acclaimed coach and currently runs a Tennis Academy in the Bay Area of California.

SANIA MIRZA

One of the thrills of playing at the top tennis centres of the world is to see the Indian flag go up whenever I'm participating in these events. That's enough motivation for any Indian who has the opportunity to perform at these tournaments.

—Sania Mirza

2015—Charleston, South Carolina, United States

It had been more exhilarating a start to the partnership than either could have imagined. The first Grand Slam event of the year had concluded at Melbourne, and then the American swing on the winter circuit had started. On that circuit, there were no tournaments more prestigious than the Premier Mandatory events (equivalent of the men's Masters 1000) at Indian Wells and Miami.

Coming together at the end of February, Sania Mirza, ranked no. 2 in the world in doubles, and Martina Hingis, one of the greatest tennis players in the history of the women's game, now on a second comeback trail, had combined to brush aside all opposition, picking up both the coveted trophies without dropping a set.

It had been a calculated risk for Mirza, the player with most at stake. Hingis was making a comeback after years in the wilderness, and Mirza, in the form of her life, was struggling with her partner Cara Black having retired at the end of the previous year. A temporary tie-up with Su-Wei Hsieh of Taiwan, also a natural deuce court player like herself, was not working as well as they had hoped, and the next combination had to be perfect with the no. 1 spot in the world up for grabs.

At this stage Mirza's father Imran stepped in with sage advice as he had done for much of her life: 'If you want to become the no. 1 doubles player in the world, you will need to play the deuce court. Martina is perfect for you as she's a master of the ad court and knows what it is to be a champion.'[179]

Four continuous weeks of tennis had exhausted the two women. Playing the lesser event at Charleston was a risk, not just from an injury standpoint, but also because there was the big adjustment to be made from the hard Plexipave courts to the green clay and the change in balls used there. But the no. 1 ranking was at stake, and they decided to go for it.

They had not expected Charleston to be easy, and it wasn't. Playing every match late at night, the Mirza–Hingis pair struggled through three tough matches, weaving together nerve-wracking super tiebreak victories in each. Finishing the semi-final past midnight on a Saturday, they were told the final was scheduled for 10.30 a.m. the next morning to enable television audiences around the world to watch the match.

Tired from lack of sleep and the continuous tennis but energised by adrenaline, the first set was wrapped up 6-0. Mirza prepared to serve for the tournament at 5-3 in the second set. Then the nerves took over, and she was broken. Casey Dellacqua was now serving at 4-5 to level the set.

Mirza recalls, 'My legs felt heavy, my arms were numb. "Will I manage to put the ball back?" I wondered. I could see the blurry tennis ball as it crossed the net and hit the surface of the court. Fault. Just missed the line.'[180] A double fault had handed the pair a 6-0, 6-4 victory. As Mirza's box erupted with joy, Hingis ran up to hug her overwhelmed partner.

It was a historic moment for Indian tennis at a location that held enormous significance for the United States. Just a few miles away from Gadsten's Wharf, where roughly half of all African slaves brought to the United States had landed to begin their life in captivity, an Indian girl from another historic city, Hyderabad, had just burst the shackles of gender perception and religious conservatism to become the no. 1 tennis player in the world.

THE UNLIKELY BEGINNING TO A CHAMPION'S JOURNEY

The journey to ultimate glory of elite sportspersons usually begins quite early, and Sania Mirza was no exception. She was just four when father Imran, a promising cricket player on the Mumbai maidans, having lost his own father early and struggling with a couple of nascent business ventures in Hyderabad, took the decision to move to Ohio in the United States, where his brother and sister lived.

Too young to get enrolled in the public school system, and her struggling father unable to afford private schooling, Mirza found herself spending her days pattering sweetly to customers at her father's print shop, and on weekends watching with immense fascination her father and cousins play tennis on the community courts.

Within a year Imran realised that there were more opportunities for him and his family back in India and decided to move back to Hyderabad. There, Sania was enrolled in tennis classes.

A month later, Imran got a call from the six-year-old's coach, Srikkanth, a twenty-two-year-old former national level player. 'You have to come, sir! She has tremendous ball sense and timing. You cannot teach that. It's pure talent.' The journey had begun.

While the coaching at various levels would continue, her father, much like T.K. Ramanathan, Robert Amritraj and C.G.K. Bhupathi had done before him, would become the main guiding light for her career.

The seven-year-old's forehand already had stunning power, and would go on to become her greatest asset. But what was clear to Imran was that to convert that asset into an awesome weapon, unbridled aggression and flamboyant stroke play needed to be inculcated in her. It was a decision that would make Sania Mirza the player she ultimately became.

Years later, her Fed Cup coach Nandan Bal would tell me, 'The reason why Sania came from nowhere to become the first Indian woman to win a Grand Slam and rise to no. 1 in the world was because on the court she displayed more guts than any Indian tennis player either before or since.'[181]

THE FIRST STEPS TO STARDOM

While Mirza had bagged her first national championship at the age of fourteen, her first ITF title by sixteen, and had a few wins on the Junior Circuit, at the Grand Slam venues success was proving difficult to come by.

At Wimbledon 2003, a piece of advice Mahesh Bhupathi gave her would change this. He walked up to her and told her not to play with Sanaa Bhambri, her usual partner. The logic was sound—their games didn't complement each other, the forehand being the mainstay for both.

On the practice courts, Mirza chanced upon a thirteen-year-old Russian girl, Alisa Kleybanova. Her strength—a devastating backhand, her weakness—she had never played doubles. After a few chats, they decided to team up. Beating the top seeds 7-6, 6-4 in the first round, the pair would go on to defeat all comers, and march into the finals of the Junior event. But first, as per tradition, the night before the final, the two excited teenagers had to choose their dresses to the Wimbledon Ball.

Mirza recalls, 'An expertly curated wardrobe was brought into the locker room. Racks of stunning dresses, shoes and handbags. We were already dreaming of strutting our stuff at the ball. We selected our clothes and went to bed that night, looking forward to the biggest day of our lives.'

The next day, somehow holding their own, the older partner covering for the nervous thirteen-year-old on crucial points, the Russian–Indian pair would prevail. For the first time, an Indian girl had etched her name on a title at a Grand Slam event. It may have been a doubles title, but in holding up the winner's trophy at Wimbledon, Sania Mirza's achievement was in every way as significant as Ramanathan Krishnan's had been back in 1954.

The glass ceiling that had long artificially constrained Indian women's tennis had been shattered decisively. The no. 1 junior doubles ranking in the world that came with the points earned at Wimbledon was merely the first candle to be lit on a long overdue celebratory cake for women's sports in India.

Mirza made the decision to turn professional in 2003, but it would take two years of grind and changes to her game before she would taste success in the ranks of the seniors.

No professional could hope to hide behind just a stunning forehand and succeed. The issues with her game could only be identified and rectified by experienced coaches. There were three glaring weaknesses—her backhand was weak, her elbow had a bend while serving, not allowing the serves to be effective enough, and finally, she didn't know how to volley.

Between Australian Bob Brett and Croatian Vedran Martic, both former coaches to Goran Ivanisevic, they not only corrected these aspects to the extent possible, but also taught her the value of physical training. Bob Brett would be almost prescient when he told her father Imran, 'Sania undoubtedly has some talent but she has plenty of weaknesses in her technique. If she works on these weaknesses and everything else falls into place, she can perhaps achieve, at best, a world ranking of 30 in professional women's tennis.'[182]

Mirza's highest career ranking in singles would turn out to be no. 27.

In 2004, making a wild card entry into the Australian Open, Mirza marched into the third round, the highest point thus far for an Indian woman at a Grand Slam singles event. There, she was to meet the formidable Serena Williams. It was great experience for the eighteen-year-old playing in a Slam event main draw for the first time, and the 1-6, 4-6 loss to the multiple Grand Slam champion was not unexpected.

Two years later, looking back at this, Nirmal Shekhar would write in *Sportstar*, 'If the Who's Who of Indian tennis was dominated by males for over five decades, then, through a scorching summer's week in Melbourne two years ago, the first bold attempt to strike some sort of gender balance was made. In the context of Indian tennis, Sania ushered in a new era in January 2005 when she made the third round of the Australian Open as a wild card before losing to Serena Williams.'

Mirza's rise in women's tennis would, however, really start in February 2005 when, ranked 131 in the world, and gaining a wild card entry into the main draw of the WTA Hyderabad Open, she stunned the whole field to win the title, beating Maria Kirilenko of Russia in the semi-finals and Aloyna Bondarenko of Ukraine in the final.

A couple of weeks later, once again with a wild card, she reached the quarter-finals of the Dubai Tennis Championships and beat reigning US Open champion and world no. 7 Svetlana Kuznetsova 6-4, 6-2. Mirza had been 0-4, 15-30 down and re-injured her twisted ankle, before making a stunning comeback. This was a match Mirza would later label 'the greatest singles match of my life'.[183]

Kuznetsova had her revenge in the second round of Wimbledon that year in a closely-fought three-setter on Centre Court. Later that year Mirza made it to her second

     Advantage India

WTA final, the Forest Hills Classic in New York, before losing to Lucie Safarova. She finished 2005 as the 'WTA Newcomer of the Year'.

Sportstar, in its annual year-end issue, wrote evocatively: 'What was the real deal was Indian, a ball-thrashing teenager with the devil-may-care attitude once associated with a fellow named Lochinvar. Sania Mirza's ascension could be told in numbers, but even her rise from no. 206 at the end of 2004 to a high of no. 31 in October 2005 did not adequately reveal the fierce confidence she owned and the desire she wore like a perfume. Here was substance that did not require any hype.'[184]

Over the next two years Mirza would continue her rise up the singles rankings and notch up significant victories against major players. Recovering quickly from a knee surgery, 2007 was her best year on the singles circuit. Winning the Asian leg of the Hopman Cup (the inter-nation mixed gender competition) in the company of Rohan Bopanna (replacing an injured Leander Paes), unexpectedly beating both Czech Republic and Croatia before finally losing to Spain in the semi-final, was a great start to the year. Over the course of a fortnight that year Mirza went on to vanquish four top 20 players, including Dinara Safina, who, just a few months later, would become the world's no. 1 singles player.

Even during this purple patch, however, tournament victories would continue to elude her. She was beaten an incredible four times on her way to titles by world no. 5 Anna Chakvetadze of Russia. As Mirza wistfully writes in her book, 'If I had found the key to beat Anna Chakvetadze that season, I would have risen higher in the rankings.'[185]

Mirza could not have known that by the time she reached her career high singles ranking of no. 27 in mid-2007, she had progressed as far as her singles career would take her. Nevertheless, her doubles results had certainly opened up the possibility of a format switch at a later date. But first would come the controversies.

THE DOUBLE-EDGED SWORD OF BEING AN INDIAN CELEBRITY

If by December 2007 Mirza had imagined that success and the universal love from fans that victories bring would stay forever, she would soon find out how fickle life as an Indian sports celebrity could be. Just as she was getting ready to step high, wide and plentiful, the year would come to a bizarre controversial end, and events of the next few months would only make matters worse.

Non-cricketing success in Indian sports is rare, and the public is consequently starved of heroes. So when someone unusual like Mirza erupts into the scene—a young Muslim girl with film star looks and bucketloads of sporting talent to top it all off, the conferring of instant celebrity status is a given.

With the status comes intense public scrutiny, the latent annoying curiosity of the average Indian about everyone else's life and a tendency to stir up controversy where none exists. Very quickly, Mirza would be subject to all of this, the honeymoon period coming to a premature end.

It started rather innocuously, as such incidents usually do. Shooting a commercial in the old city of Hyderabad that

December, Mirza was forced to temporarily take shelter in an area adjoining the Mecca Masjid (and well outside its walls) located opposite the Charminar, when word spread she was there and the crowds became unmanageable. A reporter took a picture of her sitting there with the masjid in the background and put out a story with comments from locals that she had been part of an illegal photo shoot inside the mosque. From there to charges of demeaning Islam was but a small step. Notwithstanding her innocence, a written public apology to the imam of the mosque was demanded and handed over.

This was not Mirza's first brush with the religious police. In 2005, a little-known cleric had issued a fatwa against her for the length of her skirts on the tennis court. Mirza had spiritedly retorted at the time to journalist Vir Sanghvi at the *Hindustan Times* Summit that people should focus on whether she won or lost. How did it matter whether her skirt was six inches long or six feet long? That controversy had been allowed to die its natural death as her tennis spoke for her over the next couple of years.

If religion had been the focal point of the first set of controversies, Mirza's nationalism would be the next, just a few months later.

At the World Group Hopman Cup encounter against Australia, Mirza gave India a crucial lead with a 6-2, 2-6, 6-4 victory over the local favourite Alicia Molik.* When Rohan Bopanna lost his singles, all hopes rested on the mixed

---

*Hopman Cup is an international eight-team indoor tournament which features mixed-gender national teams. It was held in Australia from 1989 to 2019 and replaced by the ATP Cup in 2020. The championship is named in honour of Harry Hopman (1906–1985), an Australian tennis player and coach who guided the country to fifteen Davis Cup titles between 1938 and 1969.

doubles. The pair would go on to win the match by prevailing 13-11 in the super tiebreak. It was, however, during Bopanna's singles match, with Mirza sitting in the players' box and cheering her teammate, that the new controversy erupted.

A photographer clicked a picture which seemed to show Mirza resting her feet on an Indian flag. In reality the 6'x9' paper flag was several feet away from her, but the angle of the photo gave the impression that her feet were on it. The media was all over the 'story'. A 'concerned' Indian filed a case against her for 'disrespect to the flag'.

A distraught Mirza, just twenty-one years old and emotionally shattered, contemplated retirement. She talks us through her thoughts at the time, 'Why do I need to go through this? I am patriotic. I have given my blood, sweat and tears to play for the country. Why do I have to justify myself to people? Why do I need to tell them I love my country over and over again?'[186]

Rohit Brijnath provided perspective in *The Hindu*: 'A girl sweats. Cramps. Sits. Puts up tired feet that have been running for India. A flag is close by, as flags often are at sports events, and this one is Indian. A photographer takes a picture seemingly from a clever angle that juxtaposes feet and flag. A case is filed in court. Someone dutifully alerts the media. And this non-issue becomes a story. Welcome to Sania Mirza's world.'[187]

Journalist Sanjay Jha wrote an emotional blog in *News18*. 'Mirza is a fairy tale story of individual determination, of being innately gritty, of fighting hard against several insurmountable barriers and achieving great success. She is only twenty-one. And has an exciting future ahead. She needs our support ... She has been mercilessly hauled up for wearing skirts, maligned for looking glamorous, and been made into a gossip feature at the slightest provocation ... We ogle Maria Sharapova and endorse her commercial deals, deifying her like a diva, but Mirza's every move is condescendingly criticised and mockingly rebuked ... For Sania Mirza the battle is a lot lonelier (than for an Indian cricket player). The double fault is her own personal anguish, as is the easy missed volley. For her, Team India means every Indian who believes in her. Has faith in her actions. Who does not cheer her shots into the bottom of the net. And sees in her success the victory of India ... India, a country of a billion people, and counting. Should we feel proud as Indians if we let that young girl out in the middle feel lonely and lost?'[188]

While pieces like these brought some cheer to the youngster, the quota of controversies had yet to run its course.

At the 2008 Australian Open, Mirza suffered an abdominal tear in addition to a wrist injury that was already troubling her. Playing a doubles match against medical advice at the Fed Cup against Hong Kong just to prevent India's relegation, Mirza then suffered a slipped disc by putting pressure on her back, trying to compensate for her torn abdominal muscles.

While she was in recovery, news belatedly leaked to a journalist that the doctor who had operated on her for a knee injury many months before had received an anonymous letter 'advising' him not to treat her knee injury as it was God's way of ensuring Sania Mirza did not play tennis anymore. A headline in the US screamed: *Treat Sania and Annoy Allah!* The Indian media then had a field day.

Tired of the never-ending controversies and feeling under enormous mental pressure from the media and her countrymen who latched onto the negativity bandwagon, Mirza announced she would skip the upcoming Bengaluru WTA tournament, inadvertently exacerbating the bad press. Former male players stood up to criticise her and question her patriotism. The rumour quickly spread that she had refused to play in India ever again. All hell broke loose. In the midst of the media mayhem, voices of reason stood up for her.

Brijnath wrote in *The Hindu* in February 2008: 'It's sad that a competitor, who recently hauled her injured, bandaged self onto court to help win a key Fed Cup match, has to keep saying, "I'm a proud Indian." It's unfortunate that in India's small tennis fraternity, older men who have no idea what it means to be seen as young, female, gifted, glamorous, a Top 30 player and role model, felt the need to criticise her decision to skip the Bangalore tournament. Even if part of the reason was some appearance fee dust-up, Sania is saying the pressure is throttling and she deserves listening to.'[189]

Barkha Dutt penned a passioned defence in *Hindustan Times*. 'What if Sania Mirza had been a man? Would she still have been at the epicentre of a strange and stormy love–hate relationship with her country? Would she still have evoked reactions that tend to swing between extremes of adulation and annoyance? .... In India though, while we have watched (in breathless awe and bewildered fright) women storm successfully into several all-male zones, the breakthrough has hardly been that dramatic when it comes to the rough and tumble of the sporting world ... Therein may lie a clue to the seemingly inexplicable and mixed up responses that the twenty-two-year-old Sania provokes. She's quite simply the only female sports icon India has ever known. And our contradictory responses to her say something about how we respond to women who are non-conformist trailblazers and not afraid to be themselves. It's almost as if we admire them and resent them at the same time.'[190]

Disturbed as she was by all the controversies, the supportive and nuanced articles from the likes of Brijnath, Dutt and Jha combined with sage advice from her friend Mahesh Bhupathi ('stood by me like the proverbial Rock of Gibraltar'), made Mirza dismiss thoughts of retirement from her mind. [191]

The adage—what does not kill you makes you stronger—would kick in. These episodes and many others like these had toughened her resolve instead of breaking it, and what Sania Mirza would do from this point on would change the history of women's sport in India.

DOUBLING UP FOR SUCCESS

By the time she reached no. 27 in the world in singles in 2007, Mirza's less-heralded doubles successes had quietly propelled her to no. 18 in that format.

'Doubles came naturally to me, as it does to most Indian tennis players,' she modestly writes in *Ace Against Odds*. As events would prove, her talent and aptitude for the format would go well beyond that. In 2007 alone, she won four titles with four different partners. In a first taste of the biggest stage, she reached the finals of the 2008 Australian Open mixed doubles event with Mahesh Bhupathi. There, much to their disappointment, they lost to Serbia's Nenad Zimonjic and China's Tiantian Sun. The multiple injuries and controversies since then meant, however, that the rest of 2008 was a virtual washout. At the Beijing Olympics the intense pain in the wrist forced her to withdraw in the midst of a singles match.

In January 2009, it was back to Melbourne, and it would be here that the fairy tale of Sania Mirza would take flight. Drafted into the tournament main draw with a wild card, despite her poor ranking due to her injury-led absence from the tour, on the basis of the runner-up finish the previous year, this time the Mirza–Bhupathi duo was determined to clear the final hurdle to greatness.

Injury, her bug bear for much of the past twelve months, once again raised its ugly head, this time through an abdominal muscle tear in the quarter-finals, and threatened to derail their campaign. But determined to climb that final step, taking painful emergency physio treatment, Mirza found herself on the Rod Laver arena for the second time in two years. This time she would not be denied, and less than two hours later, for the first time in the history of tennis, an Indian woman was at the pinnacle of the sport, holding up a Grand Slam trophy.

While the twenty-two-year-old may not have realised it then, at Melbourne that day, Sania Mirza had done much more than win a Grand Slam event. She had broken through the all-important psychological barrier that had limited Indian women from reaching for the sporting firmament. That moment, more than any other in the history of women's sports in India, would define the future. It was as if Rita Davar's failure to convert three match points at the Junior Wimbledon finals, P.T. Usha's desperate but failed attempt to breast the tape in the quest of that elusive first Olympic medal and twice world champion Karnam Malleswari's relatively disappointing Olympic bronze at the pinnacle of her career had all been leading up to this moment when Mirza stood on the podium at Melbourne.

In the years to come, Mirza herself would add to her achievements, and it would be Hyderabad, her hometown, that would become the breeding ground for female achievers in Indian sports, with first Saina Nehwal shattering the Chinese domination of badminton and then P.V. Sindhu bringing home a world championship to stamp the mark of Indian women on the sport.

Short skirts and raised trophies would become par for the course for the new Indian woman in sports. And it was Sania Mirza who had led the way, bearing the social brunt of being a pioneer, as champions down the ages have always done.

REACHING FOR THE SKY AND GETTING THERE

In his book *The Barefoot Coach*, Paddy Upton talks about bringing his South African friend Mike Horn, perhaps the world's greatest living adventurer, to talk to the Indian cricket team just before they commenced their campaign for the 2011 World Cup finals at home.

Among Horn's many outstanding achievements, probably the most incredible is his circumnavigation of the Arctic Circle. Travelling solo and without any motorised transport, he pulled a two-hundred-kilogram sled for two years and three months, covering 20,000 kilometres over two Arctic winters. This is what Horn told the team:

Guys, if you can transform the power of the mind, which we all do, when you make that will to win bigger than the fear to lose, you get rid of a lot of pressure that you yourself put on your shoulders. It's up to you ... (Remember,) it's not about being able to pull yourself up twenty times. It's about wanting to pull yourself up once ... You (need to) know one thing, and that is not to sit down when you get to the top. Because the moment you sit down is the moment you will never stand up again.

Sania Mirza may not have heard of Mike Horn when she won her first Grand Slam title, but the lessons of not resting on her laurels and believing she could go further would instinctively kick in. While injuries kept her out of the podiums and indeed the court itself for much of the next eighteen months or so, she started her comeback in mid-2010. It would take another year before she found herself back in a Grand Slam final, this time partnering Russia's Elena Vesnina on clay at Roland Garros.

The pair had a dream run through the field beating top seeds Flavia Pennetta and Gisela Dulko in the quarter-finals, but eventually lost to the unseeded Czech team of Andrea Hlavackova and Lucie Hradecka in straight sets. At Wimbledon, the Indo–Russian pair made it to the semi-finals. And after being laid up with a left knee injury for the next few months, a semi-final entry at Melbourne Park in 2012 saw Mirza's doubles ranking move up to no. 7 in the world.

In 2012, Mirza also had to take a very tough call. Her recurring injuries and multiple surgeries were taking a toll on her game. The devastating forehand would disappear when intense wrist pain took over, significantly affecting her singles game. Knees would give way as she pounded the court.

While she admits that in the first part of her career, the injuries were due to a lack of fitness, she contends that contrary to media reports and indeed some comments former players made to me in the course of writing this book, the root cause of her joint injuries was purely physiological, rather than fitness-related.

She explains in *Ace Against the Odds* that she has a chronic arthritic condition called sensitivitis, usually found in old people.[192] Her naturally hyper-mobile lax joints put her in the high-risk category for this condition. Perhaps if she had not been an elite sportsperson it wouldn't have mattered so much, but she is, and it does.

Sania Mirza decided she would not play singles anymore and would concentrate solely on doubles which put much less strain on her damaged joints. In 2012, there was another factor that weighed on her mind. To qualify for the Olympics and play for the Indian flag, Mirza needed to be among the top ten in the world in doubles. Another injury sustained through playing singles, would have put paid to that. It was a decision that would release her from constant pain, and earn her a new lease of life in the sport.

With success in the early part of the clay court season and eyes firmly set on the Olympics, Mirza once again teamed up with Mahesh Bhupathi at Roland Garros. I happened to be at Roland Garros that year and followed the progress of the Indian trio in the mixed doubles format—shuttling between the courts in Paris, watching Bhupathi-Mirza march through the draw, while Leander Paes did the same with his partner, Elena Vesnina.

Paes and Vesnina crashed out in the semi-finals but Bhupathi–Mirza marched into the finals with Bhupathi's serve and Mirza's stunning forehands waylaying all comers. After less than two hours on Court Philippe Chartier, and a scintillating display of high class doubles play, the Indian pair stood holding up their second Grand Slam title. The tricolour had rarely flown higher in the land of 'Liberté, Egalité, Fraternité'.*

It was hardly surprising, therefore, that when I asked Mirza recently about her favourite doubles partners, she answered, 'In mixed doubles I would say Mahesh Bhupathi because we won my first Grand Slam together and we then went on to win another Grand Slam after that.'[193]

THE 2012 LONDON OLYMPICS FIASCO

But if Mirza had thought that she could now concentrate on winning an Olympic medal for the country with Bhupathi, she had underestimated the capacity of the Indian tennis administrators to self-destruct the sport they are entrusted to manage and promote. She had also failed to account for the fact that her male colleagues on the team would get involved in a media-stoked public spat over Olympic doubles pairings, and she would be left stranded like the proverbial fawn on a lonely highway with headlights in its eyes.

If the end result had not been so tragic, this could well have been a Shakespearean comedy. The AITA wanted Bhupathi and Paes to pair up and give India the best shot at a men's doubles title. Paes, at the time, was the highest-ranked Indian

---

*A legacy of the Age of Enlightenment, the motto 'Liberté, Egalité, Fraternité' (Liberty, Equality, Fraternity) first appeared during the French Revolution. It was written into the 1958 French Constitution.

player on the men's circuit sitting on the no. 3 spot with Radek Stepanek as a team, so the strategy was an eminently sensible one.

On the other hand, Bhupathi and Bopanna were playing the circuit as a team and were ranked no. 6 in the world. The two Indians refused to play in the doubles at the Olympics unless they were paired together. Pushed to a corner, in desperation the AITA asked Paes, with whom they had always had a cordial relationship, to partner young and untested Vishnu Vardhan, then ranked below 300 in the world.

Wearing national pride on his sleeve as always, and acutely aware that age and the opportunity to earn an Olympic medal were slipping away, Paes countered that he would do so, but only if he was given a shot at the mixed doubles title partnering Mirza. Bhupathi, going back on his promise to Mirza, agreed to step away from the mixed doubles, presumably because he thought there was greater chance of a medal with Bopanna. It could also well be that the clash of egos he and Paes had been involved in for years clouded his judgement. Be that as it may, while all this went on, no one considered consulting Sania Mirza, caught unawares in this pincer of egos and mismanagement.

Mirza finally drafted and issued a press release. It was a desperate cry for justice that would fall on ears deafened by the din of outsized egos.

It first talked about the hurt at the betrayal from her Grand Slam winning partner from three weeks before: 'Mahesh Bhupathi has firmly stood by his commitment to play together with his men's doubles partner, Rohan Bopanna, as he genuinely believed it was good for India. However, in the process, he sacrificed the commitment he made to me to try and win an Olympic medal together for India.' This was how the poignantly penned statement began. She then turned her sights on the administrators and Paes: 'As an Indian woman belonging to the twenty-first century, what I find disillusioning is the humiliating manner in which I was put up as a bait to try and pacify one of the disgruntled stalwarts of Indian tennis. While I feel honoured and privileged to have been chosen to partner Leander Paes, the manner and timing of the announcement reeks of male chauvinism where a two-time Grand Slam champion, who has been India's no. 1 women's tennis player for almost a decade in singles and doubles, is offered in compensation to partner one of the feuding champions purely in order to lure him into accepting to play with a men's player he does not wish to play with! This kind of blatant humiliation of Indian womanhood needs to be condemned even if it comes from the highest controlling body of tennis in our country.'

It was perhaps the hardest hitting press statement any Indian sportsperson has ever made. Alas, it was to no avail as the decisions had already been made. The end result of the whole unsavoury episode was absolutely predictable.

In the men's doubles event, the seventh-seeded Bhupathi and Bopanna lost tamely in straight sets in the second round to the unseeded French pair of Benneteau and Gasquet. The unfancied Paes–Vardhan pair put up much more of a fight, but suffered the exact same fate against the second-seeded French pair of Llodra and Tsonga.

In the mixed doubles, Paes–Mirza put the angst aside and progressed to the quarter-finals. But despite their best efforts, they lost 5-7, 6-7 to the formidable top seeds and eventual winners Victoria Azarenka and Max Mirnyi of Belarus.

The 2012 Olympics were destined to remain the most public and eminently avoidable black mark in the history of Indian tennis.

BACK ON THE GLORY TRAIL

Being a truly successful elite sportsperson is often not just about winning, but having the ability and the mental toughness to win again after being knocked down.

In his book, *Finding the Gaps: Transferable Skills to Be the Best You Can Be*, modern cricket's greatest umpire, Simon Taufel, a man who knows a thing or two about operating under pressure, talks about the concept of 'bouncebackability': 'I believe the majority of any sport is predominantly played out in the space between the ears. There are three places your mind can be—past, present or future.'

He then goes on to explain how when things go wrong, the human tendency is to focus on the past, feel sorry for yourself, harbour further negative thoughts, and go down a spiral. So from his own mistakes on the field, his advice is to go through the following steps—move on and don't beat yourself up mentally; focus on the correct and robust process; acknowledge that failure happened; accept it as a part of the learning process; let it go, talk about it to release the pent-up thoughts, and then don't dwell on it; visualise the right thing to do and then bounce back.

While it would take Sania Mirza time to get out of the mental scars of the situation leading up to and the disappointment of the Olympics, bounce back she would. And how!

Working through much of 2013 with multiple partners—Bethanie Matek–Sands, Liezel Huber, Flavia Panetta and Jie Zheng, Mirza finally teamed up with former world no. 1 Cara Black from Zimbabwe.

The Black–Mirza combine was a formidable one, but a Grand Slam title continued to elude them all year. Disappointing as that was, and much against the run of play so to speak, at the WTA Tour finals in Singapore in November 2014, the pair found themselves in the finals against a Taiwanese team to whom they had lost several times that year—Su-Wei Hsieh and Peng Shuai.

Sitting on the first row at the back of the court, I watched Mirza and Black play the doubles match of their lives. It was scintillating tennis—high on drama, high on adrenaline. The famed Mirza forehand was in full flow, executing brutally powerful net-kissing shots with Black waiting at the net to put away whatever managed to sneak back into their side of the court. The serves were curling away at speed from the Taiwanese pair. Mirza would later write, 'I played an absolute cracker of a match, perhaps one of my best, as we broke the record for the least number of games conceded while winning the WTA finals.'

They may not have won a Grand Slam together, but the 'mother of all Grand Slams', as the WTA Finals is often referred to in tennis, was theirs. As Cara Black announced her retirement from the sport, the pair could not have imagined a more fitting copestone to their partnership.

There was, however, a Grand Slam title in 2014 that had Mirza's name written on it. Putting the Olympics, and Bhupathi's betrayal behind her, Mirza teamed up with Bruno Soares of Brazil before the US Open that year. Mirza's powerful forehand and Soares' brilliance at the net would take them through the draw and the pair beat Santiago Gonzales and Abigail Spears to win the title at Flushing Meadows.

All this was leading up to only one thing—the no. 1 spot in the world doubles rankings. Three months after the win in Singapore, Sania Mirza came across Martina Hingis in the locker room at the Dubai Open. Both were at a loose end as far as a partner was concerned. Mirza talks about how later that night they met in her hotel room. 'We discussed tennis, our future plans and some of our goals.' At the end of the next tournament, the Doha Open, the two decided to play together. The rest as they say, is history.

The no. 1 spot that came in Charleston was a signal of bigger things to come. Partnering Martina Hingis, Sania Mirza marched into the finals of Wimbledon in 2015. Waiting for them on the Centre Court of the most coveted Grand Slam of all was the Russian pair of Elena Vesnina and Ekaterina Makarova.

At 5-7, 7-6 and 2-5 in the decider, Hingis–Mirza looked all but out of contention. But this time Mirza had as a partner a woman who had reached for the sky and touched it. She was the only one among the four who had experienced victory at this level of the sport. She had, against her name, not one, not two, but an incredible fourteen Grand Slam titles, five singles and nine doubles. She had also never lost in the finals of a Grand Slam event in this format. As she prepared to serve at 2-5 in the third set, Hingis turned to Mirza and said, 'I don't want to lose the final.'

She held her serve, the two returned everything that came their way on the Makarova serve, with Hingis flying through the air to volley a winner and break the Russian. Then Mirza held her serve and at 5-5, the chair umpire decided to cover the roof and turn on the lights. When they came back on court, the three-game-losing streak was clearly playing on the minds of the Russians. An unexpectedly ferocious backhand down the line winner from Mirza followed by an inside-out forehand cross-court from Hingis were enough to break Vesnina. Hingis served out the match using all her years of accumulated experience.

It had been an incredible few months for Sania Mirza. She had gone from becoming the first Indian woman to be ranked no. 1 in the world in doubles to her nation's first women's Grand Slam title holder at Wimbledon. As the pair held up the trophy, the anchor's stereophonic voice said those long-awaited words: '... and for the first time, Sania Mirza, Wimbledon Champion.'[194] No fairy tale could have been scripted better.

'Every time I step on the court, I'm doing things no Indian woman has done, in tennis or in sport, back home or in that part of the world,' Mirza said after the win. 'I would like to think that I've inspired a few girls to pick up tennis rackets—not just tennis rackets, but to do whatever they believe in which is out of the box, so to say. I think that everybody [in India] knows Wimbledon; even a person who doesn't know about tennis knows about Wimbledon.'[195]

The Hingis–Mirza pair would go on to capture two more Grand Slam doubles titles—the US Open in 2015 and the Australian Open in 2016. They also added the WTA Tour

Finals trophy to their cabinet in 2015, finishing the year as the World's no. 1 ranked doubles team. During this time they stitched together forty-four consecutive victories, matching the streak that Helena Sukova and Jana Novotna had put together in 1990.[196] It had been a dream run, but in late 2016, they decided to split as a pair, having achieved what they wanted to.

Hingis and Mirza remain close friends and about their time together Mirza tells me with emotion in her voice, 'In doubles I have had some great partners but I think Martina and me had the best partnership in more ways than one. We were able to achieve so much together that has never been achieved before. So she remains my favourite partner.'[197]

Preparing for the Second Coming

In 2010 Sania Mirza had, in her inimitable way, managed to create controversy by just being herself. She had announced to the stunned media of two perennially warring neighbours her engagement to Pakistani cricketer Shoaib Malik. Notwithstanding the hate mail and the media circus, the pair got married and continued to pursue their individual careers, which saw them reach individual highs after they got together.

In 2017 Mirza announced she was leaving the circuit to have a child. Then in late 2019, like Kim Clijsters and Serena Williams before her, she announced a comeback to the WTA circuit.

Just before the pandemic hit, Mirza was back on the tour. In her first tournament in early 2020 she partnered Nadia

Kichenok of Ukraine to win the Hobart International before bowing out of the Australian Open with a calf injury. Her sights, once again, were set on the Olympics. The COVID-19 crisis and the year's delay in the staging of the greatest sporting show on earth had given her the time to recover fully.

The dream that was so brutally shattered by ego and politics eight years ago, is clearly still alive. The fire burns within, but it would not, sadly, be enough to light the flames on the Olympic torch for this incredible woman from Hyderabad.

At Tokyo, in the first round, Sania teamed up with Ankita Raina, the next highest ranking Indian woman currently on the circuit, for the doubles. The pair ran through the first set against the Kichenok sisters from Ukraine without dropping a game. Sania was in sublime form, the forehand mastery in full display, with an inspired Ankita playing out of her skin. The Ukrainaian twins, nerves now settled, narrowly won the second set in a tie break.

In the decider, with the Indian pair up 5–3 and the former World No. 1 serving for the match, the match turned on its head. Sania put in a horrendous serving game, and was broken for the first time in the match. The Kichenoks leveled the set and won the final set 10–8 in the new final set tie breaker format.

A distraught Sania knew her Olympics dream was over, and with it, sadly, had gone India's chances at a medal for the foreseeable future.

In early 2022, much to the dismay of her fans around the world, Sania Mirza announced that 2022 was going to be her last year on the circuit. But in typical Mirza fashion, that announcement has been followed by an incredible run of form, indubitably fueled by a determination to exit in a memorable blaze of glory.

This became evident when, after partnering with multiple Grand Slam winner Rajeev Ram, Mirza advanced to the quarter-finals of the Australian Open before narrowly losing to Jaimee Fourlis and Jason Kubler, 4–6, 6–7. She followed that up a few weeks later with a semi-final appearance at the Qatar Open Women's doubles partnering with Lucie Hradecka of Czech Republic. At the Miami Open she made the quarter finals with Kirsten Flipkens.

In early April, Mirza and Hradecka stepped on to the court at Charleston, South Carolina. For Mirza, this was a poignant moment in her final year on the circuit. It was at Charleston that she had, for the first time, become the No. 1 doubles player in the world.

A week later, as Mirza and Hradecka stepped on to the court to face Andreja Klepac and Magda Linette in the trophy decider, the stars appeared to be aligned for the Indian to have a fairy tale ending. Unfortunately, that was not to be. Despite playing some excellent fighting tennis, the Indo-Czech pair would go down 2–6, 6–4, 0–1 (7–10) in yet another heart breaking tie-breaker.

While a third round exit at Roland Garros in the women's doubles and second round in the mixed was a disappointing outcome, Mirza herself, and every one of her fans, had eyes on what has always been considered by Indians as the greatest stage in tennis—Wimbledon.

Partnering with former World No. 1 Mate Pavic, Mirza set off on her quest to get her hands once again on her favourite Grand Slam trophy. With hard fought victories over some of the best mixed doubles pairs in the world capped by a quarter-finals triumph over fourth seeded Gabriela Dabrowski and John Peers, the Mirza-Pavic combine faced up against the second seeds Neal Skupski and Desirae Krwaczyk in the semi-finals. Once again however, disappointment was in store for Mirza as the pair went down with a blaze of defiance, 4–6, 7–5, 4–6. It was an emotional farewell from the crowd to a former champion as Mirza exited the No. 2 court at Wimbledon for the final time in her career.

With injuries plaguing her for the rest of 2022, she stayed silent about her impending retirement before finally announcing that the 2023 Australian Open would be her last Grand Slam event and she would retire from tennis the following month after the WTA tournament at Dubai, which is now her home.

In a scene straight out of a fairy tale, on 28th January 2023, thirty-six year old Sania Mirza appeared on Rod Laver Arena alongside her forty-two year old partner Rohan Bopanna to play the final of the Mixed Doubles event. In the stands were her father, son, and her entire extended family who had been her pillars of support. While the pair did not finally lift the trophy, as Mirza would have wished, their incredible run may just have sowed the Grand Slam dream in the next Sania Mirza, watching television in a far corner of India.

Sania Mirza can be justifiably proud of what she has achieved. The simple act of a seven-year-old from the city of Hyderabad picking up an oversized tennis racquet and sending a ball across the net on a tennis court has paved the way for seven hundred million of her gender to make the journey from impossible dreams to stunning reality.

MATCH POINT

THE FUTURE OF INDIAN TENNIS
WHAT DOES IT LOOK LIKE?

As a race we are handsomely endowed with hand-to-eye coordination, which is why so many of our youngsters excel naturally at ball sports like cricket, hockey, squash and tennis. Where we fail miserably is in the legs area. Of course, I speak for myself in this respect, but unhappily I am the norm rather than the exception. We are blessed with skill, but not with speed. We are crafty, but not mobile, not at any rate by international standards. Without being unduly immodest, if I had had Bjorn Borg's legs I could have been no. 1 in the world.[198]

—Vijay Amritraj

While the nation has basked in the glory of our achievements in the doubles format over the past couple of decades, the story in singles, barring the early success of Sania Mirza, and Leander Paes' Atlanta Olympics medal, has been one of struggle and unfulfilled expectations.

In this section, before we sign off on the fascinating story of Indian tennis thus far, it would be remiss on me as the chronicler not to ruminate and indeed speculate about the future of the sport in the country. There has been overwhelming support from former players in the course of writing this book, and while the opinions expressed here are undoubtedly mine, they take into account the views of these players in laying out a likely path for the future.

It is undeniable that the modern game is very different from that played by the senior and junior Krishnan, or indeed, Vijay Amritraj. Therefore, before we turn our looking glass to the future, the immediate past and present that includes contributions of some very talented men and women who have laid the foundations for what is to come (even if their own careers in some cases pale in comparison to their more illustrious predecessors) needs to be acknowledged.

The Millenials*

Somdev Devvarman

As the sport has changed over the years and turned more physical, it has become imperative that the fitness of the players be such that it allows them to compete at the highest level, particularly in singles. It has indubitably been a major factor behind the struggles of Indian players through the years who have risen to a certain level on the back of their skills, but failed to sustain the momentum because of their fitness levels.

In 2008, this trend was bucked by a player born in the northeastern city of Guwahati in Assam, who grew up in

---

*Millenials in this context does not refer to those born in the new millennium but to those who emerged as India's tennis hopes in the new millennium.

Chennai (Madras) where he started playing tennis at the age of nine. That year, Somdev Kishore Devvarman, a student at the University of Virginia in the United States, stunned the Indian tennis diaspora by winning two successive NCAA singles titles in his junior and senior years. In his final year, his singles record was 44-1 at the NCAA Men's Tennis Championship.

The University of Virginia Today journal reported with the headline: *Devvarman Repeats as NCAA Tennis Singles Champion.* 'Devvarman ends the season with a 44-1 singles record, tying the school record for wins in a season he set a year before. He is believed to be the first NCAA Singles Champion to finish the season with one or fewer losses since UCLA's Jimmy Connors went undefeated in 1971. Since then, NCAA Champions have included Georgia's Pernfors, Stanford's John McEnroe, Stanford's Tim Mayotte and Texas's Kevin Curren, all of whom went on to be ranked in the world top twenty, but lost multiple times in college during their championship season.'

This was a remarkable achievement, and as was to be expected, Devvarman decided to turn professional on graduation from college. The one thing that already differentiated him from his seniors and peers on the Indian tennis scene was his superior fitness levels that more than made up for anything he may have lacked in the finer aspects of the sport.

A year later, coming into the Chennai Open as a wild card with an ATP ranking of 202, Devvarman threw Indian fans starved of singles achievements since the heydays of Leander Paes into a frenzy. He defeated in succession world no. 42 Carlos Moya of Spain, twice champion at the event, and world no. 25 Ivo Karlovic of Croatia. Devvarman then waltzed into the final after receiving a bye from the injured Rene Shuttler of Germany. There, Marin Cilic of Croatia would prove too good for the Indian, prevailing 6-4, 7-6. Later that year, twenty-year-old Cilic was to make his first Grand Slam quarter-finals at the US Open.

The 2010-11 period would be the period when Devvarman would come into his own as a tennis player on the international stage. Rising steadily through the rankings, he was making the main draws of the Grand Slams, but exiting in the early rounds. He ended 2010 with a break into the top hundred, becoming the first Indian male in the new millennium to do so.

During the year, while further success on the ATP Tour had continued to elude him, Devvarman had steadily become the crucial x-factor that Indian tennis had been looking for to lead the singles effort while playing for the flag. In October, he won the Commonwealth Games gold, beating Greg Jones of Australia in straight sets. A month later he picked up the singles title at the Asian Games and for good measure won the doubles as well, partnering compatriot Sanam Singh.

In 2011, Devvarman had some encouraging results on the ATP tour. At the Indian Wells Master 1000 event, he defeated world no. 22 Marcos Baghdatis of Cyprus in the second round and Belgian Xavier Malisse in the third round before bowing out fighting 5-7, 4-6 to world no. 1 Rafael Nadal in the fourth. At the Miami Masters 1000 event that followed, the Indian stunned Milos Raonic of Canada in straight sets before losing to world no. 6 David Ferrer of Spain in the third round.

In July that year, Somdev Devvarman achieved his highest ATP ranking. His world no. 62 rank was the best for an Indian male in singles since Ramesh Krishnan's no. 23 in 1985. It was, however, already becoming clear that while his fitness made Devvarman a hard competitor on artificial surfaces, on other surfaces, those with superior racquet skills made it difficult for him to be consistently effective. And his physically intensive game would soon take its toll, with a recurring shoulder injury forcing him to take a break in 2012.

In 2013, he made a comeback with his protected ranking of no. 85, but over the next two years, other than a few Challenger Tournament successes (he won the Delhi Open in 2014 and 2015), his career had fallen off the trajectory it had earlier appeared to be on.*

In 2017, at the age of thirty-one, having played his last ATP tour match at Indian Wells two years before, Somdev Devvarman announced his retirement from the sport with these words, 'I wanted to play for the right reasons. Playing for me was always super fun and passion, that was dying or slowing down.'[199]

---

*Protected Ranking: The ATP Rankings rules allow for an 'Entry Protection Petition' by an injured player 'when he is physically injured and does not compete in any tennis event for a minimum period of six months. The Entry Protection shall be a position in the FedEx ATP Rankings, as determined by the player's average FedEx ATP Rankings position during the first three months of his injury. The Entry Protection shall be in effect for either the first nine tournaments that the player competes in using the Entry Protection (excluding wild cards and entries as a Direct Acceptance with his current position in the ATP Rankings) or for the period up to nine months beginning with the first tennis event that the player competes in, whichever occurs first.

Yuki Bhambri

The man who followed Somdev Devvarman into the limelight and gave hope to fans that a bright future awaits Indian tennis was Yuki Bhambri from New Delhi.

In 2009, just as Devvarman was moving up the senior ranks, seventeen-year-old Bhambri burst into the scene winning the junior singles event at the Australian Open and becoming the first Indian male to occupy the Junior world no. 1 ranking after Leander Paes. Unlike Devvarman, whose game was dominated by his superior fitness and strong serve, Bhambri is much more of a counterpuncher from the back of the court. He is good player at the net when he comes in behind his ground strokes, and imparts heavy topspin on both forehand and backhand.

But the question that was being asked even as he transited from the junior to senior ranks was how his fitness would hold up at that level. That would soon be answered.

Bhambri's ATP career in the decade since he has been playing the senior circuit has been a matter of some disappointment given the high expectations he raised, notwithstanding the no. 83 ranking he reached in early 2018. Six first-round exits at the four Grand Slam events between 2015 and 2018, and a failure to come anywhere near the finals of any non-Challenger ATP tournaments is testimony to his yet unfulfilled promise.

The two factors that have held Bhambri back from making a mark at the highest level are those that have plagued Indian singles players down the ages—a relatively weak serve that cannot be hidden given today's brand of power tennis, and less than ideal physical fitness that has resulted in multiple injuries plaguing him throughout his career.

At twenty-seven, Yuki Bhambri is making another comeback from injury, and with age on his side given the late blooming and longevity of players on the circuit, there is still hope that he will deliver to some degree on the promise he showed a decade ago.

Ramkumar Ramanathan

In 2017, at the Antalya Open in Turkey, Ramanathan caused a major upset by defeating top seed and then world no. 8 Dominic Thiem in straight sets before losing to Marcus Baghdatis of Cyprus in the quarter-finals. The following year he reached his first World ATP Tour Final at Newport in the United States, losing to Steve Johnson in the final. It was the first ATP Tour finals appearance by an Indian since Devvarman in 2011. His ranking that year touched an all-time high of 111.

Ramanathan, now twenty-five, is one player who has had some financial support from his local association while making the transition from talented junior to consistent senior. The TNTA has consistently backed him, and his training in Barcelona is partly funded by the association. However, currently languishing at 186 in the ATP rankings, Ramanathan needs to turn around his fitness issues and display more consistency in the coming years if he wants to make it to the next level.

Prajnesh Gunneswaran

Thirty-year-old Prajnesh Gunneswaran is no spring chicken, but in a world of tennis dominated by three geniuses in their thirties, he is one of the few Indians who continues to keep fans excited. In April 2019, Gunneswaran reached no. 75 in the world, the highest since Devvarman did almost eight years ago.

At that point, Vijay Amritraj, asked about his views on the young man, opined, 'He is a big boy, serves well and strikes the ball with good aggression, especially on the forehand. I thought he had good potential but the question is two parts: whether he has the ability to work the way you need to work, and whether he is able to remain fit to put in that kind of work which is needed.'[200]

Anand Amritraj, then the Davis Cup coach, added in the same interview, 'We Indians tend to mature late and Prajnesh being a leftie, has that slight bit of advantage too as we do not see too many of them on the tour. He already has a big game with his serve and the groundies. To move to the next stage, you need to move better—this is where most of the Indian boys struggle against the westerners. He also needs to be strong so that when he has somebody down, he should be able to put them away. Third—he should become better at finishing off the points. He gains the advantage through his groundstrokes, needs to get more confident at the net and work towards cashing in on the advantage.'

Eighteen months on, Gunneswaran has dropped back to no. 142. Talking about the 2019 season, he said, 'What I did not like about it (the 2019 season) is that I got injuries at the wrong time which did not allow me to climb further up the ladder. I wasn't in great shape during the clay season. I had a shoulder injury some weeks before the French Open and so going into it, I had not practised too much, which is why I was beaten badly in the first round.'

With the forced break from the COVID-19 crisis, one hopes that Gunneswaran will heed the words of the Amritraj brothers, work on his fitness, and come back to give Indian fans plenty to cheer about in the coming years.

Sumit Nagal

In August 2019, a success-starved nation turned on their television sets to watch a first-round encounter at the US Open. This was an unusual move in itself, notwithstanding the fact that it was Roger Federer making his appearance on the Arthur Ashe stadium, for most Indian tennis fans typically start following the tournament's progress after the first week. But this was a special occasion, for lining up against Federer on the other side of the net was young Sumit Nagal, a twenty-two-year-old few had heard of before.

Two hours later, Nagal was the toast of the nation. While he hadn't upset Federer, which was always going to be a tall ask from a player who had been ranked outside the Top 350 before the year started, he had done better than any other Indian before him in talking a set off one of the greatest players in the history of the sport.

Federer would say after the match, 'I think he knows what he can bring. That's why I think he is going to have a very solid career. I think his game is based on being really consistent. He moves well, moves the ball around well. Sort of very much a clay-courter.'

In 2020, Nagal bettered his Grand Slam record by making it into the second round of the US Open. Here he ran into the eventual winner, a man in the form of his life—Dominic Thiem. A straight sets exit was the result for the young Indian, but once again his composure and game provided ample hope for the future in a sport where champions are increasingly blossoming late.

Born in Haryana, the twenty-five-year-old Nagal is ranked a disappointing 468 in the world at the time of writing this and has failed to qualify for the 2022 US Open main draw. He has had a few successes, but has miles to go if he is to move to the next level of the sport and make an entry into the top fifty at some point, and perhaps go higher. While many players, who are at the highest global levels now peaked later, after showing a lot of early promise, at twenty-five, such opportunities may be getting harder to come by for Nagal, particularly given the three-hundred place drop since that match against Federer.

As Abhinav Bindra, a man who knows what it takes to be the best in the world, had warned amidst the post-US Open euphoria at the time, 'While we rightfully celebrated the spirited show of Sumit Nagal, let's not lose perspective. We need a lot of work to do to produce a single Grand Slam champion from India. Sumit shows us we can; we must follow through on it by creating champions.'[201]

Nagal still has age on his side, but will need significant help from coaches to improve his game to consistently beat top players, and sponsors to stand by him during this period.

If he does make it to the top fifty, and if we, as a nation, rally behind him on this journey, Sumit Nagal may just be the spark the sport needed at this time to reignite the flame of hope for Indian tennis.

SECURING A FUTURE FOR INDIAN TENNIS

The pages and chapters that have come before this have shown that Indian tennis has indeed had a long history and been blessed by a series of enormously gifted players who have achieved much. Ramanathan Krishnan in the 1960s picked up from where the likes of Mohammad Sleem, Sydney Jacobs and Ghaus Mohammad had taken the sport in undivided India, and set the bar very high in singles. In the next two decades, only Vijay Amritraj and Ramesh Krishnan came close to touching it.

In the 1990s, Leander Paes chipped in with his Olympic bronze, before Sania Mirza rewrote the history of women's tennis in the country with a Top 30 ranking, not seen since the days of Ramesh Krishnan. In recent decades Paes, Mirza and Bhupathi have set the gold standard in the doubles format that every Indian tennis player hereon must aspire to reach. The likes of Yuki Bhambri and Sumit Nagal present droplets of hope for the parched throats of current Indian fans.

But what about the future? What hopes does it hold out? Indeed, does the sport in India have a future, and what would it take to secure a brighter one?

These are questions I revisited every day during the course of chronicling the story of Indian tennis. The answers to my questions from past players, ranged from guarded hope to despair. But that is human nature, for without divergent views, we would not be the creatures that we are. The picture that emerged at the end is an interesting one, and should give hope to the fans of the sport in the country.

BUILDING A TENNIS 'SYSTEM' IN INDIA

Rafael Nadal is one of the greatest tennis players the world has ever seen. It is a well-known fact that his uncle and lifelong coach Toni Nadal is significantly responsible for what Nadal has achieved today. But Uncle Toni could not have done this on his own, for there is a system in play behind it.

Often hidden in the oversized shadow of Nadal's success are the deeds of Carlos Moya and David Ferrer, two outstanding Spanish tennis players. In fact, Spain's sporting success in the past thirty-plus years is not confined to tennis alone. Anyone who has followed Spanish football or indeed any other sport will tell you that the 'golden age' of Spanish sport was born that day in 1988 when the ADO Plan, an initiative to aid elite athletes, was launched to provide a significant financial shot in the arm to sports in the country. The target was twelve medals at Barcelona 2002, up from four in Seoul the year the ADO plan was launched. It was an ambitious target. Since 1900, Spanish athletes had earned only twenty-six medals at sixteen Olympic Games.

By the time the Games closed in 1992, Spanish players had stood on the podium an incredible twenty-two times that fortnight. As *El Pais* would write twenty-five years after the Barcelona Games, 'Suddenly, those little old Spaniards were capable of competing at the highest level of sport. For fifteen days, an entire nation was left rubbing its eyes in disbelief. And sponsors—both public and private—gained new insights into the enormous potential of sports as a vehicle for advertising. Today, twenty-five years later, a Spain brand exists.'[202]

For a country that had reeled from death and destruction under a dictatorship for almost forty years (1939-75), it signalled a new future. The investment made through the ADO plan and the spectacular pay off rubbed off on the entire system, and sport would become the platform that gave pride and hope back to an entire nation. The subsequent World and European Cup successes in football united the nation, and just around the same time, Rafael Nadal stepped up to conquer the world of tennis.

This is not only the story of Spain but of every country that has achieved success in sports. Great Britain transformed the sporting landscape before London 2012. From thirty medals and tenth place at Athens in 2004, it went to sixty-five medals and third place in the standings at London in 2012. Andy Murray won both the Olympic Gold and Wimbledon that year. Coincidence? Probably not.

Closer to home, the investment of BCCI in cricket, the starting and success of IPL and the grassroots efforts put in over the past decade and more have transformed the sport in India and made the nation the cricketing powerhouse of the world. The tennis story has been a bit different in how it has played out.

Why did the two decades between 1955 and 1975 bring Indian tennis so much success? Undoubtedly some unbelievable talent came to the fore around the same time—in the form of Krishnan, Lall and Mukherjea. But it wasn't all due to individual effort. Credit must go in equal measure to the Rajkumari Amrit Kaur Coaching Scheme and the efforts of the Calcutta South Club as well as the AITA, in facilitating the Indian Winter Circuit that brought the best players in the world to India over those two decades.

Sadly, that was not to last.

Ramanathan Krishnan, writing in 1999, was not mincing words when talking about the discord between the administrators and players in *A Touch of Tennis*. 'I believe the player/administrator divide will remain. The two can never play from the same side of the net. I am talking from fifty years' experience, not out of bitterness, but merely matter-of-factly. There is always an element of suspicion, mistrust and ego-propelled nastiness.'[203]

From Vijay Amritraj to Mahesh Bhupathi, from Sania Mirza to Somdev Devvarman, the vocal critics of the body that manages tennis in India have been many.

Amritraj wrote in his book *Vijay* in 1990, 'It is impossible to escape the fact that Indian tennis has laboured under a yoke called R.K. Khanna for much of the last twenty-five years ... "Useless" is perhaps too gentle a word to use in describing the way Khanna used to run Indian tennis in the late Sixties and early Seventies.'[204]

Two decades later, in 2012, Mahesh Bhupathi would remark scathingly about Anil Khanna, the senior Khanna's son, who now ran the AITA. 'Khanna has redefined the term divide and rule. The AITA and its dictatorial attitude and its administration are harmful for the future of Indian tennis.'[205] Clearly, as far as the relationship between Indian tennis' administrators and players are concerned, it has been status quo for the past few decades.

There have indeed been others like Leander Paes who have worked inclusively with the AITA, settling differences away from the public eye, and Vishal Uppal who maintains that dialogue and settling of differences offline rather than in the media is the right way forward. But inarguably, the AITA and the government have done little to build a system and proactively arrange for sustainable financial backing of the sport in the country along the lines of Great Britain or Spain.

One of the major reasons why Indian players struggle to move up the ranking ladder is that there are not enough opportunities to collect points. In 2019, there were just two Challenger tournaments held in India, hosted by TNTA in Chennai and MSLTA in Pune. In the absence of more opportunities at home, players have to travel abroad, which is expensive, and they rarely have funding available. Across the spectrum of players I spoke to during the course of writing this book, including the likes of Nandan Bal and Nitin Kirtane, every single one lamented the lack of opportunity of playing abroad because of their financial limitations. The problem has been an endemic one for more than a century in Indian Tennis.

On 14 June 1915, *The Pioneer*, one of India's oldest newspapers, carried a piece titled 'Lawn-Tennis Form in India'. Parts of it are worth reproducing here:

'There are no first class players in India. Yet, if the best players in India are only second class, there are nonetheless among them three, or, possibly, four players who are essentially first class, in that they have been or would be, with adequate practice, in the first rank in English tournament play. These players are precluded from reaching first class form in India, because such form requires continued practice against first class players, and on a first class surface. Neither of these conditions obtain in India.'

It is a sad reflection on the failure of our ability to set things right in over a century so that the talent that is latent, and often on display when the opportunities are provided, are wasted by the collective incompetence of our administrators.

The constant, and indeed justified refrain is that the AITA fails to take responsibility for the growth of the sport in the way the BCCI or AIFF does. In that context, it is hardly surprising that the government would not go out of its way to support a sport whose administrators run it without the dynamism that one would expect. Vishal Uppal, one of the players who see more value in working together with the AITA rather than playing the blame game, asked me, 'Where will the association get the money from?'[206]

While that may echo the belief held by the AITA, getting sponsors into the sport and taking the lead in organising tournaments in the country has to be the primary responsibility of administrators who run the sport. In the same conversation, Uppal also told me that after the AITA gave the 'blessings' for him to organise a tournament in early 2020 (which had to be subsequently cancelled because of the COVID-19 crisis), the $10,000 corporate sponsorship needed had to be arranged by Uppal himself. It's not something that surprised me, for Indian corporate involvement in tennis has been largely muted in recent times, the returns from visible investments in cricket and other team sports undoubtedly appropriating the lion's share of the available resources.

Seven decades ago, in the difficult years after independence, two men, Ganesh Dey and Anadi Mukherjee, sitting in Calcutta at the South Club, thousands of miles away from the two epicentres of world tennis at the time—Europe and the United States, transformed India into the world's 'Winter Circuit', bringing the greatest players in the world to play in small centres across the country with Calcutta as the base. It improved immeasurably the standard of Indian tennis, and the likes of Naresh Kumar, Ramanathan Krishnan, Premjit Lall and Jaidip Mukherjea erupted onto the world stage.

A hundred years on, even if it cannot take the responsibility for discovering or coaching new players, the AITA can perhaps help the cause of the sport in the country by organising a series of tournaments that would give players the opportunity to earn points and face meaningful competition without the expense of months of foreign travel and the other costs involved. Surely, the genuine intent of an association in securing corporate sponsorship for the sport, were that to be demonstrated in action, is bound to succeed more than individual efforts?

Sania Mirza must count among the greatest athletes this country has produced, male or female. Her opinions have always been as fearless as her forehand, their clarity unblemished by political correctness. She sums it all up when she tells me:

> Whoever has made it until now, whether it's Ramesh or Vijay or Ramanathan Krishnan or Leander, Mahesh or myself, has made it by themselves. They have not come out of a system. So this question (about the lack of a system) would have been valid thirty years ago and even fifteen years ago. It is and has always been an individual effort and there has not been a

system in place to help these players financially or mentally or just coaching-wise to give them someone they can go to. Unfortunately, that is the truth of it.[207]

She echoes the sentiments of most of her predecessors and peers. Anand Amritraj had said much the same a few years ago. 'The boys from Tamil Nadu—Prajnesh, Ramkumar, Sasikumar Mukund (India's no. 1, 3 and 4, respectively, in the world rankings)—all three have done it pretty much on their own. Vijay and I did it on our own, so did the Krishnans. It's all individual effort, effort by the parents, it has nothing to do with the federation.'[208]

Vijay Amritraj emphasized in a recent conversation with me how expensive of a sport tennis is and the difficulty of nurturing and launching players at the highest level at a personal level. Astute businessman that he is, he used words that will resonate with today's generation: 'There is no getting away from the fact that it is the highest risk venture you could invest in if you look at a young tennis player as a startup.'

But if families don't come forward or are unable to, and a system is not forthcoming, we find alternatives in the undying spirt of Indian innovation, often derided by the term 'jugaad'. In the case of Indian sports, that has come in the form of tennis academies that were kicked off by the Amritraj brothers' BAT initiative and its success with Leander Paes, and limited private or corporate involvement with the likes of JSW Sports and Olympic Gold Quest who support elite athletes across sports.

Today, yesteryear stars from Ramesh Krishnan to Mahesh Bhupathi, Nandan Bal to Enrico Piperno and Sania Mirza run their own academies. Bhupathi has a valid point about growing and supporting tennis at the grassroots when he says, 'At the end of the day it is only when you concentrate on the eight- to ten-year old athletes and provide them with the right guidance and support that India will start churning out more and more top athletes.'[209]

Ramesh Krishnan tells me, 'You can try and create a good environment and give as many youngsters a chance as possible. Hopefully, you can keep improving the base level and if you can find an extraordinary talent, the chances of him blossoming are that much better.'[210]

Mirza agrees. 'If we don't have a few more champions coming out and playing at this level, then the chances are that tennis in India will go backwards. Which is why we are all starting our tennis academies to keep the legacy of tennis alive. We don't want tennis to go back to where it was twenty years ago. We want it to move forward and hopefully one of these girls and boys will take the next steps and make the next jump.'[211]

One can only hope this will be enough.

Emergence of a Fitter Breed of Players

Tennis has changed materially in the past few decades. It is now a much faster sport with only the players who are supremely fit surviving at the highest level.

Novak Djokovic is today the fittest player on the men's circuit. But for years, he was a deemed a talented player whose potential was always greater than his achievements. He was in the ATP top 10, but he was more famous for his collapses in crucial matches than winning them. Djokovic repeatedly withdrew from matches when the going got tough, his opponents putting it down to lack of fitness when they were being nice, and a lack of toughness in their nastier moments.

But in 2011 all that changed when he put together what was one of the greatest single seasons in the history of men's tennis, winning three Grand Slam titles and finishing at no. 1. What had changed was fitness.

Djokovic talks about it in his book, *Serve to Win*. It was July 2010, at a tournament in Croatia, and Igor Cetojevic, M.D., a holistic practitioner from my native Serbia, was explaining to me that he thought he knew why I'd fallen apart so many times in the past, and how I could change my diet, my body, and my life for the better. When my blood test (suggested by the doctor) returned, the results were shocking: I was strongly intolerant to wheat and dairy, and had a mild sensitivity to tomatoes as well. 'If you want your body to respond the way you'd like it to, you will need to stop eating bread,' Cetojevic said. 'Stop eating cheese. Cut down on tomatoes.' 'But Doctor,' I replied. 'My parents own a pizza parlour!'[212]

A diet change and a fitness regime tweak led to the emergence of a new Novak Djokovic, who, along with two other geniuses of his time, equally conscious of the need to remain supremely fit—Rafael Nadal and Roger Federer, would go on to dominate men's tennis as no trio had ever done before.

Closer to home, fitness, unfortunately, has always been an almost insurmountable problem for Indian tennis players.

Ramanathan Krishnan was born at a time when he didn't

have access to scientific fitness regimes, but on his father's advice, dragging the tennis court roller behind him had built his core back and thigh muscles. Speed would always remain an issue. 'Krish, you have to start chasing girls to be able to run faster on court,' Jack Arkinstall had once joked with him. But given the times he played in, Krishnan got away with this weakness.

By the time Vijay Amritraj came on the scene, things had already changed a bit. Amritraj would write in *Vijay*, 'As a race, we are handsomely endowed with hand-to-eye coordination, which is why so many of our youngsters excel naturally at ball sports like cricket, hockey, squash and tennis. Where we fail miserably is in the legs area. Of course, I speak for myself in this respect, but unhappily I am the norm rather than the exception. We are blessed with skill, but not with speed. We are crafty, but not mobile, not at any rate by international standards. Without being unduly immodest, if I had had Bjorn Borg's legs I could have been no. 1 in the world.'

John McEnroe's famous rant at the US Open in 1981 while struggling to get past Ramesh Krishnan in the quarter-finals on his way to the title, 'The guy serves at ten miles an hour and I still can't return it,' would perhaps never have come to pass in the modern age. As Amritraj tells me, 'Ramesh with his serve would probably not have got to where he did, if he was playing today.'[213]

By the 1990s, the need for greater fitness was beginning to hit home, and Leander Paes would emerge as the notable exception to the Indian failing on this front. With a doctor father as his mentor, fitness and understanding his body would become a lifelong obsession. The fact that he appeared at Grand Slam events at the age of forty-seven, and dreamt of the Olympic podium when he was forty-eight, is testimony to the fact that 'Indianness' is not an excuse for a lack of fitness. Devvarman showed that fitness can make a huge difference and Mirza acknowledged it as a weakness that held her back in her early years. The fact that India today is much more conscious as a nation of watching their diet and remaining fit for longer bodes well for the future of the sport.

BROADBASING THE APPEAL OF TENNIS

But in the end, the real future of an individual sport in a country is determined not merely by the facilities that exist but the inherent talent in the athletes themselves and the level of fitness that they achieve. It is as importantly a function of how many play and follow the sport.

It will come as no surprise to the many who believe that Indians have an obsession with cricket—travel platform Booking.com produced a study in 2019 that claimed forty-two per cent of Indian cricket fans would cancel their honeymoon if it clashed with their preferred team playing a big game[214]—that almost 50 per cent of the population at about 700 million follows the sport, with the Indian subcontinent making up 90 per cent of the global fan base, according to a 2018 ICC market research report.[215]

Football, a sport that has brought India far less success over the years, has 216 million people tuning in to watch the Indian Super League on television at the last count. In February 2017, the government, together with the All-India Football Federation, launched the Mission 11 Million under which football would be introduced and played in twelve thousand schools in thirty-seven cities across the country.[216]

So what about tennis, long derided as a 'rich man's sport' in India?

Contrary to all that one believes, the *ITF Global Tennis Report 2019*, the most comprehensive report ever published on the sport, supported by unprecedented data collection from 195 countries that play tennis, comes as a beacon of hope for the sport in the country.[217]

The report finds that of the 87 million tennis players in the world as reported by the various national associations, India accounts for 9.2 per cent—a staggering eight million players, two million more than cricket. There is more. The report finds that there are almost 500,000 tennis courts globally, of which 5 per cent are in India, ranking us sixth in the world behind USA, China, Germany, France and Japan in the availability of courts.

The problem on the other hand, as highlighted by this report, is that in India, while competent players are emerging from the grassroots—the country had twenty-four players among the top 250 juniors in the world—the number dropped off dramatically in the top 100. As importantly, the talent is disappearing from the courts at an early age.

Anand Amritraj said recently, 'At under-14 Indians can compete with anybody. At under-18 we are nowhere. We need more players at the grassroots level.'[218]

Zeeshan Ali was quoted in the same article, saying, 'In India, very few (top juniors) turn pro. Lot of juniors lack the financial support.' Both perspectives are valid and important to consider.

The struggle to transition from the junior to senior ranks is something every tennis player goes through. Very few make it, and in India's case that percentage has been lower than most. Ramesh Krishnan, Leander Paes and Yuki Bhambri have all been junior singles Grand Slam champions, but have found it impossible to repeat the same results at the senior level.

Krishnan came closest in terms of ATP ranking, and he tells me about transition: 'Transitioning from juniors to the senior ranks is tricky business. And it continues to be so. In fact, it is more so now with players well into their thirties performing well and staying on top of the rankings. While you say things have evolved in our society, let us not forget that they are evolving elsewhere as well. At the moment, tennis is being dominated by Europe and a youngster from India is at a big disadvantage. The cost of producing a world-class player has increased manifold.'[219]

I recently had an interesting conversation with Vijay Amritraj. He pointed out that since the BAT was shut down after seventeen years of producing top quality players, there have been no equivalent centres of tennis excellence that have come up in the country over the past four decades.

I asked Vijay why he thinks that is the case. He said: 'I genuinely have no idea. MRF spoke to us about our methods that had been so successful and set up the MRF Pace Foundation. We all know what that has achieved. Britannia had a good experience with BAT and MRF with the Pace Foundation. So why would other corporates not want to do it?'

I asked if there were no other channels for growing tennis

talent in India in a sustainable way. And to that Vijay's response was clear: 'There are so many examples of systems to follow. There is the US one, the Swedish one, the Spanish one. But for us, the only way to produce high quality singles players has been the strong support of families—the Krishnans, the Amritrajs, the Mirzas. And then there was BAT which created an ecosystem that picked up talented youngsters and took care of all their needs—food, medical, educational, religious, fitness, alongside their tennis. Then players like Leander Paes and others emerged to become Junior Grand Slam winners, Junior Asian Champions.'

Be that as it may, the conclusions we can draw about the future, based on the analysis in this section, give hope for the future.

The new golden age of Indian tennis is drawing to a close with the inevitable retirement of Leander Paes, Sania Mirza and Rohan Bopanna in the first half of this decade. The rise of a Sumit Nagal and the coming of age of Prajnesh Gunneswaran, Ankita Raina and Rajkumar Ramanathan, and the expected return to the highest level of Yuki Bhambri, are signs that the sport has continuity.

To build from here, the fact that India has a large pool of players participating in the sport, a significant number of courts available for them to play on and the legends of the recent past stepping up with their academies to provide the coaching and facilities needed to make the move to the next level are big positives. But we have to keep in mind what Vijay Amritraj said in signing off his latest conversation with me: 'None of the ecosystem that BAT built four decades ago exists today, despite the fact that there are far more opportunities—possible sponsors, CSR budgets, etc. ... Just individual academies won't do it. This is why it's hardly a surprise to see where Indian Tennis is today. Even today if someone started a BAT equivalent, there is a good chance we can create singles players who emerge with the ambition and ability to win a Grand Slam or a Davis Cup, which was the dream of every one of us who started playing the sport and were successful at it.'

The AITA needs to play their part by being proactive rather than largely reactive as they have been in the past. Corporates need to use their corporate social responsibility (CSR) funds to build champions of the future, and at the same time through sponsorships, support tournaments in the country that would enable Indian players to gain vital points needed. Tennis fans need to be patient, and they will be rewarded.

From Mohammed Sleem to Ghaus Mohammad, from Krishnan to Amritraj to Krishnan, from Leander Paes to Sania Mirza, tennis in India has gone from strength to strength and provided us with wonderful champions. The journey from Mohammed Sleem's world no. 7 singles ranking in 1921 to Krishnan's rise to no. 3 three decades later, to Vijay Amritraj, Asia's greatest and most successful singles player in the Open Era, and thirty-seven Grand Slam doubles titles between Leander Paes, Mahesh Bhupathi, Sania Mirza and Rohan Bopanna has been a difficult but glorious one.

The future will undoubtedly be brighter given the efforts in place to elevate the status and infrastructure of the sport. And it is but a matter of time before the first Indian at a Grand Slam event steps up to the podium to hold aloft the singles trophy. The wait for it may have been long, but will have been worth every moment.

ACKNOWLEDGEMENTS

To pen the history of a sport, the efforts to preserve whose past have thus far been somewhere between lukewarm to non-existent, was trying, to say the least. As a people, we in India are not good at preserving our past, but when it comes to a sport that has largely received stepmotherly treatment over the years, the information that does exist is largely confined to private collections or closely guarded newspaper archives.

I have been relentless in my efforts to track down and extract accounts that had been lost to us and tell stories of players we have forgotten, except for the names which are parroted by numerous websites without any attempt at researching their deeds. But this effort would have been largely fruitless but for the unstinting support and help of more people, from former tennis players to journalists to writers to friends and family, than I can possibly thank in this section.

Nonetheless, here it goes. If I have missed anyone the fault is entirely mine and you can rest assured that will be rectified in my next book.

My wife Anisha—She read every chapter as it was written

and gave me invaluable feedback about the content, style, length and flow. I followed a simple rule—any chapter which failed to hold her attention was re-written, and read immeasurably better for the changes. Olu, our beautiful canine daughter, lay patiently by her side wagging her tail in agreement. I like to believe the best chapters received her 'woof' of approval.

Rohit Beri—A pillar of support for my writing from the day I started. This journey to my sixth book would have been far more difficult but for his belief that writing was what I was born to do. I admit I have been a disappointment thus far, as I continue to avoid starting the fiction journey which he has long been convinced is my real calling, but I promise that I shall get to it soon, Rohit. Keep the faith, my friend!

Milind Wagle—Commentator, autograph hunter, sports history enthusiast, and most importantly, a friend and guide who went out of his way to connect me to the former tennis players who have provided such tremendous insights for the book. I am humbled by Milind's faith in me as a researcher and writer and forever grateful for his unstinting help at every stage that I needed it.

Ramanathan Krishnan and Ramesh Krishnan—This father-son duo, two of the greatest tennis players India has produced, have been a bedrock of support from the day I first reached out to Ramesh, thanks to a kind introduction from Nandan Bal. Ramesh told me not to travel from Singapore to Chennai (which I was about to do) to spend time with the two Krishnans, but instead write in and ask whatever I needed to know and he would ensure it was answered. Over the next few months, we went back and forth several times and the promptness and thoroughness with which the questions were answered, and valuable insights provided, was simply overwhelming. I am particularly indebted to the deep insights and crystal-clear views of Ramanathan Krishnan on the sport, his own game, and his seniors and peers. Thank you, sir!

Naresh Kumar—The few hours that I spent with the grand old man of Indian tennis at his home in Kolkata will forever be precious. His photographic memory of players and matches from decades ago at the age of ninety-three, the stories that he has to tell and the insights only someone with his breadth of experience can provide helped me recreate a time in Indian tennis that has all but been lost. I can only hope I have done justice to the stories he shared.

Dr Vece Paes—The Doc (as the world of sport knows him) invited me to his home in Mumbai and surprised me with Leander's presence, a bonus I was not expecting. I have rarely spent a more delightful evening discussing everything from tennis to writing to swapping Calcutta memories, than I did with the entertaining father–son duo. An abiding memory will remain—the thirty minutes or so I just listened to a dialogue between the two discussing how Leander needed to remain physically fit to lengthen his career and the changes he possibly needed to make to his racquet specifications to increase efficiency.

Leander Paes—While I would have loved to get more insights from his own career than he was willing to provide, given he intends to pen his own account someday, I thank Leander for the lovely childhood memories including hitting balls and interacting with Premjit Lall at the South Club which helped me get a better picture of Lall. I also owe Leander one for demonstrating to me a couple of shots at the net that have helped me enhance my reputation socially as a much improved doubles player. After all, there is something to be said for learning net tricks from one of the greatest doubles players of all time!

Sania Mirza and Imran Mirza—It was a pleasure interacting with Sania and her father Imran, who were professional to the core and extremely helpful and prompt in answering the questions I had. Sania's precise and insightful answers, in keeping with her straight shooting self I have always respected, undoubtedly enriched the stories I tell.

Nandan Bal and Enrico Piperno—Two former greats of the sport in India, they gave their time and insights generously and put me in touch with others in the fraternity. But for this chain of introductions, this book would never have been completed.

A special shout out to Enrico Piperno for sharing rare personal photos from the famous Frejus Davis Cup victory against France which enrich the chapters that speak of the tie.

Seema Misra and Gaurav Misra—The daughter and son (and a former national champion himself), respectively, of the great Sumant Misra, were so generous in the time they spent with me and the photos from the personal albums and rare newspaper cuttings they shared that helped enrich the chapter on the early greats of the sport in India.

I owe a debt of gratitude to Phillip Jacob, the grandson of Sydney Jacob, India's first Grand Slam semi-finalist and one of the most incredible personalities the sport has thrown up. Philip reached out to me, and over the past few months that Westland and I have discussed this updated edition, he has selflessly shared from Sydney Jacob's personal scrapbook, priceless historical material that has been lost to us—newspaper articles from India and England, personal photographs from Davis Cup and the French Open, and trophies won at once prestigious tournaments in India, whose existence has been all but forgotten. As I told Philip, Sydney Jacob deserves a standalone book for his tremendous achievements on and off the court, and perhaps we shall get to work on it together someday!

Gulu Ezekiel—Journalist, writer, collector—a big shout-out to Gulu for his unstinting support for my writing, and sharing valuable articles from his enviable collection of sports magazines which are otherwise inaccessible. At least one chapter of this book would not have been completed without his inputs.

Rohit Brijnath—A writer whose ability to string words and emotions together continues to leave me awestruck, whose encouragement made me write this book and sage advice to 'tell a story on at least every third page' I have tried to follow. My thanks to Rohit also for lending me a few invaluable and rare books from his own collection for my research and suggesting people I ought to speak to for insights.

Nitin Kirtane—A man who is an inspiration for his love of the sport, continuing to play tennis at a high level and winning tournaments when most have switched to coaching or a social game or two. Nitin's insights into the financial struggles of making it from the domestic circuit into the international one was invaluable in shaping how I looked at this aspect of the sport's history in India.

Abbas Ali Baig—A true great of Indian cricket and one of the nicest men I have had the honour and privilege of calling a friend these past several years. His inputs on his uncle S.M. Hadi were invaluable in capturing the essence of the player and the times, and his recollection of playing Ghaus Mohammad in Hyderabad helped me complete the picture of this remarkable pre-independence giant of Indian tennis. At eighty-two, Abbas' memory and love for cricket and tennis continue to be a thing of joy.

My friends, Ananthakrishnan and Chinmoy Jena, have been enormously encouraging about all my books and indeed sports writing. The friends and family who have encouraged me to keep writing through my five books are too many to name, but you know who you are!

A sad goodbye and thanks to a dear friend K.K. Murali, one of the greatest supporters of my writing. A die-hard tennis fan, he was waiting eagerly for this book, but lost patience with life itself before it could see the light of day. Thanks for all the love and support over the years, Murali, and hope you enjoy this, sitting in a cosy corner of the celestial library.

Research sources—The gross inadequacy of the search engine when it comes to Indian tennis was fully exposed as I wrote this book, simply because of lack of digitisation. If it had not been for the yeoman work done by the likes of Tennisarchives.com (free) Ultimatetennisstatistics.com (free) and Britishnewspaperarchives.co.uk (paid), valuable insights and previously untold stories in this book would never have come to light. The *Sportstar* archives available online were useful reference for the past two decades of the sport. Thanks to Ayon Sengupta, editor, *Sportstar*, who offered access to

The Hindu archives if I could visit their Chennai offices. On the other hand, outright refusals to access their archives from some of India's other leading newspapers were disappointing indeed.

The newspapers, journals and websites who continue to support my writing: *Sportstar, The Cricketer Magazine, ESPN Cricinfo, Hindustan Times, The Print, News9 Live, Cricket Soccer, Cricket Writer, Firstpost, County Cricket Matters, Fountain Ink* and *The Roar.*

And finally, thanks to the editor of the original edition of this book, Karthik Venkatesh, publisher V.K. Karthika and the team at Westland who reposed faith in a entrepreneur-by-day and sports writer-by-night to pen the history of Indian tennis much before the release and eventual acclaim and awards for *Wizards,* the first book they had commissioned. Karthik has been a bedrock of support and become a good friend who was always there with an encouraging word, a reinforcing ego boost and new ideas whenever doubts crept in over the course of the many months of researching and writing this book.

I am delighted that Westland has emerged stronger and with even more determination to publish 'good' books across genres. I look forward to working together with Karthika V.K., Gautam Padmanabhan and the team on more collaborations across genres in the years to come.

NOTES

The Origins of Tennis

1. Gary Morley, '125 Years of Wimbledon: From Birth of Lawn Tennis to Modern Marvels,' CNN Sport, 22 June 2011, http://edition.cnn.com/2011/SPORT/tennis/06/14/tennis.wimbledon.125th.anniversary.museum/index.html

2. *The History of Tennis*, History Channel UK, https://www.history.co.uk/history-of-sports/history-of-tennis

3. Julian Norridge, *Can We Have Our Balls Back Please?: How the British Invented Sport*, 2008, London, Allen Lane (an imprint of Penguin Books)

4. Ibid.

5. The History of Tennis, History Channel UK, https://www.history.co.uk/history-of-sports/history-of-tennis

6. Elizabeth Wilson, *Love Game: A History of Tennis, from Victorian Pastime to Global Phenomenon* (Serpent's Tail, Profile Books Ltd., London, 2014)

7. Ibid.

8. Robert D. Osborn: *Lawn Tennis: Its Players and How to Play* London: Strahan and Company, 1881

SECTION ONE: THE BEGINNINGS OF THE SPORT IN INDIA

Indian Tennis: The Journey Begins (1885–1947)

9. This was renamed the Calcutta Cricket & Football Club after it moved from Eden Gardens to Ballygunge in 1950.

10. Cota Ramaswami, *Ramblings of a Game Addict*, 1966, Madras, Privately Published, p. 36

11. The 3rd Punjab Rifles was a part of the Indian Defence Force. During the First World War compulsory service was deemed necessary and the Indian Defence Force Act was passed in 1917. The volunteer corps became units of the IDF and were redesignated. European British men between the ages of eighteen and forty-one were subject to compulsory service within India. The IDF was disbanded after the war ended. 'Auxiliary Regiments,' Fibis, https://wiki.fibis.org/w/Auxiliary_Regiments and *The London Gazette*, 5 November 1918, https://www.thegazette.co.uk/London/issue/30992/page/13015/data.pdf

12. He would be 126 in the unlikely event he is reading this book today with a glass of whiskey by his side.

13. In 1956, Lew Had of Australia defeated fellow countryman Ken Rosewall in the final, 6–2, 4–6, 7–5, 6–4, to win the gentlemen's singles tennis title at Wimbledon.

14. University of Southampton Special Collections, https://specialcollectionsuniversityofsouthampton.wordpress.com/2017/03/08/celebrating-the-contribution-of-women-lady-swaythling/

Mohammed Sleem: The First Indian Tennis Superstar

15. This author found no recorded evidence of such a victory or indeed the existence of such a grass court tournament from the archives. Given the difficulty of obtaining old records, it is possible that his participation at Craigside in older records refers to the Welsh Covered Court Championships held in 1913. If that is the case, it can be said with some certainty that he came nowhere close to winning the title.

16. William T. Tilden, *The Art of Lawn Tennis*, 1950, Simon and Schuster, New York

17. Cota Ramaswami, *Ramblings of a Game Addict*, 1966, Madras, Privately Published, pp. 36-37

18.   The Tennis Base https://app.thetennisbase.com/?enlace=
playern&player1=SLEEM,%20MOHAMMED

19.   The 1924 records list the Gleneagles Championships
in Scotland as the only tournament of the name between
September 15-20. Sleem's victory has thus far always been
incorrectly recorded to be in the United States during those
dates. '1924 Results,' *Tennis Forum*, https://www.tennisforum.
com/1551-yearly-results/415450-1924-results-3.html

20.   *The Illustrated Sporting and Dramatic News*, 30 August 1924,
Courtesy—British Newspaper Archives, 30 August 1924.

21.   The Lawn Tennis Review by 'No Mad' in the *Portsmouth
Evening News*, 6 July 1934 Courtesy—British Newspaper
Archives, 6 July 1934.

22.   *Belfast Telegraph*, 14 July 1934, Courtesy—British Newspaper
Archives, 14 July 1934.

23.   *Yorkshire Post and Leeds Intelligencer*, 15 December 1933,
Courtesy—British Newspaper Archives

24.   Khushwant Singh, 'In the Name of God,' *The Telegraph, India*,
19 Aug 2006, https://www.telegraphindia.com/opinion/in-
the-name-of-god/cid/1025942

Sydney Montague Jacob: Civil Servant to Grand Slam Semi Finalist

25.   Donald Lehmann, 'Sydney Montague Jacob,' http://www.
myjacobfamily.com/favershamjacobs/sydneymontaguejacob.
htm

26.   Ibid.

Ghaus Mohammad Khan: The Pre-independence Giant of Indian Tennis

27.   'Veteran's Gallery: Ghaus Mohammed,' *Sportsweek*, 4 July
1974, p.

28. Rima Kashyap, 'There's No Power in Tennis Now Says Ghaus Mohammed', *The Sportsweek Annual*, 1973
29. Ibid.
30. *The Scotsman*, 1939, Courtesy—British Newspaper Archives, 1939.
31. In personal conversation with the author in 2019

SECTION TWO: INDIAN TENNIS COMES OF AGE

The Big Three: Independent India's First Men of Tennis— Dilip Bose, Sumant Misra and Naresh Kumar

32. Victory Tests: The five-match first-class series between the Australian servicemen based in Europe and the best available England side started less than a fortnight after Germany surrendered in May 1945. Three 'Tests' took place at Lord's, given the transport problems and the fact the only major usable venue immediately available. It's worth mentioning that Old Trafford, the scene of the final match, was still being repainted and renovated by prisoners of war on the eve of the game. The series was drawn 2-2, but legends like Keith Miller, who famously remarked about pressure on the cricket field— 'Pressure? There's no pressure in Test cricket. Real pressure is when you are flying a Mosquito with a Messerschmitt up your arse'—emerged from this series.
33. In 1946 and 1947, Wimbledon was held before the French Championships. The Australian Championships were held in January that year, becoming the first Grand Slam event to be held after the end of the war.
34. In private conversation on email with the author in September 2019
35. Ibid.
36. Ibid.

37. Tom Brown and Tyler Lee, *As Tom Goes By*, SCB Distributors, 2011

38. In private conversation with the author in November 2019

The 'Golden Age' of Domestic Tennis

39. Ramanathan and Ramesh Krishnan, *A Touch of Tennis—The Story of a Tennis Family*, 1999, Penguin Books India (P) Ltd. p. xxii

40. Ibid. p. 34

41. Dhiman Sarkar, 'South Club and Tennis: Still Love-all at 100,' *Hindustan Times*, 15 February 2020

42. William Tilden, *Aces, Places and Faults*, 1938, Robert Hale Limited, London

43. Georgina and Premjit Lall, *Down the Line—The Premjit Lall Story*, 1978, Rupa & Co, pp. 14-27.

44. Krishnan (1999)

45. Ibid. pp. 101-2

46. Lall (1978) p. 15

Ramanathan Krishnan: The King of Indian Tennis

47. Lall (1978) p. 28

48. *Coventry Evening Telegraph*, 10 March 1954, Courtesy—British Newspaper Archives, 10 March 1954, https://www.britishnewspaperarchive.co.uk/viewer/bl/0000769/19540310/289/0021

49. Krishnan (1999)

50. Ibid.

51. Ibid.

52. Ibid.

53. In personal conversation with the author in September 2019

54. Krishnan (1999)

55. In personal conversation with the author in September 2019

56. In personal conversation with the author in November 2019
57. In personal conversation with the author in September 2019

The 'Bengal Twins': Premjit Lall and Jaidip Mukherjea

58. Lall (1978)
59. Ibid. p. 1
60. Ibid. p. 2
61. Dhiman Sarkar, 'South Club and Tennis: Still Love-all at 100,' *Hindustan Times*, 15 February 2020
62. Sreemoy Talukdar, 'Trapped in a Body That Limited Him,' *DNA India*, 26 January 2009
63. Lall (1978), p. 87
64. Ibid. p. 33
65. In personal conversation with the author by email in September 2019
66. 'Wimbledon,' Twitter, https://twitter.com/Wimbledon/status/482216765804773376?s=20
67. In personal conversation with the author in September 2019
68. Krishnan (1999)
69. *Birmingham Daily Post*, Courtesy—British Newspaper Archives, 28 December 1966.

Vijay Amritraj: The 'A' of Tennis

70. Kent Hannon, 'Any Day Could Be a Vijay Day,' *Sports Illustrated*, 24 September 1973, https://www.si.com/vault/1973/09/24/618063/any-day-could-be-a-vijay-day
71. https://www.si.com/vault/1986/03/31/628966/tennis-player-vijay-amritraj-is-as-fine-on-film-as-he-is-on-the-court
72. Vijay Amritraj, *Vijay! From Madras to Hollywood via Wimbledon*, 1990, Libra Mundi, London, pp. 57-58.
73. Ibid. pp. 42-43
74. Ibid. p. 64

75. *Liverpool Echo*, Courtesy—British Newspaper Archives, 14 May 1974.

76. Dave Seminara, 'The Year the Davis Cup Felt Empty,' *The New York Times*, 28 November 2009, https://www.nytimes.com/2009/11/29/sports/tennis/29davis.html

77. Amritraj (1990), p. 66

78. *The New York Times*, Courtesy—New York Times Archives, 1 November 1974.

79. In personal conversation with the author in 2014 in Singapore

80. David McMahon, David, *Wills Book of Excellence: Tennis*, 1985, Orient Longman Limited, Hyderabad. p. 82.

81. Ragav S. Dipak and Keerthivasan K. 'Vijay Amritraj: How a Racquet Rocketd Him to Fame!' *Sportstar*, 29 January 2018

82. In personal conversation with the author in 2014 in Singapore

83. Krishnan (1999), p. 59

84. Amritraj (1990), p. 66

85. Ibid. p. 209

86. Michael Mewshaw, *Short Circuit: Borg, McEnroe and Connors, The Era of Bribes, Match-Fixing and Drugs*, 1984, 2011, Penguin Books, New York

87. In personal conversation with the author in 2014 in Singapore

88. Amritraj (1990), p. 101

89. Ragav S. Dipak and Keerthivasan K. 'Vijay Amritraj: How a Racquet Rocketed Him to Fame!' *Sportstar*, 29 January 2018

Ramesh Krishnan: The Master of Touch Play

90. Krishnan (1999)

91. Krishnan (1999), p. 159

92. In personal conversation with the author in November 2019

93. Ibid.

94. Ibid.

95. Krishnan (1999), p. 160

96. Amritraj (1990), p. 182

97. Krishnan (1999) pp. 143-4
98. Amritraj (1990), pp. 182-3
99. In personal conversation with the author in 2014 in Singapore
100. In personal conversation on email with the author in September 2019
101. Krishnan (1999), p. 124
102. In private conversation on email with the author in September 2019

The Almost Men

103. Balbir Singh, 'Keep Learning to Be a Successful Coach: Akhtar Ali,' *Sportswire*, 28 January 2012
104. In personal conversation with the author in September 2019
105. In personal conversation with the author in March 2020
106. Krishnan (1999)
107. Phalguna Jandhalya, 'An Ace in Showing Movies' *Business Standard*, 6 February 2013
108. 'S.P. Misra Is Non-playing Captain,' *The Hindu*, 5 July 2012
109. 'AITA Removes Zeeshan Ali, S.P. Misra from Senior Selection Committee,' *The Indian Express*, 15 November 2018
110. 'Gaurav Misra Edges Out Krishnan to Win National Tennis,' *Sports India*, 12 March 1972
111. In personal conversation with the author in March 2020
112. Dave Seminara, 'The Ghost of a Lost Final,' *Open (The Magazine)*, 26 November 2009
113. In personal conversation with the author in July 2019
114. Ibid.
115. In personal conversation with the author in June 2019
116. In personal conversation with the author in November 2019
117. Kamesh Srinivasan, 'Vishaal Uppal, Former Tennis Player and Now Coach, Talks about His Career and Why the Game Is Not All about Skill,' *The Hindu*, 12 August 2019
118. In personal conversation with the author in April 2020

SECTION THREE:
DOUBLES: INDIAN TENNIS FINDS ITS PLACE

What Is It about Indians and Doubles?

119. Sania Mirza, *Ace Against Odds*, 2016, HarperCollins Publishers, Noida, p. 120

120. In personal conversation with the author in November 2019

121. Pete Sampras, *A Champions Mind: Lessons from a Life in Tennis*, 2008, Crown Archetype, p. 84

122. All numbers include the ATP tour, Grand Slam events and Davis Cup.

123. Press Trust of India, 'I Have Guts to Go After My Goals: Paes' *The Hindu*, 12 September 2015

124. Mirza (2016), p. 41

125. The original quote from Sujit Mukherjee in his book *Playing for India* read: 'Perhaps some aspect of our national character, especially as evolved in almost a half century of new nationhood, finds fullest expression in handling the cricket ball in a hundred slow and devious ways.'

The Genius of Leander Paes

126. As of January 2020

127. Rohit Brijnath, 'Leander, 1996, and the Teary Game,' *Mint*, 11 August 2011

128. Ibid.

129. Andre Agassi, *Open: An Autobiography* (HarperCollins, 2009), p.

130. Shayan Acharya, 'Leander Paes: Passion Undoused!' *Sportstar*, 5 November 2019, https://sportstar.thehindu.com/magazine/leander-paes-interview-tennis-doubles-grand-slams-olympics-hingis-navratilova-sampras/article29888494.ece

131. At a corporate motivational talk

132. Gautam Bhattacharyya, *Leander: Portrait of a Never Say Die Indian*, 1996, Fourth Estate Publications. Calcutta

133. In a personal conversation with Enrico Piperno

134. PTI, 'Mahesh Bhupati Flouted Selection Criteria, Says Angry Leander Paes,' *Deccan Chronicle*. 6 April 2017, https://www.deccanchronicle.com/sports/tennis/060417/mahesh-bhupati-flouted-selection-criteria-says-angry-leander-paes.html

135. In personal conversation with the author in October 2019

136. Marc Malinowski, 'Biofile with Leander Paes,' *Tennis-Prose.com*, 26 November 2010

137. In a personal interview with the author in October 2020

138. Rohit Brijnath, 'Under 6 Feet Indian Ace Beat Wimbledon finalist,' *India Today*, 15 October 1995, https://www.indiatoday.in/magazine/sport/story/19951015-under-6feet-indian-ace-beat-wimbledon-finalist-807806-1995-10-15

139. Shuma Raha, 'I Don't Believe That I Am a Talented Tennis Player,' *The Telegraph*, 15 August 2010

140. Naresh Kumar, 'A Special, Winning Partnership,' *Frontline*, 19 June-2 July 1999, vol. 16, Issue 13

141. Paul Oberjuerge, 'Leander Paes and Mahesh Bhupathi Cause Double Trouble,' *The National*, 25 January 2011

142. In the author's personal conversation with Enrico Piperno

143. Nicholas Brulliard, 'A Doubles Pair Reunited, and It Feels So Good,' *Wall Street Journal*, 26 January 2011.

144. Amitava Das Gupta, '"Proud" Martina Navratilova Urges Leander Paes to Go for More,' *The Times of India*, 10 September 2013

145. 'Leander Is My Favourite Mixed Doubles Partner: Martina Navratilova,' *Hindustan Times*, 28 November 2015

146. 'Martina Inspired My Longevity: Leander Paes,' *Indian Express*, 16 October 2019

147. Ishan Sen, 'Leander Paes: The Legendary Architect of Indian Tennis,' Sportskeeda, 26 May 2013, https://www.sportskeeda.com/tennis/leander-paes-the-legendary-architect-of-indian-tennis

148. Vishal Menon, 'Leander Paes and Me Are Like Brothers from Different Mothers: Radek Stepanek,' *Indian Express,* 15 September 2015, https://indianexpress.com/article/sports/tennis/leander-paes-is-my-brother-from-another-mother-radek-stepanek/

149. Lokendra Pratap Sahi, 'Bond with Martina Will Remain Very Special,' *The Telegraph*, 28 October 2017

Mahesh Bhupathi and Rohan Bopanna: The Unlikely Twin and the Worthy Successor

150. Deepti Patwardhan, 'Paes and I Conquered the White Man's Game: Mahesh Bhupathi,' *New Indian Express*, 20 April 2020

151. Kristijan Breznik, 'Revealing the Best Doubles Teams and Player in Tennis History,' *International Journal of Performance Analysis in Sport*, December 2015

152. Sampras (2008), p. 84

153. Prakash, 'Mary Pierce: Leander Paes Is a Legend: Big Fan of Mahesh Bhupathi,' *Tennis World*, 21 February 2020

154. Nicole Chia, 'WTA Finals: Hingis Happy to Slam Door Shut,' *Straits Times*, 29 October 2017

155. In personal conversation with the author in March 2020

156. Mirza (2016)

157. 'India Bans Pair from Davis Cup for Two Years over Leander Paes Row,' *Agence France-Presse, The National*, UAE, 16 September 2012

158. 'Bhupathi Bristles after AITA Acts Tough,' *The Telegraph*, 16 September 2012

SECTION FOUR: THE RISE OF THE INDIAN WOMAN

The Early Pioneers of Women's Tennis

159. *Bexhill-on-Sea Observer*, British Newspaper Archives, 6 September 1924

160. Ramachandra Guha, 'The Sporting and Unsporting Politician,' *Hindustan Times*, 10 September 2010, http://ramachandraguha.in/archives/the-sporting-and-unsporting-politician-hindustan-times.html

161. *The Sphere*, Courtesy—British Newspaper Archives, 24 March 1923

162. Deeksha Bharadwaj, 'Rajkumari Amrit Kaur, the Princess Who Was Gandhi's Secretary and India's First Health Minister,' 2 February 2019, https://theprint.in/theprint-profile/rajkumari-amrit-kaur-the-princess-who-was-gandhis-secretary-indias-first-health-minister/186245/

163. P.K. Datta, *A Century of Indian Tennis*, (Publications Division, Government of India, 2001), pp. 82-83.

164. Datta (2001), p. 83

165. *Aberdeen Press and Journal*, Courtesy—British Newspaper Archives, 26 May 1929

166. *Yorkshire Post and Leeds Intelligencer*, British Newspaper Archives, 23 May 1929

167. *Lancashire Evening Post*, British Newspaper Archives, September 1930

168. *The Hull Daily Mail*, British Newspaper Archives, September 1935

169. Datta (2001), p. 86

170. Sidin Vadukut, 'The Remarkable Life of Leela Row Dayal,' *Mint*, 30 June 2018, https://www.livemint.com/Leisure/hL3EjZctOHVopSB5TCOQUK/The-remarkable-life-of-Leela-Row-Dayal.html

Women's Tennis Comes of Age

171. Khushwant Singh, 'Daughter of Controversies,' *The Telegraph*, 23 February 2008, https://www.telegraphindia.com/opinion/daughter-of-controversies/cid/622053

172. In personal conversation with the author in September 2019

173. Datta (2001), p. 208

174. In personal conversation with the author in January 2020

175. Balraj Shukla, 'First Queens of Indian Tennis and the Reign of Rita Davar' *The Bridge*, 10 January 2019

176. In personal exchange with the author in December 2019

177. Mihir Mankad, 'The Top 10 Mankad Family Athletes,' https://mmankad.wordpress.com/2012/02/27/family-legacy/

178. Nirupama Vaidyanathan, *The Moonballer*, Self-published, October 2013, p. 22

Sania Mirza

179. Mirza (2016), p. 214

180. Ibid.

181. In conversation with the author in July 2019

182. Mirza (2016)

183. Ibid. p. 74

184. Kamesh Srinivasan, 'In the Big League,' *Sportstar Year End Issue*, 31 December 2005

185. Mirza (2016), p. 119

186. Mirza (2016), p. 129

187. Mirza (2016), p. 133

188. Sanjay Jha, 'Sania, Bhajji and Mera Bharat Mahaan,' News18, January 2008

189. Rohit Brijnath, 'Sania Will Have to Manage Her Awkward World,' *The Hindu*, 7 February 2008

190. Barkha Dutt, 'Disadvantage Sania,' *Hindustan Times*, 9 February 2008, https://www.hindustantimes.com/india/

disadvantage-sania/story-cT6XQBt8V7bpDpTcuqRjqN.
html

191. Mirza (2016), p. 139
192. Mirza (2016), p. 179
193. In personal conversation with the author in April 2020
194. Wimbledon 2015 Highlights Reel, Youtube, https://youtu.
be/BXYSC_3AXA8
195. Stephanie Livaudais, 'Wimbledon Flashback: Hingis, Mirza dominate at Wimbledon in historic triumph,' *WTA Tennis*, 7 July 2020, https://www.wtatennis.com/news/1714057/hingis-mirza-dominate-at-wimbledon-in-historic-triumph
196. Marc McGowan, 'Australian Open 2016: Martina Hingis and Sania Mirza win women's doubles,' *Herald Sun*, 29 January 2016, https://www.heraldsun.com.au/sport/tennis/australian-open-2016-martina-hingis-and-sania-mirza-win-womens-doubles/news-story/1e1c351f5eb149dae6e86c023bf5e7aa
197. In private conversation with the author in April 2020

SECTION FIVE: MATCH POINT

The Future of Indian Tennis: What Does It Look Like?

198. Amritraj (1990), p. 116
199. 'Somdev Devvarman Quits Professional Tennis, Says, "No Fun, Passion Dying."' *Hindustan Times*, 2 January 2017
200. 'Has the Right Kind of Ingredients in His Game: Tennis Veterans Share Thoughts on Prajnesh Gunneswaran,' *The Bridge*, 3 February 2019
201. 'Sumit Nagal Has Triggered a Debate on Tennis in India,' *The Economic Times*, 28 August 2019
202. Jose Samano, 'The Games That Changed Spain: 25 Years on from Barcelona '92,' *El Pais*, 25 July 2017
203. Krishnan (1999), p. 85

204. Amritraj (1990), p. 128

205. 'AITA's Dictatorial Attitude Harmful for Indian tennis, Slams Bhupathi,' *India Today*, 18 September 2012

206. In personal conversation with the author in April 2020

207. In personal conversation with the author in March 2020

208. Deepti Patwardhan, 'The Lone Warriors of Indian Tennis,' *Mint*, 14 December 2019

209. Ashish Magotra and Abhijit Kulkarni, 'The JSW Model: Is the Group's Steady Success in Indian Sport a Blueprint for Other Corporates?' *Scroll*, 30 May 201

210. In personal conversation with the author in September 2019

211. In personal conversation with the author in March 2020

212. Novak Djokovic, *Serve to Win*, 2013, (Zinc Ink, Penguin Random House, Canada, 2013), p.

213. In personal conversation with the author in 2014 in Singapore

214. '42% Indians Will Cancel Honeymoon for Cricket Final: Survey,' *The Quint*, 27 November 2019, https://www.thequint.com/sports/sports-buzz/indians-survey-honeymoon-cancel-for-cricket-world-cup-final

215. ICC Media Release, 'First Global Market Research Project Unveils More than One Billion Cricket Fans,' International Cricket Council, 2018, https://www.icc-cricket.com/news/759733

216. Nirmala Ganapathy, 'While Cricket Still Rules, Football Is Winning over More Fans Amid Moves to Boost the Sport,' *The Straits Times*, 12 August 2017, https://www.straitstimes.com/asia/south-asia/indias-new-goal

217. ITF Global Tennis Report 2019, October 2019, http://itf.uberflip.com/i/1169625-itf-global-tennis-report-2019-overview/0?

218. Y.B. Sarangi, 'Indian Tennis Stalwarts Rue Lack of Financial Backing,' *Sportstar*, 15 February 2020

219. In personal conversation with the author in September 2019

BIBLIOGRAPHY

1. Andre Agassi, *Open: An Autobiography*, 2009, HarperCollins
2. Cota Ramaswami, *Ramblings of a Game Addict*, 1966, Madras, Privately Published
3. David McMahon, David, *Wills Book of Excellence: Tennis*, 1985, Orient Longman Limited, Hyderabad
4. Elizabeth Wilson, *Love Game: A History of Tennis, from Victorian Pastime to Global Phenomenon*, Serpent's Tail, Profile Books Ltd., London, 2014
5. Gautam Bhattacharyya, *Leander: Portrait of a Never Say Die Indian*, 1996, Fourth Estate Publications, Calcutta
6. Georgina and Premjit Lall, *Down the Line—The Premjit Lall Story*, 1978, Rupa & Co
7. Gordon Forbes, *A Handful of Summers: A Memoir*, 1978, William Heinemann, Johannesburg, South Africa
8. Julian Norridge, *Can We Have Our Balls Back Please?: How the British Invented Sport*, 2008, London, Allen Lane (an imprint of Penguin Books)
9. Michael Mewshaw, *Short Circuit: Borg, McEnroe and Connors, The Era of Bribes, Match-Fixing and Drugs*, 1984, 2011, Penguin Books, New York
10. Nirupama Vaidyanathan, *The Moonballer*, Self-published, October 2013
11. Novak Djokovic, *Serve to Win*, 2013, Zinc Ink, Penguin Random House, Canada
12. P.K. Datta, *A Century of Indian Tennis*, 2001, Publications Division, Government of India
13. Pete Sampras, *A Champions Mind: Lessons from a Life in tennis*, 2008, Crown Archetype
14. Ramanathan and Ramesh Krishnan, *A Touch of Tennis—The Story of a Tennis Family*, 1999, Penguin Books India (P) Ltd.

15. Robert, D. Osborn: *Lawn Tennis: Its Players and How to Play, 1881,* Strahan and Company, London
16. Rod Laver, *A Memoir*, 2013, Pan MacMillan Australia, Sydney
17. Rod Laver, *The Education of a Tennis Player*, 1971, Simon and Schuster, New York
18. Sania Mirza, *Ace Against Odds*, 2016, HarperCollins Publishers, Noida
19. Simon Taufel, *Finding the Gaps: Transferable Skills to Be the Best You Can Be*, 2019, Pan Macmillan, India
20. Sydney Jacob, *Favour for Fools in a Decadent Empire*, 1972, London, Privately Published
21. Tom Brown and Tyler Lee, *As Tom Goes By*, 2011, SCB Distributors
22. Vijay Amritraj, *Vijay! From Madras to Hollywood via Wimbledon*, 1990, Libra Mundi, London
23. William T. Tilden, *The Art of Lawn Tennis*, 1950, Simon and Schuster, New York

9 789395 767859